Where there appears to be only dirt,
there may be the root system of some kind of insistent thriving.

CAMILLE T. DUNGY

VERMONT ALMANAC

STORIES FROM & FOR THE LAND

Vermont Almanac is an editorially independent initiative that's published once a year by For the Land Publishing, Inc. This is our second volume – we hope each annual edition will form a collection for readers to enjoy and re-enjoy. We're immensely grateful to the sponsors who help make this work happen. And a special thanks to the hundreds of people who have donated to the cause. The reality of publishing in the 21st century is that we can't subsist on sponsorship revenue and bookstore sales alone, and our continued existence depends on donations and pre-buys. If you like what you read and want to see another volume next fall, please contribute at:

WWW.VERMONTALMANAC.ORG

We Are:

Sugarmaker & Editor
DAVE MANCE III

Christmas Tree Grower & Editor
PATRICK WHITE

Business Manager
AMY PEBERDY

Forester & Editor
VIRGINIA BARLOW

Graphic Designer
LISA CADIEUX | LIQUID STUDIO

FOR THE LAND PUBLISHING
BOARD OF DIRECTORS
Marjorie Ryerson, President
Trevor Mance, Vice President
Chuck Wooster, Secretary
Kate Whelley McCabe

BEHIND THE SCENES
John Douglas, Chris Doyle, Marian Cawley, Giom,
Lora Marchand, John K. Tiholiz, Tamara White

Volume II: Copyright 2021 For the Land Publishing, Inc.,
PO Box 514, Corinth, Vermont 05039.
For purchase inquiries, or to sponsor our work,
please contact amy@vermontalmanac.org.
Direct all editorial correspondence to
dave@vermontalmanac.org. (802) 439-5651.
For the Land Publishing, Inc., is a 501 (c) (3) public benefit
educational organization.
Printed in Milton, Vermont.

COVER PAINTING
Kate Gridley

The cover image was excerpted from a larger painting entitled *The Sport*. "In a biological sense, a 'sport' is a mutation, or change," writes artist Kate Gridley. "I spent months looking into the form and function of these tools, at the diverse edges and patinas, the interplay of objects and shadows. I ponder the hands that held them, the bodies and minds that sweated, hammered, plowed, drilled, harvested, hauled, and cut in order to construct lives and alter a world."

MONTHLY PAINTINGS
Amy Hook-Therrien

"I have always been drawn to birches," writes artist Amy Hook-Therrien. "They are like ghosts of the forest. They bring a sense of tranquility and fragility to a landscape. They sit quietly, giving a hint of color and their personality as their bark curls away. I thought I might get bored, eventually, painting the same tree time after time. I didn't. I think I could paint birches for the rest of my life and be wonderfully happy."

TANIA AEBI lives in Corinth and still hopes to get her beehives through winter.

VIRGINIA BARLOW has worked as a forester, writer, and editor in Corinth.

A lifelong farmer and agricultural advocate, **DR. TERENCE BRADSHAW** is director of the University of Vermont Fruit Program and Horticultural Research & Education Center. He was raised on a dairy farm on West Hill in Chelsea.

MARK BUSHNELL is a long-time Vermont journalist who switched from editing newspapers to writing about history because he enjoys time travel. His books include *It Happened in Vermont* and *Hidden History of Vermont*.

LISA CADIEUX was born and raised in Swanton and spent her childhood in the woods creating imaginary wildlife habitats. As an adult, her creative work includes book design, interior design, metalsmithing, cooking... liquidstudiodesign.com

AARON CARROLL is a beginning farmer, photographer, and entrepreneur living in Underhill. He is passionate about landscape horticulture and seasonal outdoor activities with his family.

JEFF CARTER has been the UVM Extension Agronomist for Field Crops in Addison County for the past 36 years. He is currently living in Bristol with his wife Pam and sharing his love of the land with both children and grandchildren alike.

MICKI COLBECK lives in Central Vermont with a couple of little brown dogs who take her on hikes up into the hills to look at stuff – mostly mosses, ferns, birds, and rocks – and who help her write about them later. mjcolbeck.com.

JENN COLBY owns and operates Howling Wolf Farm, LLC with her husband Chris Sargent, where they produce lamb and pork as well as hosting farm stays and events. She has worked in and around Vermont dairy and livestock agriculture for more than 25 years.

SARAH CAOUETTE is a writer from Vershire whose recent work focuses on the discovery of place and identity through storytelling, and through engagement and experiences with one's environment. Her one-year-old son has given her a new way of seeing the world.

C.E. CROWELL is a poet, economist, entrepreneur, and educator. Having operated Goshen Gore Farm, a sheep and commercial hay operation in Plainfield for 11 years, his current projects are Vermont Saffron and the Center for Agricultural Innovation.

TONY D'AMATO is a Professor of Silviculture and Applied Forest Ecology and Director of the Forestry Program at the University of Vermont. He lives in Williston with his wife, Jess, son, Quinn, and dog, Otis.

Professional photographer **JL DAMON** lives on a hill with his wife, two amazing daughters, dogs, chickens, cats, ducks, the occasional rescued critters, and a constant stream of friends and family.

DR. HEATHER DARBY is a Professor of Agronomy at the University of Vermont. She has been conducting outreach and research on industrial hemp since 2016. More information about Darby's research can be found at www.uvm.edu/extension/nwcrops.

SYLVIA DAVATZ has been saving seeds for over 25 years. Her main interests are preserving rare or locally adapted varieties, grain diversity, season extension, and experimenting with crops such as upland rice. She loves cooking the garden's bounty and practices totally unscientific permaculture.

JUDY DOW is a nationally known activist, basket weaver, and teacher of traditional Abenaki culture and native practices.

BILL DRISLANE is a board member of Sundog Poetry Center, lives in Jericho with his wife botanist Liz Thompson, and when he's not digging in the garden, writes, fiddles dance tunes, and presents and recites poetry at cafes and festivals.

OWEN DUFFY is a fiction writer who loves to spend time outdoors with his family in their home state of Vermont.

WENDELL DURHAM lives on his family's diversified farm in wild West Corinth. He spends his days helping on the farm, wood carving, baking, running, nordic skiing, and tending to his small orchard.

MEGAN DURLING and **NATHAN BRADSHAW** are teachers and lifelong learners who help steward a small high school in East Burke. They are building their first house in the town of Newark, where they have chosen to settle down with their two dogs and soon to be firstborn.

KARA FITZBEAUCHAMP operates Evening Song Farm with her partner, Ryan, in hopes that their work can be a small piece in the puzzle to shift the climate crisis. When she is not farming, she is often swimming with her kids.

SHANTA LEE GANDER is the 2020 recipient of the Arthur Williams Award for Meritorious Service to the Arts. Her debut poetry compilation is *GHETTOCLAUSTROPHOBIA: Dreamin of Mama While Trying to Speak in Woke Tongues*. Shantaleegander.com.

Vermont State Climatologist **DR. LESLEY-ANN L. DUPIGNY-GIROUX** is also a professor of Geography at the University of Vermont and president of the American Association of State Climatologists.

KATE GRIDLEY'S studio is in Middlebury, where she's been painting since 1991. She's currently working on two projects, both funded by the Vermont Arts Council and The Vermont Community Foundation, which involve sound, words, and paintings.

EDITH FORBES has worked as a computer programmer, house renovator, farmer, and writer. She is the author of four novels and the upcoming memoir *Tracking a Shadow: A Lived Experiment with MS*.

KRISTEN FOUNTAIN lives with her family in Albany, where she writes, supports community projects, and dreams of a cutting garden.

WILLIAM HART, Professor Emeritus of History at Middlebury College, is the author of *For the Good of their Souls: Performing Christianity in Eighteenth-Century Mohawk Country*. Bill is currently writing a biography of Alexander Twilight.

Strafford native **DAISY HEBB** created the *Seasonal Garden Series and Natives & Their Pollinators Series*. Both are artistic, watercolored, learning tools to help people understand our ecosystems. The new *Keystone Species Series* is a collaboration with entomologist Doug Tallamy.

MIKE HEBB is a Vermont native naturalist following interests in horticulture, beekeeping, bryology, violin building, lathe work, antique motorcycles, and trail design in Strafford.

ROBERT HOAR researches Vermont history at the Bennington Museum Library, volunteers at the Bennington Monument, and works at the Bennington Battlefield. He grew up in Shaftsbury in an old house built by a militia captain.

AMY HOOK-THERRIEN is a Vermont watercolor artist originally from Chelsea. She attended the University of Maine in Orono where she received her BFA. Her main focus is on the New England landscape and the fragility of nature.

MARY HOLLAND is a lifelong naturalist/environmental educator/writer/nature photographer who spends her time looking for interesting finds in the woods to photograph and put on her blog, www.naturallycurious withmaryholland.wordpress.com.

MARK ISSELHARDT, University of Vermont Extension, draws on degrees in forest management and plant biology and 26 years of experience in maple to provide research-based education on issues from trees to syrup jug.

KATHRYN KRAMER's most recent book is a memoir, *Missing History: The Covert Education of a Child of the Great Books*. Her November essay is partly taken from a nearly completed book about Vermont, *The Rise and Fall of the Republic of West Delphi*.

CHRIS KURDEK lives in the small town of Stannard and is a meteorologist and science educator. He enjoys homesteading and being outdoors – skiing, hiking, paddling his canoe, and taking his snow machines out for a rip.

BETTE LAMBERT is a mother of six and grandmother of twenty. A long time dairy farmer, she currently works with son, Paul, and daughter, Marilyn, at Silloway Maple in Randolph Center.

JOHN LAZENBY is a photojournalist based in Montpelier.

SYDNEY LEA, author of 23 books, is the 2021 recipient of Vermont's Governor's Award for Excellence in the Arts. A Pulitzer finalist and winner of the Poets' Prize, he was the founding editor of *New England Review* and Vermont's Poet Laureate from 2011 to 2015.

TED LEVIN is the author of several books about the natural world. *Liquid Land* and his most recent book, *America's Snake: The Rise and Fall of the Timber Rattlesnak*e, won the Burroughs Medal. He divides his time between the deck and the road. He lives in White River.

Raised in Island Pond, **PAUL LEFEBVRE** is a reporter for the *Chronicle*, a weekly paper in Barton. He has four books, of which three are collections of his columns and a memoir, *Crossing Jack Brook*. He lives in Newark.

DIANA LISCHER is an award-winning poet, professional grant writer, avid gardener, and chicken whisperer living in Dummerston. She grew up on a flower farm, co-owned a sheep farm, and currently works seasonally at an orchard farmstand.

BEN LORD is writer, naturalist, and high school science teacher who lives and forages in southeastern Vermont. You can find him at progressivelylesswrong.com.

If attention is the beginning of devotion, then **DAVE MANCE III**'s devotion to the natural world was formed in large part by the hunting, fishing, and trapping he did in his formative years.

MARY MATHIAS is a retired Social Worker, formerly a dairy farmer at Frog Run Farm in the Northeast Kingdom. Now she enjoys the climate of Vermont's 'banana belt,' in Brattleboro.

JACK MAYER is a writer and pediatrician who has written about his practice and about Vermont's Long Trail. He has published *Life in a Jar: The Irena Sendler Project, Before the Court of Heaven*, and *Poems from the Wilderness*, which won the 2019 Proverse Prize for poetry collections.

A co-founder of the Vermont Center for Ecostudies, **KENT MCFARLAND** is a conservation biologist, photographer, writer, and naturalist. He's co-host of Outdoor Radio, a monthly natural history series on Vermont Public Radio.

RACHEL SARGENT MIRUS is a freelance teaching artist and science writer. She lives and works in the Green Mountains.

GARY W. MOORE is a native of Bradford. He and his wife, Linda live in a home they built in 1973. He enjoys working the 58 acres of forest they own that was once part of the family farm.

SUZANNE OPTON is author of *Into the Light Cellar*. She often asks a small performance of her subjects as a window into their circumstances. She's best known for her images of soldiers between tours of duty in Iraq and Afghanistan.

Throughout his various careers as a Protestant minister, state senator, utility regulator, and energy policy consultant, **SCUDDER PARKER** has been writing poetry. His first book of poetry, *Safe as Lightning*, was published in June of 2020. scudderparker.net

BRYAN PFEIFFER is a writer, educator, and consulting field naturalist specializing in birds and insects. He lives with his partner Ruth and their English shepherd Odin on a hillside in Montpelier. www.bryanpfeiffer.com.

VERANDAH PORCHE is a cultural worker: poet, songwriter, mentor, scribe, and selectboard member, based in Guilford. Hear songs and poems on www.patreon.com/pattyandverandah verandahporche.com. A new album is in the works.

JULIA PUPKO fell in love with the natural world at a very young age, learning about plant medicine from her mother and spending hours exploring the forests with her father. She pursued a degree in Environmental Sciences at UVM and graduated with honors in 2019.

ROB RINALDI JR is a father, husband, son, handyman, artist, photographer, publisher (www.n-news.com) poultry farmer, fixer, problem solver, caregiver, community builder, a maker of small rocks from big rocks, wood hauler, pizza maker, non-believing believer.

JODY SCHADE is a devoted gardener and canner, with more than 25 years practice. She lives on 35 acres on Sheffield Heights in the Northeast Kingdom with her husband, two boys, an assorted flock of chickens, and Harley the cat.

For much of his life **JOHN SNELL** has been using a camera, either visual and thermal versions, to see this amazing world and share his vision of the wonder of it all.

LAURA SORKIN is a writer, former farmer, and present co-owner of Runamok Maple. She lives in northwest Vermont with her husband and two children. In her spare time she enjoys growing unlikely Vermont plants such as lemons, pineapples and carnivorous flowers.

BRETT ANN STANCIU published *Unstitched: My Journey to Understand Opioid Addiction and How People and Communities Can Heal* in September, 2021. She lives on a hillside in Hardwick with her two daughters.

ALESSANDRA RELLINI is a farmer, butcher, and psychology professor who was born and raised in Italy. She and her partner Stefano raise pigs, sheep, and chickens at Agricola Farm in Panton. agricolavermont.com

ARI ROCKLAND-MILLER is co-founder of The Mushroom Forager. He shares his passion for mushroom hunting through the written word, guided forays, presentations, and interactive workshops. themushroomforager.com

State Game Warden **MIKE SCOTT** has been a member of the Vermont Warden Service since 2014, currently providing Fish and Wildlife law enforcement services in eastern Orange County. In his off-duty time, he is an active sportsman and dabbles in maple sugaring and farming.

LI SHEN grew up in London, UK. She spent several decades in medical research in London, then Cleveland OH, and at Dartmouth Medical School, before jumping ship into sculpture, photography, and writing.

TOM SLAYTON was editor in chief of *Vermont Life* from 1985 to 2007. During his tenure, the magazine earned more than 90 awards for graphic and editorial excellence.

LETTIE STRATTON is a freelance writer + creator of Wild Wanderer, an outdoor adventure site for the LGBTQ+ community.

Born and raised in the Champlain Valley, **LEATH TONINO** is a freelance writer and the author of two essay collections from Trinity University Press: *The Animal One Thousand Miles Long* (about Vermont) and *The West Will Swallow You* (about everywhere else).

BILL TORREY is a woodsman, author, and storyteller who worked forty years slaying tall timber from the wooded ridges of Vermont where his family has lived since 1767.

CATHERINE TUDISH lives in Corinth. Her third book, a collection of short stories called *A Thousand Souls*, will be published by Brighthorse Books in 2022.

JOAN WALTERMIRE was in her first of many years as Curator of Exhibits at Montshire Museum of Science when she wrote her most important poem – about opossum reproduction. This attracted her long-time mate. They live in Vershire.

BRAD WHEELER lives in Corinth. When he's not looking at soils around the State, he spends his time in the woods appreciating the vast diversity of the world around him.

PATRICK WHITE is an editor at *Vermont Almanac* and runs Meadow Ridge Christmas Tree Farm in Middlesex with his wife, Tamara, and son, Aidan.

DAN WING has been baking bread for 50 years – a progression of white sandwich, quick Cuban, kitchen-oven sourdough, and now, for 25 years, wood-oven sourdough and pizzas. He went out from his home in Corinth to meet some Vermont growers and millers.

CHUCK WOOSTER owns and runs Sunrise Farm in White River Junction, where he lives with his wife, two dogs, and assorted sheep and chickens.

October 2020–September 2021

*A content index of the many people, places, and topics
covered in Volume I is available online at vermontalmanac.org.
A similar index for Volume II is in the works.*

PREAMBLE

Last December, the *Rutland Herald/Times Argus* wrote a gracious editorial about Volume I of *Vermont Almanac* entitled: "How to Vermont." That title captures, in three words, the spirit of this project.

Some of this how-to work is literal: The proper angle of a water bar on a woods road is 30 degrees. Citronella candles don't work; use a fan, instead, to keep mosquitos away from your patio dinner table. Use a rubber mallet to drive a cleaver through your lamb chop in the exact place you want the bone cut. We can go on and on (and do, in the pages that follow).

But, really, our work is in service of bigger, more abstract how-tos: How to appreciate the rural skills and wisdom that we've been blessed to inherit. How to re-invent agriculture in ways that are both financially viable and environmentally sustainable.

The photos on the previous pages are of the people who helped write and illustrate this book, but if you also consider the sources for their work, and the sponsors, and donors, and every one of you who plunked down money to buy the book, we have a tribe of thousands. There's strength in these numbers. Strength in the idea of people who put the land at the center of their identity.

The stories we tell about ourselves define us; in the same way, the stories we tell about where we live come to define a place. As Vermont changes with the times, and as an influx of new residents, prompted by the pandemic, move to the state, articulating the enormous value of farming, forestry, homesteading, and other land-based pursuits is more crucial than ever. Let the stories in this book stand as a declaration: *This* is Vermont.

OCTOBER

October

As a kid, I loved ice cream, dogs, swimming pools, basketball, sledding, Christmas presents, summer vacation, *Star Wars*, and raking. This last one, I'll admit, didn't top the list, but neither did it rank at the very bottom. Ah, the smooth-grained handle and flexy metal tines! Ah, the cool air and hard ground and rhythmic scratching! Ah, the so-called boring chore!

To be clear, not just any type of raking tickled the ivories of my soul. Grass clippings held no appeal, twigs were a royal pain in the butt, and unlike some Zen monk who lavishes attention on his temple's rock garden, pebbles struck me as best left in place, undisturbed. What I loved as a five-year-old, a nine-year-old, and a twelve-year-old was specifically – and exclusively – raking autumn's rainbow of leaves.

This annual pastime had absolutely nothing to do with productivity, with tidying and organizing, with sculpting messy nature into neat piles, and absolutely everything to do with a running start and face-first plunge. Or a belly-flop. Or a catastrophic cartwheel – whatever's clever. Breathing heavily, sweating, head bowed in focus, I hauled and heaped, heaped and hauled, struggling to build each bomb bigger than the last. A wild ROYGBIV explosion – foliage shot skyward, darting and whirling, sneaking into my collar and sleeves, foliage *attacking* me – was the ultimate fall fun.

And it still is, sort of.

These days, when I think back to the exuberant, reckless yardwork of my youth, I discern the seed of a different, related hobby: bushwhacking. Oh yes, the adult me loves bushwhacking (especially bushwhacking October's kaleidoscopic color bonanza) with the same intensity that the childhood me had for hours of unpaid landscaping labor. Here's why: *Boom!*

In my experience, bushwhacking approximates the ROYGBIV explosion, the flailing bliss of leaves packing your nostrils and ears and mouth, surrounding you, overwhelming you. As kissing is to sex, pot is to LSD, and a Bic lighter is to fifty gallons of diesel and a blowtorch, so the civilized stroll is to the arduous backcountry 'shwhack. Hiking a manicured trail is nice enough, but bushwhacking is, well, nasty.

Of course, nastiness is precisely what repels many sane people. *Why stumble and tumble, thrash and crash? Why tear my trousers, rip my jacket, ruin my backpack with stickers and thorns? Why donate blood from the knuckles, ankles, and cheeks? Why bang a shin and nick a cornea? I enjoy the woods plenty. I'm pleased with the calm, safe, designated path. What kind of freak needs the forest to smother him, to abuse him?*

Hi, pleasure to make your acquaintance. My name's Freak, er, Leath.

I could offer an easy dozen arguments in support of bushwhacking – you re-inhabit your ancient animal self, you encounter the local topography and ecology without mediation, you learn to relish being lost – but that's unnecessary. A single word covers the various bases, a word Henry David Thoreau deemed so important that in his book *The Maine Woods*, he repeated it, echoing himself, even adding little *yippees* in the form of exclamation points. Hollers Henry: "Contact! Contact!"

Okay, but what does the word mean exactly? My dictionary provides the following pair of definitions: 1) the state or condition of physical touching; 2) the state or condition of communicating or meeting. Put the definitions together, let them intertwine, and you arrive at the simple yet profound realization that pressing flesh to bark, to petiole and blade, is in fact an avenue to understanding, a route to intimacy.

Ultimately, then, bushwhacking is an invitation to discover the environment somatically *and* mentally, with body *and* brain. An invitation to *know* our rainbow world by *feeling* our rainbow world. An invitation to get a running start, leap from the trail, and plunge into color.

October: Vermont's greatest month? Probably. Ah, the chilly nights and frosty dawns. Ah, the wool sweaters and down vests. Ah, the garage, where a trusty rake waits patiently for its annual tour of the yard. Lucky 'shwhackers, here we are again, like last year and the year before, here in the season of leaves. Sometimes, we rake them. Sometimes they rake us. —*Leath Tonino*

Sort of Normal

After an abnormally dry and hot summer, an average amount of rain finally came in October. Temperatures throughout the month were also around normal, at least when you look at the month-end average. But averages don't always tell the full story.

If you had to ask a Vermonter what the normal October temperature is, they would likely struggle with an answer. Large swings in temperature are typical throughout the month, as it is in the heart of a transition season. The northern jet stream starts to make its southern push, and summer features such as the Bermuda high retreat south.

This year was true to form. Two periods of well-above-normal temperatures were observed during the start to the middle of the month, with Burlington almost hitting a balmy (for any season) 80 degrees. Then the end of the month offered well-below-normal temperatures, with lows in the teens and 20s. As is often the case, the notoriously colder Northeast Kingdom recorded its first freeze on October 12, a good month before Burlington.

October is accompanied by a sense of urgency, as many of us wrap up the growing season and finalize preparations for winter. Processing and preserving becomes a major focus as we work to ensure that the root cellar or cupboard is stocked for the winter and no product is wasted. This is the time of year that freezers are also stocked, and in recent years it has become nearly impossible to find a meat processor with openings, unless an appointment is booked around a year prior. The declining light adds to the sense of urgency: around an hour and a half of sunlight is lost over the course of the month. —*Christopher Kurdek, Fairbanks Museum and Planetarium*

October 1, 2020, at Elmer Farm in Middlebury: Harvest complete, the sandbags that held down row covers all growing season were just removed.

JENNIFER BLACKWELL / ELMER FARM

NATURE NOTES

NINE DRAGONFLY SPECIES in North America are known to be migratory. The ones that breed in New England, like this common green darner, are now shipping out.

VT CENTER FOR ECOSTUDIES/JOSH LINCOLN

OCTOBER 5, 2020.
The male catkins on beaked hazelnuts are fully formed. Good to know that somebody's thinking about spring.

JOSH FECTEAU

Leaving Leaves

Pete Amber, an arborist from Chelsea, advocates leaving the rake in the garage and the leaves where they fall for the sake of the trees, because leaves are the best, most natural way to increase soil fertility.

But there are other reasons, you could say millions of other reasons, if you could count the myriad creatures that thrive among fallen leaves in winter. According to the Xerces Society, an organization that promotes invertebrate conservation, most butterflies and moths use leaf litter to protect their eggs, larvae, chrysalises, or adults from the cold. Great spangled fritillaries and wooly bear caterpillars, among others, nestle into leaves for protection. Swallowtail and luna moth chrysalises look like the leaves they hide in. Some bumblebees need leaves for protection.

Lace bugs, snails, worms, beetles, millipedes, spiders, and other small animals overwinter in leaves and some will be food for birds, snakes, amphibians, and small mammals in the spring.

We live in a small opening in the woods and never rake leaves, even the thickly piled ones. Come spring and you might think we were the tidiest leaf rakers in town. The leaves are gone. —*Virginia Barlow*

Self-Digestion

MARY HOLLAND

Shaggy mane, *Coprinus comatus*, is one of a group of mushrooms known as inky caps. Both of these common names reflect the appearance of the mushroom at different stages of its development – the cap has white, shaggy scales, and as the mushroom matures, its gills liquefy into a black substance that was once used as ink.

Most inky caps have gills that are very thin and very close to one another, which does not allow for easy release of the spores. In addition, the elongated shape of this mushroom does not allow for the spores to get caught in air currents as in most other mushrooms. The liquefaction/self-digestion process is a strategy to disperse spores more efficiently. The gills liquefy from the bottom up as the spores mature. Thus the cap peels up and away, and the maturing spores are always kept in the best position for catching wind currents. This continues until the entire fruiting body has turned into black ink. *—Mary Holland*

I n Underhill, Vermont, trees are monitored at the base of Mount Mansfield each fall, and the timing of peak fall color and leaf drop is recorded. In the fall of 2020, the timing of peak color for most species at upper elevations was earlier than the long-term average. Peak color was close to the long-term average for those trees at 1,400 feet. The color developed rapidly, and leaves fell quickly – both symptoms related to drought. The growing season length for sugar maple at 1,400 feet was four days shorter than the long-term average, and nine days shorter than last fall. *—Vermont Department of Forests, Parks, and Recreation*

MARC FORMEISTER

When this photo was taken on October 2, peak foliage had already passed on the upper elevations of Mount Mansfield.

AT HOME

(Re)Learning the Secret to Successful Canning

Normally, as the growing season approached, I'd be busy preparing my garden as I had done for more than 20 years. But 2020 was different. My husband had taken a job nearly 200 miles away, our house was on the market, and we were moving at the end of the school year. For the first time in an awfully long time, I had no plans to plant.

So in late summer, I found myself with idle hands. It was the first time in recent memory that canning wasn't my primary occupation during that time of year. I confess it wasn't all bad. It gave me the opportunity to adjust to my new life in the Northeast

G. JOHANSEN

Kingdom, but by the time apple season arrived, I was anxious to make applesauce.

On a crisp autumn afternoon, I dragged my canning pot out of the basement and washed the months of dust off it and a dozen pint jars. Bent over the compost bin, I peeled apple after apple. Soon, I found myself standing over a steaming pot, inhaling the spicy, sweet aroma as I stirred. For the first time in months, I felt grounded. Solid. Our lives had been in chaos for quite some time, and I hadn't realized how out of balance I'd felt until then. Nor had I remembered how happy canning made me and how much I'd missed it. Clearly I wasn't alone, as there was a rush on canning supplies that resulted in shortages during the pandemic.

Whatever you're canning, there is no hurrying along the food in the pot. Jam cooked too quickly will be gritty because the sugar doesn't fully dissolve, and the jam won't set properly if you haven't cooked it to its gelling point. Jars rushed in the canning pot won't seal properly. There is an intentional, joyful slowing down. Of being present. Of being aware of the smell of the food cooking. Of its texture and thickness. Of the part you play in bringing out its sweetness and goodness.

Gone are the days when a successful and bountiful harvest was canned as a means of surviving the winter. Now our gardening and our canning has the space to become a labor of love. Be it strawberry jam that you make as a gift for friends and family or chutney you've discovered that you just can't eat a pork chop without, what you put up doesn't have to consume you or your kitchen.

There is something so incredibly delightful about having a homemade jar of something on any table you set, and whether you put up 6 jars or 600 in a season, the secret to doing it well is joy. Each jar is a gift – a gift of time, of labor, and of love. It is a tangible representation of our own happiness – one that we can share. —*Jody Schade*

Foraging Wild Nuts in the Northeast

A s a modern-day forager, I see nuts as the Holy Grail of wild plant foods. Mankind cannot live on greens alone – or on stalks and shoots, for that matter. As nutritious and tasty as these foods may be, the foundation of a foraging menu must be dense in energy, rich in calories, and satisfying for the kind of hunger that one develops during a day on foot looking for things to eat.

Nuts have a complex chemistry, and like any food, some of nuts' chemicals are great for you while some of them are not. Hickory nuts, butternuts, and hazelnuts are all palatable right off the ground and require no more processing than the removal of their shells. Beechnuts are a tasty autumn nibble, but they contain the mildly toxic compound fagin. No need to worry about it. It would take an awful lot of beechnuts to make you sick, but it's probably one reason beechnuts were traditionally pressed into an oil, which does not contain the offending substance. Acorns, the Northeast's most abundant nuts, contain large concentrations of tannins that must be removed. Anyone who has tasted cakes or breads made of acorn flour, however, will tell you that time invested in tannin leaching is worthwhile. —*Ben Lord*

ROB ROUTLEDGE/BUGWOOD.ORG

PAUL WRAY/BUGWOOD.ORG

USDA FOREST SERVICE

GMIHAIL CC

NUT	NOTES
AMERICAN BEECH *(Fagus grandifolia)* [1]	Nuts usually fall easily from their prickly husks. In large quantities, try roasting or pressing for oil.
AMERICAN HAZELNUT *(Corylus americana)* [2] BEAKED HAZELNUT *(Corylus cornuta)*	Ripens in late summer. Dry until husks shrivel, or bury and rot husks for about one month. Remove husks by hand or work in a sack until husks separate. Eat straight from the shell or roast.
SHAGBARK HICKORY *(Carya ovata)* [3] MOCKERNUT HICKORY *(Carya tomentosa)*	Dry to split husks, then remove by hand. Some foragers claim that striking the correct place on the shell leaves the kernel intact. Hickory milk is a soup stock made by crushing the shells and kernels together, soaking them for several days, and decanting the liquid.
OAK *(Quercus spp.)* [4]	All acorns must be leached of tannins either by boiling the coarsely chopped nuts in multiple changes of water or by soaking and decanting finely ground nuts in cold water. Leaching is complete when the nuts are no longer bitter. Dry and grind into a flour that, when mixed with wheat flour, makes remarkable baked goods.
EASTERN AMERICAN BLACK WALNUT *(Juglans nigra)* [5] BUTTERNUT *(Juglans cinerea)*	Rot husks off in a shallow container over several months and break off what remains. (Caution: Inky dye in the husks stains clothes and skin.) Shells are hard – some people run over the nuts with a car to crack them. Using wire cutters and nut picks helps to remove stubborn kernels. Delicious raw: butternut is reminiscent of banana.

Most nuts store well in the shell at room temperatures without special preparation, with the exception of acorns, which should be dried before storage.

✿

Making Corn Husk Dolls with Linda Sheehan

Kwalaskonigan kamgwahôzo nônnoak minitak kezabadak ala nônnôkaw minitak tkebagak. (Soak corn husk for 5 minutes in hot water or 10 to 15 minutes in cold water.) *Ligba–pikawtaha Kaskakwalaskonigan pabasiwi.* (Fold a wide husk in half lengthwise.) *Niga, pikawtaha pabasiwi memhôwigan ta tasahôwigan.* (Then fold in half from bottom and top.)

Kwalaskonigansis wlitôzo w'dep. Pikôgna dasto aligwigwek w'dep. Pona waskijigek pikawtahwôganek. (Take a small husk to make her head. Bend it over and squish it to head size. Place it in the long husk up at the top of the fold.) *Kelabido wiwniwi wkwedôganek wji wjat chitamiwi.* (Tie sinew tightly around the neck.) *Waji wlitôzikil mpedinal, Kaskakwalaskonigan kaskak ta kwana, Segweskôbassem nhenol chichigwigekkil pesigiaal nanôwiwi.* (To make the arms, take a wide and long husk, tear

one end in three narrow pieces to the midpoint of the husk.) *Niga chitamôbageniga ta kelabido wiwniwi wji wjat matanaskiwi wlitoan melji.* (Then braid the husk tightly and bind it with sinew at the end to make the hand.) *Mpedin pidigato Kwalaskoniganek kwahliwitta wkwedôganek.* (The arm is put inside the cornhusk [body] right near the neck.) *Chitamôbageniga agômiwi ta kelabido wiwniwi wji wjat matanaskiwi waji wlitôan melji.* (Braid the other side tightly; bind it with sinew at the end to make the hand.)

Waji wlitôzikil mkôdal ta mdolka, kadawaka pazegwen kwenak kwalaskonigan. Winato nisnol nitkwaljial; pona kwalaskonigan wji pemaiwi pasojiwi wdelegwi. Kelabido wiwniwi wji wjat wlitôan mdolka. (To make the stomach, use one long cornhusk. Take a longer husk; circle it around two fingers. Place it into the [body] husk on the side near the armpit.

Bind it with sinew to make the stomach.) *Nikwôbi mkôdal.* (Now legs.) *Chebahla pôjiwi kwalaskoniganal nhenol pesigiaal, niga chitamôbageniga ta kelabido wiwniwi wji wjat matanaskiwi wji wlitoan mezid.* (Separate left-side cornhusks into three pieces, then braid them tightly and bind them with sinew at the end to make the foot.) *Awaka pahami kwalaskoniganal waji tôtadbeskwaikwanikhaman wji mkôdal.* (Use more cornhusks to create the exact same length for the legs. You may need to add some narrow husks as you braid so the legs will be of equal length.) *Chitamôbageniga agômiwi ta kelabido wiwniwi wji wjat matanaskiwi waji wlitoan mezid.* (Braid tightly the other side and bind it with sinew at the end to make the foot.) *Kelabido wiwniwi tmezna noskigek wjat.* (Cut off the extra sinew.)

K'dagwagwihô Kwalaskonigan-igejokôn! (You're finished making a cornhusk doll!)

Alnôbaiwi, which roughly translates to, "In the Abenaki Way," is a 501(c)(3) nonprofit organization whose members include inter-tribal indigenous citizens, friends, and allies. Members come together to participate in living history, song, dance, gardening, fellowship, and ceremony, all while creating content for the Vermont Indigenous Heritage Center to preserve the knowledge of Vermont Abenaki culture.

Garlic and Curiosity

I come from an Italian-American family where the big multifaceted, labor-intensive project is king. Whether it be making dinner, working on a collaborative art project, or building a barn, these undertakings are driven by a strong sense of curiosity and the desire to have multiple generations work together to achieve a common goal.

My family's enterprises have had two major themes: building things and growing things. Nearly 30 years ago, my Uncle Gerard and Aunt Vaughn started growing garlic on a hill farm in Chelsea. Though my uncle had never been a gardener, my aunt loved working in the dirt. Gerard was oriented toward the culture of farm life and the ordered nature

PHOTOS BY ROB RINALDI, JR.

The garlic harvest: A 1951 Ford 8N, pulling a low trailer, helps move a few hundred heads.

of that world. He had great respect for the hard but rewarding lives of farming families. He was also the guy who started *N-News* magazine 36 years ago, after having a 1951 Ford 8N tractor pretty much appear before him like a saint.

At the time, he didn't think he needed a tractor, but he was curious about the 8N's agricultural history. Growing garlic was a way of connecting to Vermont's agricultural traditions while linking other interests together – tractors, family, and, of course, cooking. They started with 300 plants but quickly ramped up to 2,000. I would go and help out with the major jobs – planting and harvesting, preparing the ground with the tractor, adding manure, rotating plots, making the planting hills, walking with the dibble wheel.

Growing up, garlic was an ingredient in most of our dinners. But our family embraced it even more closely once we started growing it. Roasted garlic, garlic soup, garlic pizza, pesto (both traditional and scape pesto) – our family got hooked. Fresh garlic has a sticky, sugary, garlicky-ness and an intensity and depth that store-bought garlic can only dream about. The only thing I can compare it to is the difference between February's store-bought tomatoes and the red, juicy globes purchased at the farmer's market or picked from the garden in late summer. Something like 70 to 80 percent of garlic consumed in the United States comes from China, so that's what you're likely purchasing at your grocery store.

Garlic is a "backwards crop." You plant it in the fall, two to three weeks before frost, and harvest it in July, when most other crops are still growing. As with tomatoes, there are many varieties of garlic, but they break into two major categories: softnecks and hardnecks. "Neck" refers to the part of the leaf stalk that grows up out of the bulb just above the ground. Softneck varieties have a floppy stalk that can be braided easily. Softneck heads have two or three rows of cloves, with very tiny cloves in the center. Hardneck varieties have rigid stalks with one row of large cloves per head. Hardneck varieties also produce a "scape" that needs to be trimmed off in June in order to put energy into the bulbs. Each variety has a different

Left: Garlic is one agricultural product that is easily packaged and shipped; Rinaldi Garlic sells to customers around the country. Right: After planting in late October, garlic is covered with straw, hay, or leaves. Here Bailey Rinaldi, Jill Morton, Nilla Rinaldi, and Jay Rinaldi cover the garlic rows.

taste, different environmental preferences, and different longevity when stored. Looking for milder garlic? Stick with German White. Want something garlicky-strong? Try Georgian Fire or Crystal. Need something that handles a damper growing climate? Try growing Montana.

Though hardneck garlic could be grown by planting the offspring of the scapes, the most efficient way to produce garlic is to propagate it asexually. Each year, we hold off the largest heads of a particular variety and save them for seeding the fall planting. In doing so, we are constantly high-grading our own varieties for our own plots.

Garlic seems to offer some kind of magical properties. There are hundreds of antidotes that involve garlic. I don't believe garlic is a cure-all, but I do believe there is something there. I know when I feel like I am getting a cold, I make a slice of toast with butter and thinly sliced raw garlic on it, then I melt a little asiago cheese on top of that. Maybe it is in my head, but I believe garlic has helped fend off many colds.

When my parents, my wife, and my young daughters took over the garlic enterprise in 2005, we started ramping up the number of plants (now 10,000) and varieties (8). Planting, shepherding, and harvesting garlic is a big job. With the exception of soil preparation, which we do with a tractor, it is all done by hand. Cloves need to go in with the pointy end up in order to make a plant that grows straight. (Think about planting a tulip bulb – same idea.) Rows have to be weeded in May and July. And when you're harvesting, each plant has to be pulled out gently, one variety at a time, and then hung up to cure for six to eight weeks. Organizing to plant, harvest, hang, and then take down and clean 10,000 plants is overwhelming. At times, I have considered ways to mechanize the process, but I have yet to come up with a way of doing it on a small scale. Maybe if we were tending three or four times the quantity we grow, it might make sense to invest in some expensive planting and harvesting equipment, but then the harvest would become an entirely different animal.

For me, garlic is a metaphor. It represents a paradigm shift in my thinking – like when you finish a long hike or a hundred-mile run, you feel somehow differently about things after you grow a thousand garlic plants. Maybe it has something to do with planting it in cold ground in late October. It seems impossible that anything good could happen in the dirt from November through March, especially in central Vermont. But garlic is really the first thing out of the ground. Its little, thin, spiky leaves poking up through the bed of mulch that we put down to give it some protection and hold back early weeds offers the first rays of springtime hope. Those spikes of green declare victory over another long, dark Vermont winter. —*Rob Rinaldi, Jr.*

A LOOK BACK

A Journal

It's easy to romanticize earlier generations of Vermonters – those who lived in a simpler time without all the stresses and challenges of modern life. Heck, if it weren't for worrying about freezing or starving to death in the days before electricity and central heat, or fears of becoming sick or injured in an era before vaccines and anesthesia, those old-timers wouldn't have had a care in the world.

The reality is that our ancestors who made their living off the land worried about exactly the same thing that many of us do today: namely, how to make a living off the land. Mike Batten of East Orange loaned us an old journal kept by farmer Ernest Magoon of West Topsham from 1914 to 1917. What struck me in reading it was that there are no vignettes of rocking peacefully on the porch, pipe in mouth, or idyllic scenes of Magoon taking a beautiful Saturday afternoon off to go canoeing (though he did occasionally fish). No, it's just page after page of cold reality – descriptions of hard work done (how many loads of manure he hauled, how many trees he cut, when he sheared his sheep, how many pounds of milk he brought to the creamery) and a detailed tally of how much money was earned, paid, or borrowed in the process.

Another striking bit: I could not find anywhere where Magoon recorded even a single complaint or grievance. Certainly during those three years, Ernest must have been hobbled by some aches and pains, been disappointed by a harvest, been worried about something. Certainly there must have been some emotions around these two entries from early 1917:

February. 2:
Ernest, Doris, and I was up to see Mother today.
She passed away at 9:15 at night.

February 5:
Ernest, Doris, and I went to Mother's funeral.

But, ever the tough old Yankee, none of those emotions were deemed worthy of sharing, even with himself. In today's age, when so many people want to immediately share their every thought and feeling with the world on social media, it is refreshing to find someone who didn't feel the need to do that.

Reflecting on the true reality that Ernest Magoon and other previous generations lived shouldn't disillusion us; if anything, it should make us feel more connected to them. Rural life is different now, but it hasn't really changed.
—*Patrick White*

October 1915

1 I drew 2 loads of wood to school house for F. E. Bagley

2 Harry and I went over to East Barre Dr. C. Jones paid me $13.28 for 2 sheep & 2 barrels of apples I paid $1.57 for grain rained most all day

3 I went over to C. Button & salted sheep 5 left

4 I paid C. Button $20. I drew 1400 ft of lumber to H. D. Stevens he paid me $108.10 by check and $70. by note to be paid in 60 days Roux Granite Co paid me $40. all to date

5 Rained I sent $154.11 in checks to the Peoples Bank I drew 1 load of wood to school house Frank Mason paid me $1. on wood

6 Pearl Dow paid me $3. for 3 cords of wood W. Gillis 3 cords of wood me $4.50 for

6 I drew 1 load of wood to Frank Mason and 1 load to school house

7 Harry and I drew 2 loads of wood to school house and killed 2 sheep Clarence Moulton stayed here

8 I carried 1 sheep & 1 lamb to Dr. C. Jones 62 & 42 lbs at 14 and 13½ cents per lb he owes me $13.03 I owe F. I. Sargent $6.55 cents for grain

9 Harry B. and I drew 1 load of wood and to school house & 1 to Frank Mason John Bixby paid me 1. he owes me $3.98 for lumber

10 Harry and I went up on Clark place O K Clarence Moulton stayed here all night

11 Harry and I drew 3 loads of wood to Frank Mason Clarence Moulton take 3 pigs of me he is to pay me $6. and a horse rake he take a load of wood to C. H. Martin

Mushroom Cultivation in Vermont

Beneath the forest canopy, inoculated hardwood logs burst with shiitake mushrooms. Mulched paths hold the regal king Stropharia, while toothy lion's mane and fleshy oysters erupt from round, stacked totems of beech and poplar. Even in this managed forest farm, surprise visitors make unannounced appearances – wild golden chanterelles hiding in the shade of the stacked shiitake logs; giant puffballs popping at the periphery.

This landscape shaped my awareness of mycological abundance when I managed an educational agroforestry demonstration site at Cornell University over a decade ago. Forest farming provides a resilient, integrated outdoor system here in the Northeast, but indoor cultivation offers a longer season and increased control over

1000 STONE FARM

Kyle Doda and Betsy Simpson of 1000 Stone Farm.

environmental variables.

Here in Vermont, mushroom cultivation takes place both inside and out, on diversified farms as well as enterprises that focus exclusively on cultivating edible or medicinal fungi. Mushrooms can be nutritious and economically valuable, but new cultivators should have realistic expectations.

Kyle Doda, owner of 1000 Stone Farm in Brookfield – a diversified produce operation that grows shiitake, blue oyster, king oyster, pioppino, lion's mane, and chestnut mushrooms indoors on a year-round basis – provides a balanced assessment: "It is a very tricky enterprise, with many swings in market demand and production, but as we have gained experience, things have gotten better and more sustainable as a part of the farm." Doda notes that Vermont's climate presents mushroom growers with both opportunities and challenges. While our springs and falls offer optimal conditions, he cautions that Vermont winters and summers can create "production situations which need to be creatively solved."

Karen and Brian Wiseman, co-owners of Peaceful Harvest Mushrooms in Worcester, have found a niche in the increasingly competitive market by focusing on cultivating and crafting their own certified organic, Vermont-based, double-extraction mushroom tinctures year-round. Over the past six years, the Wisemans have leveraged their engineering and pharmaceutical industry backgrounds to hone in on regulated, climate-controlled indoor mushroom cultivation systems that can withstand Vermont's unpredictable weather. Karen Wiseman notes that selling fresh cultivated or wild

Karen Theriault Wiseman and Brian Wiseman of Peaceful Harvest Mushrooms

mushrooms as a standalone crop in rural Vermont can be a tough market, but that focusing on tincturing six key species adds value and minimizes risk of loss of a highly perishable fresh product.

Mark Krawczyk, who with Ammy Martinez co-owns Valley Clayplain Forest Farm in New Haven, uses logs from selectively managed timber stands on the farm to grow mushrooms. Over the past five years, Valley Clayplain Forest Farm has inoculated over 1,000 logs, focusing on log harvest and inoculation in late winter "when we aren't as busy with other farm-related activities." Their outdoor mushroom cultivation systems, which have expanded to include shiitake as well as oyster and lion's mane, have proven fruitful, but Krawczyk cautions aspiring new growers not to expect an immediate windfall. "If you want to make a go of it, you need to anticipate losses, knowing that in time, things will get easier," Krawczyk explains. He adds, "But if it's something you want to do, it's worth staying the course and making adjustments as necessary."

Mushroom cultivation is not only a business model in Vermont; it can also be a hobby. For those interested in getting started with outdoor cultivation, whether just one log or one thousand, shiitake is a reliable and proven species, with a history of innovative cultivation in Japan and increasing prominence globally including here in New England.

Minimal space is needed to get started – this spring, my family inoculated 60 locally-sourced beech and hophornbeam logs on our small lot in Richmond village,

Mark Krawczyk and Ammy Martinez of Valley Clayplain Forest Farm

which we laid in crib stacks in a shady, previously neglected corner of our property. As we eagerly await our first flush, our logs are being quietly colonized by shiitake spawn. Once spawn run is complete, shiitake offers a distinct advantage over most other species grown outside: logs can be shocked, or soaked overnight, to force fruitings at predictable intervals.

Mushroom cultivation is a deeply rooted, yet dynamic field, evolving to fit particular niches, environments, and market demands. Yet, despite the remarkable innovation and expertise of growers, it is also a humbling enterprise. We are grateful to Vermont's myriad mushroom growers for their contributions toward freshness, seasonal availability, and consistent yields, diversifying our diets while fostering innovative land use practices. —*Ari Rockland-Miller*

FUNJ SHROOMING COMPANY
Urban Mushroom Farming

Two lefts off Route 7 in St. Albans, tucked behind shopping plazas, is an example of a growing trend in urban farming: the FUNJ Shrooming Company. FUNJ is headquartered in the back few rooms of an old barn, but despite its unassuming location and tiny operational footprint, this youthful company is blooming. Or, rather, *fruiting*.

FUNJ is a craft mushroom-growing farm, part of the emerging industry of small-scale mushroom cultivation. Mushrooms historically have been marginalized as produce because of their short shelf lives and delicate constitutions. Most mushrooms can't sit in a shipping box being jostled for weeks without dissolving into a gooey mess. The species

You can teach an old barn new tricks. Kevin Melman in the retrofitted (with the addition of plastic sheeting and temperature-, humidity-, and airflow-regulation systems) St. Albans barn that is now home to FUNJ.

Agaricus bisporus, which is sold as button or crimini mushrooms when small and portabellas when large, is a common grocery store exception. With this uninspiring choice of mainstream offerings, craft mushroom growers have found a niche by providing quality local-variety mushrooms.

FUNJ founder and owner Kevin Melman currently cultivates oyster mushrooms (*Pleurotus spp.*), from snowy white to eye-catching salmon pink. He also grows bushy clumps of lion's mane (*Hericium erinaceus*). With an exclusively local operation, he ensures that his product is at peak quality when it reaches customers, whether they're chefs, shoppers at local retail stores, or CSA members. Melman finds that many are willing to pay extra for the quality he can provide at a local, small-batch operation. One of his chef regulars told him that opening a new delivery of FUNJ mushrooms "is like Christmas morning."

Melman began FUNJ in August 2019. With an interest in sustainable and urban farming and teenage experience foraging mushrooms, Melman was aware of the growing popularity of small-scale mushroom cultivation. A night of insomnia led to Craigslist browsing and the realization that he could find all the equipment he'd need to start his own operation.

Melman's first harvest was in January 2020. His original business plan was to deliver directly to local chefs, but the pandemic shut down restaurants that March, forcing him to pivot quickly to local grocery stores and farmers' markets to make his early sales. He now provides about half of his mushrooms to chefs and has a growing CSA membership.

Melman grows all his mushrooms following the same careful process, which starts in the outer room with the combining and wetting of his substrate, a high-nutrient 50–50 mix of hardwood sawdust and organic soy hulls, waste products from local organic farmers. The blocks of substrate are packed in biodegradable plastic bags and sterilized using an atmospheric steam sterilizer.

Top: FUNJ grows its mushrooms on a substrate made up of hardwood sawdust and soy hulls from local organic farmers.
Bottom: Packaged for sale to restaurant, farmers' market, local retail and FUNJ CSA customers.

On my visit, I noticed that much of Melman's equipment is on wheels, allowing the steam sterilizer to be carted into the lab with its cargo of ready-to-inoculate substrate. The lab is a small room full of wheeled shelving units packed with substrate blocks. The whole room – even the ceiling – is lined with plastic for easy cleaning. Along the back wall, Melman has a homemade airflow hood capable of removing 99.97 percent of particles in the air larger than 0.3

microns and effectively eliminating the spores of any other fungi that might contaminate his substrate. In front of the hood, he mixes a small amount of mushroom "spawn," the spores that are the pure source of a mushroom species, into his substrate blocks.

Melman grows multiple species and varieties of oyster mushroom because they develop through the next cultivation steps quickly. Substrate inoculated with oyster mushroom spawn sits in the lab for about a week before it is moved to the fruiting room. At this point, fuzzy white halos of the fungus's mycelium appear throughout the substrate.

The fruiting room is an indoor tent with a monster humidifier. I expected it to be warm, but Melman had the heat off when I visited; he told me that most of his mushrooms grow best under 60 degrees. The fruiting room is also packed with wheeled shelves filled with substrate blocks, now with clumps of mushrooms at various stages of growth bursting out of them.

*Golden enoki fruiting (top) and
fresh blue oyster mushrooms.*

In the fruiting room, an oyster mushroom block will need another week of growth before it is ready to be "initiated"; Melman slits the plastic and lets fresh air into the substrate. The first sign that mushrooms are starting is a "bubbling up" of what is called "primordium" near the slit. The primordium will turn into baby-sized mushrooms ("pins") at around day 10 in the fruiting room. After that, the mushrooms double in size every day, and Melman typically harvests them by the end of their second week. The spent substrate is saved and sold as compost.

After harvest, Melman considers his mushrooms to have a one-week shelf life. He aims to deliver mushrooms within a day of cutting. Before I left, he gave me a few blue oyster mushrooms. They were the fattest, most colorful oysters I'd ever seen, and when we added them to pizza a day later, they had a richer umami flavor than the oyster mushrooms we buy from the store.

Melman sees opportunity in the growing trend of home food delivery and emphasizes connecting directly with customers. "CSAs are the most beautiful thing for a small farmer," he says and he plans to expand his own program. Melman also plans to increase his variety of products by adding outdoor hoops where he can inoculate logs for shiitake mushrooms (*Lentinula edodes*). Shiitake are harder to farm because they grow slowly, with an eight-week cycle, and the inoculated logs take up space in the meantime. And space is a precious commodity in urban settings. He's also considering medicinal reishi (*Ganoderma lingzhi*), hen-of-the-woods (*Grifola frondosa*), and enoki (*Flammulina velutipes*), all known to be slow or tricky to cultivate.

With a small physical footprint, a mushroom farm can provide quality produce in any location following sustainable methods. Melman's primary food mushroom, the oyster, is also a star in mycoremediation, where mushrooms are used to efficiently break down otherwise intractable waste. Mushroom cultivation synthesizes urban farming, sustainable food production, and mycoremediation. The net result is that a mushroom farm can use waste discarded from other agricultural industries (like hardwood sawdust and soy hulls), make nutritious food in a small area, and produce useable compost as a byproduct. It's no wonder young agriculture entrepreneurs like Melman see mushroom farming as the future. —*Rachel Mirus*

Growing Mushrooms at Home

Like commercial craft mushroom farming, home mushroom growing is a rising trend. The easiest way to break into growing your own mushrooms is to order a grow kit. Many mushroom cultivators also offer home kits, including FUNJ Shrooming.

"Kids love them," said owner Kelvin Melman, and my two-year-old was indeed excited by the two kits I ordered. The kits weren't much to look at: two compact cardboard boxes completely filled with brown substrate encased in clear plastic. One was white lion's mane and the other pink oyster mushrooms. The pink oyster mushroom block arrived plain brown, but even through the plastic I could see that the lion's mane had begun making primordia – small white bubbles of mycelium that will become the mushrooms.

Instructions for kit care are simple. Leaving the substrate block in the box, we made an X-cut through the plastic with a clean knife. (This is easier said than done with a toddler head-butting in.) The sudden access to fresh air stimulates the fungi to fruit, and the mushrooms will push right through the plastic slits. The budding mushrooms need fresh air, but they also shouldn't be allowed to dry out. To keep humidity up in the box, I flipped up the flaps and taped them to prevent too much air circulation.

The instructions said to spritz the cut plastic three to five times a day until the primordia appear.

An illustration of the pink oyster mushrooms.

We started out spritzing and then had the bright idea to move our kits to an unused shower, along with our small humidifier. At first, we over-humidified, so when I checked on the kits the next day a wall of fog greeted me when I opened the shower door. Everything was dripping with condensation. Mushrooms need humidity, but water droplets sitting on the young mushrooms can kill them. So we found a humidity setting that kept the

ART & PHOTO BY RACHEL MIRUS

Mushrooms from our kit at two weeks (pink oyster left, white lion's mane right).

shower steamy, but not dripping.

At first I was worried about the condition of the kits, because the shipper left the boxes without notice during a cold snap and they sat outside for an unknown amount of time. It quickly became clear the lion's mane had come through its shipping ordeal, but the oyster mushroom substrate initially appeared inert. While the lion's mane primordia began doubling and tripling in size into full-fledged mushrooms, it was over a week before I noticed small salmon-pink blotches on the oyster mushroom block.

Once the pink oyster mushroom primordia appeared, though, they raced to catch up with the lion's mane and within two days turned into "pins," or miniature mushrooms. At this stage young mushrooms double in size daily. My daughter began asking to see the mushrooms multiple times a day.

When to harvest home-grown mushrooms depends on personal preference. The instructions recommend picking lion's mane after they develop stubby hairs but before the hairs reach a full centimeter in length. Oyster mushrooms should be cut while the cap edge still curls under.

The FUNJ kits can produce up to three batches of mushrooms, if they are kept in humid conditions. After that, the substrate and the plastic casing can be composted. And even after that, Melman mentions that it's worth checking the compost area – mushrooms can pop up when least expected.
—*Rachel Mirus*

JL DAMON

NOVEMBER

November

I've wondered when I stopped being a summer person and became a resident. (Not a "real Vermonter" – not opening that can of controversy.) *Summer people* – it's a term with moralistic overtones. Fair-weather friends; they skip the character-building winter. Where will they be when your car gets stuck in the mud or you have an ice dam on your roof and water is running down into your kitchen? Summer people, living in summer houses.

That's what we did, my parents, brother, and sister and I: driving up the sweaty East Coast, till at last, in the gathering dusk, we'd burst out of the car, breathe the cool night air, and rush in, our trial-by-turnpike rewarded by that inimitable smell: old wood, decomposed mice, and mold – the very elixir of peace.

It felt like home to me long before it actually was. But when did that happen? Was it the March I came up, earlier than anyone in the family had, and sat a foot from the woodstove? I was playing my recorder when a small mouse emerged from behind the woodbox and came to sit on the toe of my boot.

Or was it the April when, after I'd built my own house, there'd been a sudden thaw, and commuting home from work, I took the quick way down a back road and the car sank up to its axles in mud and I had to walk the four miles home in the dark? Singing – in order to ward off any bears or skunks who might be waking up and stumbling across my path: battle hymns, of course.

But then came the first November. It's so quiet in November. Different from the quiet of deep midwinter, when nothing can speak. Now, it's as if it's chosen not to. If it hasn't already, it will soon snow, and when the whiteness blankets everything it is so silent that, lying in bed in the dark, all you hear is the tide of your own blood in your ears, as if everything in the universe has condensed to the single point that is you, darkest implosion of your most solipsistic dream.

It's in winter that you're lost without other people. In summer you can forget that you need them, so gentle does the world seem on sunny days: the trees listing in the wind, scripting their eloquent speech against the sky. Woe betide the person in winter who has no neighbors, no one to call upon if your battery is dead or you get stuck in a snowdrift.

That fall I first stayed on, awaiting a manuscript that my neighbor Porky Senecal threatened to drive down in his son-in-law's lavender school bus to Manhattan to fetch from my recalcitrant editor (he was going to "take care of that woman"), the water had been shut off so I took baths in the brook through November, and when I couldn't stand it anymore took showers then at friends' houses; every day I carried water up from the village for cooking and washing.

I was alone, but not lonely. I worked on another book during the day, oblivious of my actual surroundings to the degree that once, rereading the line, "A knock came on the door," I got up out of my chair and went to open it. If I wanted company I'd go down the hill, visit Eleanor Burroughs, who fed me doughnuts while we played Yahtzee. Visit Tom Watkin or Lyle Shepperson and Annick Leymarie, who'd stop what they were doing and make coffee. Hike up to Sunny Johnson's to get honey. And in the evening go to the Carriers' barn, so warm and welcoming in the early winter dark, and walk back and forth with David from barn to milkhouse as he emptied the milking machines that looked like giant tea kettles into the bulk tank.

Not one of those folks is here anymore. Several have died, the rest have moved away, but I still remember how, when I walked down our winding road lit by moonlight, I'd stop and look across the wide expanse of snow-smoothed fields and the lighted squares of windows were like beacons across a body of water. I'd continue on down and through the village, the snow squeaking as I trod on it, gaze through the uncurtained windows and see my friends and neighbors, or know who was inside if I couldn't see them. I could knock on any door at all and it would be opened and I would be greeted warmly and asked to come inside. —*Kathryn Kramer*

Deer Season Dud

While October is a very defined transition month in Vermont, November is usually more of a waiting period. Lake and river temperatures are a bit too chilly to enjoy a paddle or swim, and summer biking and hiking have mostly come to an end. Winter activities are on stand-by, as a solid snowpack does not usually come until the end of the month, if it comes at all. Deer hunters are eager to see snow on the ground because deer are much easier to track, plus they stand out against a white backdrop. Deep snow also means deer need to forage harder for a meal and are prone to travel more to find food.

Unfortunately for hunters and winter enthusiasts, things didn't work out this year. Cold temperatures and snow were tough to come by in November 2020, as the late summer and early fall pattern of warm and dry conditions prevailed through much of the month. The mean monthly temperature for Burlington was well above normal, with the mean high temperature running around 6 degrees higher than usual. Although a record low was recorded in Montpelier at the start of the month, record-breaking warmth through the middle more than counteracted that brief cold snap. Montpelier observed daily record high temperatures between November 8 and 11 as highs topped out in the lower 70s each day. About a third less precipitation than normal fell throughout the month, as well. —*Christopher Kurdek, Fairbanks Museum and Planetarium*

Ralph Hewett of Woodbury with his 189-pound, 8-pointer.

RALPH HEWETT

20 YEARS OF DEER SEASON OPENING WEEKEND WEATHER NOTES
(The second Saturday of November, southwestern Vermont.)

2001	cold, snowy
2002	6" snow, bitter
2003	cold, blustery
2004	cool, snowflakes
2005	sun, 60s
2006	sun, 60s
2007	cold, wind
2008	drizzle, 60s
2009	overcast, 60s
2010	sun, 60s
2011	cool blustery then warmup
2012	cool then stupid hot
2013	warm, 60s
2014	cold, highs in 30s
2015	cool, 40s
2016	cool, 40s
2017	cold, 10-30 degrees
2018	cold, 30s
2019	abnormally cold, highs in 20s
2020	cool, 40s

JEFFERY DAVIS @WHITETAILVT FACEBOOK GROUP

CAMERA 1   22 NOV 2020 08:04 am

Above: Generally warm, snow-free conditions through mid- to late-November benefitted deer more than deer hunters.

NATURE NOTES

A Year of Winter Finches Ahead

In November 2020, it was predicted that the finch species that nest and winter here would be joined by an unusually large number of their more boreal brethren. Winter finches rely on tree seeds in winter, and when these are scarce, the birds will be on the move. Most of these finches usually come south, but some species, like white-winged crossbills and sometimes pine siskins, may move east or west rather than south when food is scarce.

It's easy to foretell the status of the boreal seed crop by mid-summer, well before the seeds have matured, by the number of visible cones on tamaracks, the spruces, and hemlocks. White pine seeds take two years to mature, so estimates can be made of the seed crop both for the coming winter and the next one by counting the new small cones and the larger, nearly mature ones.

You might think that a poor seed crop, though good for us birdwatchers, would be terrible for the finches, but tree seed crops have always had big ups and downs and the birds that depend on them are used to and good at being nomads. In many years, Christmas bird counters in Algonquin Provincial Park in Ontario have found fewer than a hundred finches of all stripes, while almost 13,000 were counted in 1989.

Thanks to The Finch Network for these forecasts. —*Virginia Barlow*

PINE SISKIN

Pine siskins nest to the north of us and they often come this far south in winter unless there's a big crop of conifer seeds back home. We can expect to see more of them than usual this winter.

REDPOLL

The birch and alder seeds that redpolls like are in short supply this year and because of that, many redpolls have already shown up here and more are likely to arrive. They'll eat goldenrod and aster seeds until the snow is deep. When there's an exceptionally large crop of paper birch seeds, redpolls may stay put in the north. [2]

RED CROSSBILL

Perhaps later in winter, when they have finished off the supply of white pine seeds, red crossbills will head south. Typically, most of them don't migrate. [3]

N. LEWIS/NPS

MATLACHA/FLICKR

DON FAULKNER

ANDY REAGO & CHRISSY MCCLARREN

C. WATTS

WHITE-WINGED CROSSBILL

We might well see a lot of white-winged crossbills this winter because spruce and tamarack cone crops are poor. [4]

AMERICAN GOLDFINCH

Many more American gold-finches winter in our area now than in the past, perhaps because of the ever-growing number of well-stocked birdfeeders to be found. Absent birdfeeders, they, too, rely on tree seeds in winter, when thistles and the many other composites that they eat in summer are buried in snow. By late February or March even the boreal stay-at-homes may head our way if they run out of food. [5]

CEPHAS/CC

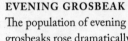

CEPHAS/CC

EVENING GROSBEAK

The population of evening grosbeaks rose dramatically during the severe spruce budworm outbreak in the 1970s and '80s and has recently increased again – along with a new outbreak of spruce budworms. Both adults and chicks eat budworm caterpillars in the summer, but in winter it's mostly deciduous tree seeds from sugar maple, box elder, and ash. They may deplete this resource and show up here in large numbers. [6]

PURPLE FINCH

Current spruce budworm outbreaks in the north have enabled purple finches, like the evening grosbeaks, to fatten up many nestlings. There may be too many purple finches in the north for the available food supply. [7]

PINE GROSBEAK

Because there's a good supply of mountain ash seeds (it seems that the birds spit out the berry skins and much of the pulp), pine grosbeaks are likely to stay in the boreal forest, which they often do. They don't migrate unless they have to. [8]

RON KNIGHT

KENT MCFARLAND

Wingless Winter Moths

On even the darkest, coldest days of November, there are still signs of lepidopteran life if one looks closely enough. Two moth species of the genus *Operophtera*, known as the Bruce spanworm moth *(O. bruceata)* and the introduced winter moth *(O. brumata)* manage to survive in conditions that would kill most other moths and butterflies.

Incredibly, these moths can fly in temperatures as low as 27 degrees F. How do they do it? Morphology (the study of the form, shape and structure of living organisms) appears to provide the answer.

The male Bruce spanworm moth has one of the lowest wing loads (total weight divided by wing area) of any moth measured. This both reduces the number of wing beats and lowers the energetic cost required to sustain flight. These little moths also have one of the highest flight muscle to body size ratios. These surprisingly bulky muscles are able to compensate for the reduced muscle contraction associated with cold temperatures and continue to generate enough tension to power each wingbeat.

The female Bruce spanworm moth has also adapted to survive in low autumn temperatures, but in a completely different way. Females are flightless and have no wings at all. When they emerge in October and November, they laboriously crawl up the lower trunk of a host tree, where they solicit flying males with a chemical cocktail of pheromones.

It's likely that these adaptations occurred in response to predation. By late October and November, most of the insectivorous birds have migrated south and bats have migrated or gone into hibernation. With their most significant moth predators out of the picture, these moths have free reign of Vermont's forests. —*Kent McFarland*

Above: Operophtera bruceata, *in flagrante delicto.*

CROSSING PATHS

Bones of a woolly mammoth unearthed in Mount Holly in 1848 during the construction of a railroad line from Rutland to Burlington ended up scattered in several places, including at the Hood Museum at Dartmouth College. Nearly 170 years later, Nathaniel Kitchel, a post-doc at Dartmouth, found some of this mammoth's bones at an off-site museum storage facility and sent a fragment of the animal's rib bone to be radiocarbon dated. He found that it lived about 12,800 years ago.

Previously thought to have been extinct for a longer time in the Northeast due to environmental changes, it now seems that this elephant coexisted with this area's first human residents. Kitchel and his Dartmouth colleague Jeremy

MAURICIO ANTÓN

DeSilva, an anthropology professor, have no evidence that humans eliminated mammoths here, although that appears to have been the case in other parts of the world.

Woolly mammoths are the best known of any prehistoric animal because of the many frozen specimens that have been discovered. They lived on Wrangel Island until about 4,000 years ago and are most closely related to present-day Asian elephants. Another analysis of the bone suggests that this very large vegetarian fed on spruce and alder. —*Virginia Barlow*

JERRY HAM

BIRDFEEDING IS OKAY. Those of us who fret about leaving chickadees without seeds in the birdfeeder when we go away in winter can calm down, according to a new study. Thirty years ago, scientists removed birdfeeders that had been faithfully filled for 25 years and found that the neglected, formerly pampered chickadees survived just as well as their unfed cohorts. More recently, experimenters clipped the wing feathers from some chickadees and left others unclipped. The clipped birds could fly but the change in wing loading increased the amount of energy needed for flight. But chickadees whose wing feathers were clipped didn't come to feeders for handouts more often as you might expect; they were okay at finding food without human assistance.

Birdfeeding may have unintended negative effects, such as increasing disease transmission, but even if it's not a necessity, overall it does contribute to winter survival and reproductive success among the bird species that eat from feeders. —*Virginia Barlow*

AT HOME

❦

Making Raw Hide

Above: A deer hide that's in the process of being de-haired.
Note the deer ticks that are embedded in it.
Below: Rawhide cordage.

It's important to most deer hunters to use as much of the animal as they can. But there are only so many tanned deer hides you can have in your house or camp. An alternative use for the hide is to process it into rawhide, which has myriad uses, from strapping to parchment to dog chew toys. The hair removal process is relatively simple:

STEP 1: Remove the hide from the deer (the sooner you do this, the easier it will be). Once removed, scrape off all the meat and fat. You can use a commercial fleshing knife, which has a sharp edge for cutting and a dull edge for pushing, or make do with a sharp knife and a blunt object, like a tablespoon or a piece of slate. It's important to get all the flesh off, though you needn't fuss about removing every last bit of membrane.

STEP 2: Prepare a de-hairing soak by adding hydrated lime (calcium hydroxide) to 10-15 gallons of water. You can buy lime at any masonry supply store. Add one cup of lime for every gallon of water. (And wear gloves when you're handling the lime.) Mix well and add the fleshed hide. Cover it with rocks or firewood so it's completely submerged. Let it sit for one week.

STEP 3: Remove the hide from the tub. If it's ready, the hair will pull out in clumps. If not, add more lime and soak some more (it's hard to overdo it). Using a scraper, remove all the hair. When finished, turn the hide over and remove any stray bits of flesh you might have missed in the fleshing process. Then neutralize the lime by rinsing the hide in running water for two days or by soaking for eight hours in a baking soda solution. (Use two cups of baking soda for every five gallons of water.) When done, stretch the hide in a cool, arid place and allow to dry. —*Dave Mance III*

Venison Osso Buco with chef Jessee Lawyer

Jessee Lawyer is an enrolled citizen of the Missisquoi Abenaki Band out of Swanton, Vermont. While his Native roots don't particularly influence his cooking at Sweetwaters American Bistro in Burlington, where he's Executive Chef, they have a huge impact on the cooking he does at home. Foods like bear fat maple popcorn (a favorite of his son's), three sisters stew, and osso buco are staples at Lawyer's home table. "I like low and slow dishes, especially during hunting season in the fall and winter when you want something warm and hearty to warm you up," he says.

So what makes Abenaki food Abenaki food? Lawyer says it's all about the things that were specifically used by his ancestors. "What makes indigenous food is the cultivars – the wild game and wild edibles that were indigenous to this area prior to colonization," he says.

These things differ from region to region and tribe to tribe. "There could be corn, beans, and squash [in Vermont], and then corn, beans, and squash in the Southwest, but they're different varieties and they have their own wild game and wild edibles to go along with that," Lawyer explains. Moose, bear, deer, ducks, geese, and small game fish, along with berries, wild greens, mushrooms, and sunchokes are just a few typical elements of Abenaki cooking.

While some native chefs choose to cook without using any "colonized ingredients" (think flour and cream), Lawyer prefers a broader approach. "It helps my cooking to just be free and cook what I want while keeping the Abenaki ingredients at the center of the plate," he says.

However, Lawyer is quick to note that neither way is right or wrong. "I think within the spectrum of indigenous cuisine, from cooking-to-decolonize to contemporary indigenous cuisine, there's value in both."

If your mouth is watering after hearing some of the meals that grace Lawyer's table, the recipe at right will let you try one of his dishes in your own kitchen: Osso Buco with Grits and Fiddlehead Gremolata.

—*Lettie Stratton*

OSSO BUCO

1 venison shank cut into three 2-inch pieces
Flour for dredging
½ cup bear fat or another high-temp oil
1 carrot
1 small onion
2 celery stalks
1 bay leaf
Thyme
Rosemary
Parsley
2 Tbsp. tomato paste
¾ cup of wine
3 cups of chicken, beef, or game stock
Salt and pepper

FIDDLEHEAD GREMOLATA

2 cups fiddleheads, blanched
1 clove garlic
1 cup parsley
1 lemon, zest & juice
Salt/pepper to taste
3 Tbsp. bear fat or olive oil
Pinch red pepper flakes

Preheat oven to 300 degrees. Heat bear grease in Dutch oven over medium-high heat. Salt shanks well and dredge in flour to coat. Brown them well. Remove and set aside. Add the carrot, onion, and celery and sauté until slightly browned, about 7 minutes. Pour in the wine and use it to deglaze the pot. When it comes to a boil, add the stock, herbs, and tomato paste and bring to a simmer. Return the shanks to the pot and turn to coat. Cover the pot and move to the oven. Cook until tender, around 2 to 4 hours depending on the size of deer. Serve venison on top of grits and garnish with the gremolata.

Can Deer See Colors?

While pondering the complete collection of hunting catalogues you've accumulated over the past four months, you might find yourself wondering why during archery season, clothing companies try to sell you camo patterns that make you invisible to deer, but then during rifle season, the same companies try to sell you glowing blaze orange suits – but don't worry, deer can't see colors anyway.

Over the years I've had hunters tell me that deer can too see color, and that the conventional deer-are-color-blind thing is a white lie dreamed up by well-meaning government officials who were tired of hunters shooting one another. (There is overwhelming evidence that wearing bright colors during rifle season saves human lives.) On the other hand, there's a similar conspiracy theory that holds that maybe it's just the clothing companies that are blurring the truth here, as it's in their best interest to sell you two sets of hunting clothes, one for each season.

Fortunately there's a significant scientific record we can turn to to separate rumor from fact. Deer vision has been studied on a molecular level using DNA cloning, electroretinography, and scanning electron microscopy; it's also been studied in more old school ways using positive and negative stimulus tests on live, captive animals. What researchers have found is that deer can see colors, though they don't experience them in the same way we do. They can pick out short- (blue) and middle- (green) wavelength colors, but they're less sensitive to long wavelength colors such as red and orange. "They're essentially red-green color blind," said Brian Murphy, a wildlife biologist and the CEO of Quality Deer Management Association. Murphy participated in research done at the University of Georgia in the 1990s, where different wavelengths of light were emitted into the eyes of sedated deer and researchers measured the deer's brainstem responses.

If you're a hunter or nature photographer who's trying to be inconspicuous in the woods, it seems that the worst color you can wear is blue. Deer eyes lack the ultraviolet light filter that human and other longer-lived animals have, which means they see blues and other short-wavelength colors about twenty times better than we do. "Blue jeans are much more vivid to a deer than blaze orange," said Murphy. Color-conscious outdoorspeople should be aware, too, that clothing companies and laundry detergent manufacturers often add UV dyes and enhancers to their garments and cleaning products, so clothing can take on an ultraviolet glow regardless of color or pattern.

The takeaway seems to be that there's nothing conspiratorial going on when a fish and wildlife department urges hunters to wear orange – in fact, hunters should feel free to wear orange during archery season, too. If you're more inclined towards cool colors, avoid blue and anything that's UV brightened. And if you're a young hunter feeling overwhelmed by the advice being dispensed by clothing manufacturers and the self-appointed experts in hunting magazines, keep in mind the big picture here. A deer's sense of smell may be 1,000 times better than ours, their hearing is at least as good as ours, and as a prey species, their brains have been hardwired over millennia to pick up on the slightest movement in the woods and associate it with danger. In short, what color your hunting clothes are is pretty insignificant in the grand scheme of things. —*Dave Mance III*

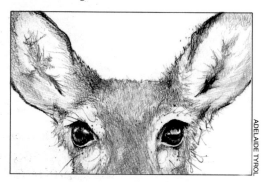

ADELAIDE TYROL

VERMONT'S 2020 DEER SEASON BY THE NUMBERS

Reported deer kill:
18,991

Previous year's (2019)
reported deer kill:
16,550

Number of antlered bucks
reported in 2020:
9,256

Number of adult does:
7,892

Number of fawns:
1,843

Percentage of harvest that occurred
during the new novice season:
1

Percentage of the harvest that
occurred during the new October
muzzleloader season:
10

Percentage of the harvest that
occurred during bow season:
32

Percentage of the harvest that
occurred on youth weekend:
6

Percentage of the harvest that
occurred during December
muzzleloader season:
14

Percentage of the harvest that
occurred during rifle season:
37

Average number of hours hunters
spent afield in rifle season:
44

Average number of deer sightings
per 10 hours of hunting:
2.0

Average time spent hunting before seeing a buck:
36 HOURS

Number of towns that had deer
harvest totals among their 10 best:
29

Number of towns that had deer
harvest totals among their 10 worst:
24

Number of reported deer exceeding 200 pounds:
122

Heaviest deer weighed on a
certified scale (in pounds):
263

Number of licensed hunters:
85,050

Estimated number of active hunters:
72,000

Percentage increase in hunting
license sales from previous year:
10

Number of individual successful hunters:
15,053

Approximate number of venison
servings generated by the harvest:
3.8 MILLION

It's the People You Know

The absurdity of containing a hunting camp fire with buckets of water should have occurred to me sooner than it did. But it didn't. It may have been because of an unwillingness to believe what was happening. Or a reluctance to credit the possibility I could be misled by desperation. Or maybe alcohol was a contributing factor. It doesn't matter. In the end there was only a hole in the ground where there once was a camp, and a consuming sense of loss and dread. Days later I found the words I needed in a novel by Jeffrey Lent, *Lost Nation*, and copied them down in a notebook of phone numbers, appointments and quotes: "He pushed on knowing the worst lay ahead. That fact alone delighted him, now faced with the worst, he had the opportunity to wrestle himself from it." Even so, as Lent acknowledged, it is "a grim delight."

The fire occurred on the eve of opening day of deer season – a time in November when seasons past camp had been full of friends looking forward to spending some time together in the woods and in a place unlike any other: no electricity, no indoor plumbing, heated only with wood and lit with only gas and kerosene lights. But change had been in the air. Over the prior few seasons the numbers of campers had dwindled until there were only two and then one. On Friday I went into camp with the dog and high hopes. It was possible that someone might be coming in later to stay the night, but in any event, the camp was ready and stocked with a minimum of three days of food. The woods were wet from days of rain and snow, and if no tracking snow came in overnight, at least the ground would be quiet and soft for opening day.

Once settled inside camp there were passing bouts of nostalgia, but I was feeling content: the camp was warm, the wood box was full and I had gathered enough water to do the after-supper dishes and make coffee in the morning. An hour or so before dark, Fast Eddy and a pal stopped by on their way to his camp on the mountain. We had a drink over the hope of eating venison before the week was out, and they were soon on their way, leaving me with my newspaper and books in a one-room camp that was feeling large and regretfully empty.

I still hadn't decided what to have for supper when Savoy and Val showed up. Val whipped up a cocktail sauce to go with the cooked shrimp she had brought from home, and we sat at the table and drank and ate and talked about the out-of-the-way places we had been – the trails, the streams and ponds – occasionally turning to the topographical maps that were mixed within pictures of people who had spent time in camp and now looked up at us from under a sheet of table-top Plexiglas that had been a fixture long as I can remember.

It was nearly eleven when they left. I watched their lights flash through the trees as they went down the trail, grateful for their visit and looking forward to the mid-week ride that Savoy and I were planning to take through the woods on the East Branch Road. Their departure suddenly left me feeling tired and I lay down on the bunk, leaving the overhead gas light lit by way of reminding myself to get up and feed the stove before turning in for the night. I woke up startled. The camp was full of smoke that was making my eyes smart and water. At first I thought the smoke was coming from the stovepipe; we had had problems before with the draft on the cook stove, drawing smoke up and out from a low burning fire. But this time the draft wasn't the problem. Once I got to the stove I saw flames coming out of a smoldering hole in the floorboard about the size of a dishpan. I grabbed the fire extinguisher that we kept behind the door and doused the flames. The fire went out as fast as a candle. But the smoke continued curling up and around the rear base of the stove. I kept pouring water that I had gathered earlier in pails until the pails were empty and the floorboards were still smoking. I don't remember how many trips I made to the brook, or when it became evident I didn't have enough pails, enough water, enough stamina, enough of anything to make a difference. Let it be, let it go, I told myself. At some point I stopped carrying water and the camp burned down.

I walked out of the woods while the fire was still burning under a tin roof that had collapsed and buckled. I saw no need to call the fire department; nor did I want to. What's the point? The camp was gone; why pretend it could be any different? By the time I drove downtown, I realized I should report the fire; a realization that became increasingly urgent when I walked into the Brighton Garage and told Craig what had happened, that all was lost. "Use our phone," he said. "You've got to report it. It's the law."

I waited until after the fire trucks went by before going back into the woods and parking on the high road, about a 15-minute walk to camp. A scene of twisted metal, smoldering timbers and an enormous bed of cherry red embers glowed where there had once been a cord of dry firewood. A crowd of Mountain Street neighbors were gathering, and Fast Eddy and his brother, Beau, were using Vice Grips to pull sheets of hot roofing tin out of the ashes, offering help to build again. I left a short while later and went home with questions that had no answers. Rose arrived with a bottle of whisky, and invited me back to her house for supper.

I went back into the woods Sunday afternoon with a rake, on the off chance I might find something worth salvaging. At first I didn't see her, sitting over by the stone fire circle smoking a cigarette. Years ago we shared a short marriage and managed to remain close friends after it ended. Her presence alone might have sent me into a tailspin, but I had the rake and there were all those ashes. "You going to take anything, a keepsake?" she said, before announcing she was going to take one of the camp stones lying about to put in her garden. "I have a lot of good memories about this place," she said, allowing a moment of silence to come and go before adding something I had never heard her say before. "This is where I fell in love with you."

I turned away and stared back into the gaping hole as if to see where everything – the stove, the bunks, the table with the railroad caboose armchairs were before the fire. I didn't want her to see me cry, or come to grips with any feelings I was having. Once out of the woods we took a ride, had a long talk, and she fed me a supper of exceptionally good leftovers. I drove home feeling better than expected. It's the people you know who will save you and make life at its darkest less grim. —*Paul Lefebvre*

DAVE HOEFLER

DOUG MCGRADY

Ginseng – An Eastern Forest Legacy

Fifty years ago I acquired 10 acres on a steep Vermont hillside that lends itself to many uses. Over that time it has heated my house, cooked my meals, and provided an excess of maple syrup. I had occasionally heard about a small but valuable herb called ginseng, and read up on it in the Foxfire books. The impression I got was that my hillside was a habitat the plant might like, but for 20 years I could never find it.

When my son Ben got to be about nine years old he read the Foxfire books, too, and he asked me about ginseng. I told him it seemed like we might have some but I could never find it. A week or so later he yelled to me "Come out and look at something, Dad." He had found it. Not one but a dozen or more plants and he had marked each one with a colored tape circle so I would avoid it while working in the woods.

Four hundred years ago, before the major changes that Europeans brought to our forests, this unpretentious but abundant little herb called ginseng was already valued by Native Americans for its healing qualities. Amazingly, even though it can usually only live under a full deciduous forest canopy, ginseng has survived the many cycles of cutting and recovery that have taken place over the past century. It has also survived the heavy foraging that has come because of ginseng's commercial value, though over-harvesting has made the plant increasingly harder to find.

A "CURE-ALL"

There are two ginseng species in eastern North American forests. American ginseng *(Panax quinquefolius)* grows a root that is highly valued medicinally; *Panax trifolius* (better known as dwarf ginseng) has a much smaller root and hence less value. They are both herbaceous perennials with palmate compound leaves that each have five leaflets.

The genus name *Panax*, like "panacea," is from a

Greek word meaning cure-all. Chinese records indicate that ginseng has been in use for over 5,000 years for its medicinal virtues, in infusions, as a food like a vegetable, and as powdered or extract additives in Korea and China. Studies have corroborated some of the claimed benefits, including improved concentration and mental performance, lowered blood sugar, improved sexual performance, and strengthened immune system.

GROWING YOUR OWN GINSENG

There are two primary ways to grow ginseng. Cultivated roots can be grown in as little as five years with sufficient fertilizer and care: the large acreages covered with slated shading or fabric frames look, at first, like tobacco farms. But ginseng feeds heavily, and ginseng monocultures create the same soil and growing problems that all monocultures create. Commodity ginseng must also compete with large farms in China, which affect US markets.

It's probably safe to say that most of the ginseng harvested commercially in Vermont is wild simulated, a propagation method whereby the plants are grown in a natural forest environment. New and stratified ginseng seeds are available, as well as young roots for propagation. In addition to shaded forest soils, good drainage is necessary. Ginseng does not like soggy ground. Seeds are dispersed by hand and get little help during their growth. Sometimes fertilizer is used, but not fungicides or pesticides. Once established, the plants should be left on their own for 7 to 10 years. The resulting roots are considered to be superior to cultivated ginseng. While attrition from deer, rodents, competition, disease, and weather will reduce the population of plants, the biggest threat usually comes from thieves. Deer will nip off the tops and set the plants back but the incipient terminal bud will usually sprout again the next season. Rodents will eat the seeds before they even emerge.

While long a dominant supplier of ginseng, one thing that China doesn't have is the natural environment the US does for growing wild ginseng. Their forests were stripped long ago for agriculture and wood, so North America has an edge when it comes to growing wild ginseng because our forests have been allowed to recover.

WILDCRAFTING

Hunting for wild ginseng is still practiced in Vermont. While it's not as big a cultural thing here as it is in Appalachia, 'sangers have been hunting roots here for generations. Folktales and stories of the biggest root or the biggest patch abound. Current prices for fresh, exportable wild ginseng are between $500 and $600 a pound, so there is an economic incentive.

Ginseng gathering and sales are controlled by the individual states, which all must conform to CITIES (Convention on International Trade in Endangered Species) regulations in order to monitor the health of ginseng populations. Licenses are required and regulations are in effect regarding how harvesting is done. In Vermont, it can be dug only from August to October. Landowner permission is required, and all plants harvested must have three or more prongs and the seeds must be replanted in the same ground. Finally, the roots must be presented for inspection if sold. No collecting is allowed in parks or wildlife management areas; a different permit is required for dealers along with record-keeping requirements.

In general, the older generation of ginseng collectors is not being replaced by younger generations. Differing interests and the scarcity of plants probably explain this. On a positive note, fewer people can identify ginseng when they see it, which should reduce the risks of theft when starting your own wild-simulated patches.

For 300 years in this country ginseng has been a real contributor to our health and income. This little herb could stand your help in preserving and repopulating its former territory. —*Mike Hebb*

Ginseng Identification

AMERICAN GINSENG thrives in the shade of a full deciduous forest canopy, under the likes of maple, ash, and beech. Its seeds require two seasons to germinate and the plants mature in four years. The first year it has a single compound leaf referred to as a prong with three leaflets. The second year it will have five leaflets.

At maturity it reaches a foot or more in height, will have three to four prongs, and will bear fruit. The prongs originate from a single point on the stem. The three to five leaflets on each prong originate from one point as well. Mature plants produce a flowering umbel on a central stem.

American ginseng seedling

Above: American ginseng flowering, July, West Hartford, Vt. Right: Ginseng berries.

Hunt the hardwood forests with plenty of shade and mature canopies. Wild ginseng is said to like land that has never been cultivated. Where you find one, look for others. —*Mike Hebb*

Insect pollination results in a cluster of green berries that ripen to red by late August. Each berry contains one to three seeds. This is a good time to spot them, though they are similar to jack in the pulpit berries.

The berries drop by October to restart the cycle. They may roll downhill a short way but seldom fall far from the parent. Over decades, the new plants spread slowly. But since a ginseng plant can live as long as 100 years, this results in a local community of many generations all living together. To the early diggers this was a gold mine, and few large groups still exist.

To find ginseng, go out in August and look for the clusters of red berries and leaf structures matching this photo, or go in October and look for the yellow leaves still on their stems.

On Foraging

One of the pleasures of foraging for hard-to-find plants and fungi is the treasure hunt quality of it all. An experienced 'sanger will see the wisdom in Mike Hebb's advice (prior page) to look for forestland that has never been cultivated, and to search hardwood forests with deep shade. But to many, it will all sound unsatisfyingly vague.

The more you observe practiced foragers – and the more you forage yourself – you'll come to see that the hunt is guided by a fusion of contemporary and traditional knowledge. A good forager enters the forest with a logical foundation of information, but then the intuitive knowledge kicks in. They'll walk and walk, covering a lot of ground fast because it doesn't seem right. Then they'll get to a spot that feels ginseng-ey, or mushroom-ey, and slow down, and there it'll be. It's not dissimilar to the way a practiced fisherman can read water he's never fished before and intuit his way to trout.

The reason this sounds annoyingly mystic is that most of us were taught to accomplish tasks through concrete steps – the means to a specific end. We were given a blueprint, knowledge was doled out brick by brick, and we built our intellect like you'd assemble a wall. But this kind of thinking doesn't translate all that well in the natural world. It's agrarian thinking – it's why our forefathers and mothers cut down the forests and turned them into land they could cultivate. "Take this seed. Now do this and this and this and you'll have food." That order, that blueprint, was easy to practice and share. The native peoples didn't think like this – "go to where the deer are; go to where this plant grows" – they'd honed their hunter-gatherer minds in an intuitive way.

My partner's a teacher and she says that "synthesis" is a buzzword in education these days; basically, they're trying to build and strengthen intuition in kids. They want to keep giving them bricks, but they don't want them to build walls that end up obscuring their views. Our European notions of learning have taught us to value order over feeling, but when a place feels ginseng-ey, it's not that the forager's mind has stopped working well, it's that it's working so fast the thinking seems unconscious. It's taking all these disparate bits of data that were acquired from all these different experiences and synthesizing them into something applicable to the moment.

"So can this be taught?" I asked her. "Or is it just something you acquire through repeated exposure?"

"That's the million dollar question," she said.

—Dave Mance III

Forestland that was never cultivated will often have pit and mound topography, which is created by ancient blowdown events. Notice how the hemlock in this picture is growing on a mound, and the windward side has settled into a pit. It's an indication that this earth has never seen a farmer's plow.

A LOOK BACK

Ginseng Diggers

Editor's Note: The following article appeared in the Vermont Phoenix *on October 31, 1902.*

Two Brattleboro residents derive handsome profits from the sale of ginseng root. While many more people have successfully hunted the root for the past three or four years, the work entailed seems to have gradually discouraged them, until, dropping out one by one, they have left the field to two or three persistent diggers, who, having become experts, find their searchings not only remunerative, but likewise fascinating in the open-air exercise which their efforts require.

We all remember how our grandfathers, many years ago, dealt extensively in the root, employing in many instances their neighbors in the season of ginseng digging, sending their product to Boston by team.

In those days if the crop brought 75 cents to $1.25 a pound, the diggers considered themselves fortunate, though it is probably true that the root was more easily found than today, when a digger must traverse a wide

A map of Brattleboro from 1860 shows "Ginseng Hill."

CHARLES W. GRAU

territory, and oftentimes spend several days in securing a very few pounds of the root which however, brings much higher prices than were paid half a century ago, while the demand has constantly increased.

To the many New Englanders who possibly have never heard of the enormous profits realized from the traffic in ginseng, the story of its digging and marketing by one who has made a business of it, and the fact that this valued commodity flourishes, as it were, at their doors, affording to those who know and seek it a most satisfactory income, will be of interest.

Vermont's ginseng product is said to be of a superior quality, commanding, like the ginseng of certain sections of Canada, Maine and northeastern New York, the highest market price. Vermont's crop is generally marketed in Boston or New York, and is supposed ultimately to find its way to China, where the great bulk of all the ginseng raised is sold.

Here in Windham County there are half a dozen dealers in the root, most of whom do their own digging and who have so quietly pursued their vocation as to attract little or no attention, though the results of their labors are shown in sizable incomes.

One of the most successful "diggers" in this section of the state is George Whitney, whose farm is located on the old turnpike which leads off from the stage road about four miles west of Brattleboro village. Mr. Whitney has dug ginseng for the past 11 years, during which period he has familiarized himself with the hills and dales of Windham and Windsor counties, having travelled over nearly every farm in both.

About nine years ago Mr. Whitney secured his largest crop, gathering in the months of September and October a large quantity of the root, which, when thoroughly dried, as it must be before sold, amounted to about 75 pounds, for which he was paid $3 a pound by White Bros. of Boston. This was considered a good price then, though since that time ginseng has increased in value, until, last year Mr.

Whitney sold his crop for $6.75 a pound, and hopes to do as well, or even better, this year. [Editor's Note: It's tricky to calculate for inflation that far back, but a spitball estimate is that $6.75 in 1901 would be about $200 a pound today.] Brattleboro 10 years ago was considered a great locality for ginseng. The Aldrich, Clark and Miner farms were, to quote Mr. Whitney, "literally alive with the root." At that time he was supposed to be about the only digger in this vicinity, though Paul Willis, a war veteran, and Orrin P. Shepardson, the old carriage maker, hunted the root. J. J. Barnes of Westminster, has gathered ginseng for years in connection with his farm duties.

The most Whitney ever found in one locality was on the farm of Mrs. W. H. Bigelow, in the west part of Brattleboro, just northwest of Round mountain, where he dug steadily for at least two weeks with most satisfactory results. When he began, it was his custom to pick off the little fibres of the root before shipping, but now that it has been ascertained that these little feelers are well nigh invaluable, the buyers invariably require the fibres to be left on the root.

Ginseng is generally found in woodlands, among hardwood timber, butternut timber land being the best locality for it, although it is indigenous to the soil of old-growth ash and maple where the land is partly shady. The roots grow in all shapes and lengths, and Mr. Whitney reports finding as many as nine roots to one stalk, though it generally grows with two or three roots. Whitney's best find this year has been a root that weighed nine ounces.

After digging the roots are washed and dried as much as possible before shipping, but the seller must await another and more thorough process of drying by the buyer before it is finally weighed, when he gets his money. The root is dug with a little hook-like contrivance attached to an ordinary walking-stick, and great care must be exercised not to cut or break the root, for such damage takes from its selling price.

For the past two or three years ginseng has been reported as scarce, owing, it is supposed, to too much hunting and the fact that cattle and sheep seem to be very fond of it, and where they graze it is difficult to find enough to pay for the digging. Mr. Whitney says he has never dug less than this year, but then he was late in getting at it and some other fellow, evidently, had got there first.

Ginseng is of slow growth and takes five years, at least, for the root to mature from the seed. A Newfane

Ginseng was a valuable product by the end of the nineteenth century.

man is engaged in growing ginseng under cover. The Newfane patch is fenced in and protected, according to common report, by a system of electric bells, which ring whenever the wire fence is touched. This grower is said to have sold recently over $300 worth of ginseng berries to different ones, who will attempt to cultivate it as is done in the West.

Ginseng is pleasantly aromatic and probably slightly stimulant. The celestials value it highly and consider it a specific for almost every trouble from which they suffer. It has been used in China for 40 centuries, where the product is one of great commercial importance. Imperial ginseng raising is a government monopoly, being grown in the royal parks and gardens, where a death penalty is visited upon those who steal the plants. This product sells as high as $200 [$6,350 in 2021 dollars] a pound, and is used by the aristocrats of China.

We know, of course, that Americans are given to the use of ginseng, believing in its efficacy in severe bowel complaints. Some people habitually keep it in their homes as a medicine and consider it a great tonic, while others chew it as they would gum, the taste being very pleasant.

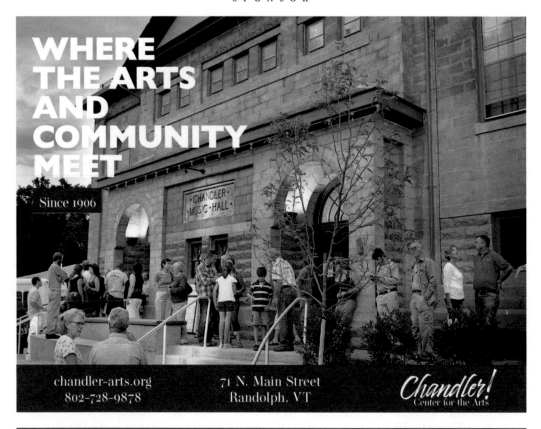

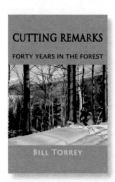

Tapping in 1947
Inset: Tapping the same tree in 2014

Here's to family breakfasts.
Here's to food that tastes like the place it came from.
Here's to craft that's passed down through the generations.
Here's to local products made by local people.
Here's to the resilience that keeps rural industries afloat.
Here's to the hope, and ambition, and hard work
behind new endeavors.

MANCE FAMILY TREE FARM
is proud to support the *Vermont Almanac.*

We Ship! Order today at MANCEMAPLE.COM

MANCE FAMILY
TREE FARM

Amy Hook-Therrien

DECEMBER

December

While I had always assumed Robert Frost wrote his best known poem, "Stopping by Woods on a Snowy Evening," in Vermont, I never knew until we moved here that he wrote it in summer.

When we arrived here in December four years ago, via the South, we hadn't experienced a winter in years. It was a shock to look out our window and see snow falling every day.

We would drive past Frost's home in Shaftsbury and wonder how he stayed warm when we never felt warm. The walls of that house are stone, and in pictures taken in the home, Frost is wearing multiple sweaters and sitting in a chair by the fireplace. I still wonder if he slept in that spot, as well.

Frost was a transplant here, too, no doubt shocked by frozen woodpiles and snowed-in doorways. People of his era experienced a different type of winter – likely colder, in un-insulated houses that may never have gotten truly warm. Nights of hot water bottles in beds and ice on the insides of windows. Seeing your own breath when you awakened each morning.

And I, hauling in firewood that first winter, feeding a hungry woodstove and knowing the feeling of a house's growing cold when it goes out, also had to get hip to the multi-sweater look. Because in winter, a house can never be warm enough.

Friends who saw pictures of our snowy woods made references to *The Shining*, and maybe we did, too – although it wasn't funny to us. I found myself like *Frozen's* Olaf, dreaming of green grass, blooming flowers, and trees. The beach in summer. Warm waves breaking over me.

Of course, we learned to love winter. We now hang Christmas lights on our house even though no one can see them but us. We clear our own driveway of snow. We bought snowshoes. We ski. We stop in the woods, too, to watch them fill with snow.

So it seems fitting that Frost would have felt nostalgic about winter in July, when he could shed the layers, when he wasn't in the midst of feeding an endless fire or shoveling a walkway or seeing his dinner invariably go cold before he could finish it.

In summer, when the weeds are tall and lush and the woods feel as if they are closing in on you, a Vermont winter can suddenly feel romantic. With its red barns dolloped with snow, its rolling hills that sparkle in the sun, its bare mountains that turn red at sunset.

Frost must've been struck by a similar thought as he walked through his field that one summer morning – but quickly tempered it with his knowledge of the cold and its dangers to water-filled pipes and to warm bodies, and how urgent and vital it is that whatever promises we make in winter – far more than in summer – must be kept. —*Owen Duffy*

Records Both Ways

Overall you can expect Vermont winters to be snowy, cold, and cloudy, but there's also significant variability in terms of temperature and precipitation over short periods. Things can warm up only to be followed by crashing temperatures; we can get snow daily and then have things dry out for a week, or turn to rain. Really, the only guarantee when it comes to December weather in Vermont is a lack of daylight. December offers just around nine hours of daylight each day, bottoming out on the Winter Solstice on December 21. This lack of light can be a struggle, and I often wonder how our neighbors to the far north deal with the even stronger imbalance of sunlight throughout the year.

Further reinforcing the lack of sunlight theme is

This photo was taken on December 17, 2020, in East Wallingford. Photographer Carolyn Haley writes: "The total dump was somewhere between 40 and 42 inches, starting from bare ground the night before. It was all gone within seven days, though at the time of this shot temps were subzero."

the abundant cloud cover that is typically observed at the start of our winters. The indirect culprit for the generally gloomy conditions is the Great Lakes upstream (to our west). The interaction between colder air flowing over the relatively warmer and unfrozen waters of the Great Lakes prompts plenty of clouds to form and drift east.

December 2020 started off with a significantly lower than normal amount of snow over the higher terrain, and little if any snow in the deeper valleys. The Mount Mansfield Snow Stake, just below Vermont's highest point, is the go-to for weather-watching Vermonters interested in gauging how deep the snowpack is compared to average. At the start of the month, the reading at the stake was close to zero, not a hopeful sign for the rest of the month. Recording-setting temperatures to start the month did indeed keep snowpack levels down: record warmth was observed over northern Vermont on the first day of the month, with Montpelier, St. Johnsbury, and Burlington all setting daily high records in the 60s. A high of 66 degrees saw Burlington almost tie its all-time high December temperature of 68. Following up on November's warmth, December saw Burlington's mean temperature above normal by 5.5 degrees. The end of the month also provided record warmth as Santa delivered a big lump of coal for the snow lovers. A record high of 65 degrees was observed on December 25, accompanied by a rainstorm – hardly a white Christmas.

Amazingly, this record-breaking warmth came during the same month that we saw record-breaking snowfall. The state 24-hour snowfall record was broken in Peru on December 17, as 44 inches of white gold came down, breaking the old record dating back to 1995 held by the notoriously snowy Jay Peak. Much of southern Vermont, in fact, got walloped by the gigantic storm. December 2020 saw Vermont's weather variability on full display. —*Christopher Kurdek, Fairbanks Museum and Planetarium*

NATURE NOTES

Changing Snow Patterns and Freeze-Thaw Cycles

We often talk about the effects of climate change in the future tense. For instance, Vermont is predicted to have a 4.8-degree Fahrenheit increase in December's average temperature between 2039 and 2069 as compared to the average temperatures that were reported between 1968 and 2000.

But climate change is already affecting Vermont. Our December average temperatures, like our annual average temperatures, have been trending upward for decades. In December, this means more fluctuations between freezing and above-freezing than we've traditionally had and less snowpack depth and cover.

When there's consistent snow early in the season, before the soil fully freezes, the soil is able to stay at or slightly above freezing throughout the winter. With little to no snow, soil is subject to increased freeze-thaw cycles, which can increase the amount of water in the soil and the soil temperature on warmer days. This can increase microbial growth, and the microbes quickly deplete the limited oxygen supplies in the soil, causing it to become anaerobic. In soils with high nitrogen content, like farm fields, freeze-thaw cycles create the perfect conditions for denitrification, a process that leads to the release of nitrous oxide. Nitrous oxide is a greenhouse gas almost 300 times more damaging than carbon dioxide. So a feedback loop can form, wherein an increased number of freeze-thaw cycles causes an increase in N_2O emissions from the soil, which in turn raises greenhouse gas concentrations in the atmosphere, causing more freeze-thaw cycles.

In the forest, one of the big risks of increased freeze-thaw cycles is to tree roots. A deep freeze when the soil is bare can damage fine tree roots. The trees will have to allocate more resources to root growth and repair during the growing season to compensate for the fine-root loss during the winter. Abnormal warmth followed by deep cold can also increase the risk of crack formation where there are wounds in a tree's trunk.
—*Julia Pupko*

How do researchers know that freezing and thawing damages tree roots? Because they do controlled experiments, like this one at Hubbard Brook Experimental Forest, using electric coils to manipulate soil temperature.

Grouse Snowshoes

These photos of a bird's foot might make you think they come from two different species. But both belong to the ruffed grouse. As days shorten, modified hairs on each of a grouse's toes begin to grow. The comb-like protuberances, called pectinations, nearly double the surface area of the foot, allowing the bird to walk on top of soft snow. As photographer Susan C. Morse has noted, "this is a vital adaptation for a bird that spends much of its time walking." In winter, a grouse's legs become more fully feathered as well, providing needed insulation. In spring, both the leg feathers and the pectinations are shed. ⓥⒶ

SUSAN C. MORSE

AMY HOOK-THERRIEN shared this December picture of a wild turkey. This rare mutation is referred to colloquially as "smoke phase." The turkey has no brown pigment in its feathers.

AMY HOOK-THERRIEN

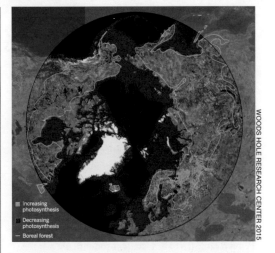

Increasing photosynthesis
Decreasing photosynthesis
Boreal forest

WOODS HOLE RESEARCH CENTER 2015

WARMER TEMPERATURES are known to increase photosynthesis in the higher latitudes, and Siberia has been getting greener. This isn't working so well in boreal North America, where stresses such as fire, pests, and drought have made things browner overall.

SUSAN C. MORSE

The Stuff's Just Awful

It's long been known that mouse poison (roden-ticide) has a way of trickling out of the house or barn and harming wildlife. Most stories about this involve birds of prey who feed on poisoned mice before they die. Now there's evidence that the damage extends far beyond owls and raptors.

December is fisher trapping season in Vermont, and all trappers must submit their carcasses to the Fish & Wildlife Department for examination. In 2019, the state sent 30 fisher livers to a University of Pennsylvania lab to be tested for rodenticide exposure. When the results were in, it was demoralizing to learn that all 30 fishers had poison residue in their livers.

In all, there were five different compounds that turned up: chlorophacinone, diphacinone, broma-diolone, brodifacoum, and difethialone. Twenty-six out of the thirty animals had more than one poison in

their livers – one had all five.

The old axiom "The dose makes the poison" applies here, and since different animal species have different tolerances to different poisons, and since the levels found in a liver don't necessarily represent all that's been ingested, it's hard to say exactly how compromised the fishers were. But if we compare the amount of poison residue in the Vermont fishers to dead California fishers whose toxicology was measured in another study, there's overlap.

"We can say that these were potentially lethal doses in the Vermont fishers," said Chris Whittier, a researcher at Tufts University who was involved with the study.

Even more disturbing is that much of the poison was second-generation rodenticide that mammal bodies don't easily metabolize. *Kills 'em dead in one feeding!* the ad copy proudly proclaims. Eighty-three percent of the fishers had brodifacoum – one of the so-called "single dose" poisons – in their livers. (Levels ranged between 0.01 and 0.19 ppm). There are scores of scientific papers online that give a sense of the effect this chemical has on non-target animals. Brodifacoum residues were detected in the livers of 234 non-target mammals from eight species in a study block where the poison was being used in bait stations to control invasive possums in New Zealand. Another study recorded how it crossed the placenta from a Great Pyrenees to her puppies.

The second-generation chemicals are so noxious that they're not allowed to be sold over the counter in small packets in hardware or grocery stores. The bureaucratic logic here is that by making them "professional class," they'll be available to exterminators but not widely available to homeowners. But in practice, what it means is that you can't buy a little bit of the poison: you can only buy a lot. Eight-pound pails of brodifacoum are sold on Amazon, and they'll deliver it right to your front door.

Fishers have a reputation of being a forest animal, so how have these poisons moved from the home and barnyard to the woods? Whittier said that poisoned fishers in California were tied to illegal marijuana farms on national forest land. Maybe there's some of that here. Maybe it's a case of selection bias, and the 30 fishers were, by virtue of the fact that they were trapped, from a pool of animals with ranges that overlap with human environments. It seems that the thousands of deer camps sprinkled throughout the state must be a vector.

Whittier said that researchers are revising their study parameters to be able to better answer these questions and, further, that plans are in the works for a region-wide study. —*Dave Mance III*

A fisher raiding a wood duck box.

ALFRED BALCH

DAVE MANCE III

28.77 inHg↑ 🌡 29°F) 12/11/2018 08:36PM CAMERA1

There's this idea in some circles that fishers are deep-woods creatures; bobcats, too. But the woods are only so deep in this tiny rural state, so there's plenty of opportunity for human interface with pretty much every mammal species out there. Here, a bobcat mother and her grown kitten loiter in a Vermont barn. If there were poisoned rodents in the barn, there would be poisoned bobcats. Somewhere out there is a picture just like this with fishers in it.

AT HOME

❧

Better Mouse Trapping

It's probably safe to assume that people turn to mouse poison because it's easy, an idea that relates to the fact that mouse trapping can be hard. But when we consider the environmental ripple effects poison has, it's clear that we ought to try to get better at trapping so we don't have to poison the ecosystem in and around our home.

There are lots of tips online aimed at helping you improve your skills – like everything on the internet, some are good and some are useless. Some good ones include wearing gloves to keep concentrated human scent off the trap, using small amounts of smear baits, like peanut butter or bacon grease, that are hard for the mouse to remove without triggering the trap, and setting the trap perpendicular to a wall with the bait up against the wall.

The basic underlying principle to always keep in mind is you want the mouse to be centered when it goes to take the bait. This is why perpendicular to the wall trap placement is best practice: because mice run along walls, it puts the bait squarely in their path. With this in mind, you can make further improvements by adding blocking to funnel the mice away from the back of the trap.

Another basic underlying principle to keep in mind is that mice are good at staying alive, and so they'll soon realize you're trying to trap them and learn to avoid the traps. So it makes sense to really try to make the most of your first night. Set a dozen traps, not just one or two. And do it on a night when you're staying up late watching a movie or football game, so you can hear them go off and empty/reset them in real time.

With gang setting and a concerted early push,

Mice fear danger from above, so will almost always run along the inside wall underneath a stove or cabinet to access food in the kitchen. This trap placement ensures the bait is square to the mouse, and that it can be accessed under cover, where the mouse feels secure. It's a great set.

Mice can be surprisingly good at stealing bait from the old wooden-style traps. One trick to prevent this is to place the trap vertically, about 5 inches up a wall. This forces the mouse to commit its head in a way that a flat set doesn't.

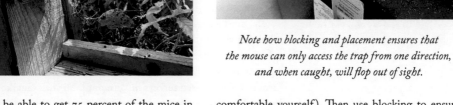

Note how blocking and placement ensures that the mouse can only access the trap from one direction, and when caught, will flop out of sight.

you should be able to get 75 percent of the mice in the first few nights. Once the population has dwindled down to educated mice, you'll need to trap more stealthily. Change your style of traps and your bait to give them a new look. Identify countertop or fridge-top locations where mice are comfortable feeding (if you pre-bait such areas with food and unset traps, you can get them used to an area and make them comfortable yourself). Then use blocking to ensure that when a trap set in this area goes off, the mouse and the trap will fall off the counter or refrigerator and out of sight. This technique effectively hides the dead mouse and keeps the other mice who visit the site comfortable. Repeat this process until you have your kitchen back and your partner likes living in the country again. —*Dave Mance III*

CLEAN CHOPS WITHOUT A SAW

If you've ever butchered a pig or a lamb at home, you undoubtedly wished for a band saw when it came time to cut through the spine and separate the chops. Lacking one, you probably used a cleaver and did a terrible job, thinking to yourself: my God, how on earth do people swing this thing and hit that tiny notch in the bone? They don't. Take your cleaver and carefully find the right notch and the right angle, then use a rubber mallet to apply the force that will break the bone. Thanks to Mary Lake for sharing this slick butcher's trick.

A LOOK BACK

Marching Turkeys to Market

I f you want something to be thankful for, be glad you weren't a Vermont farmer in the early 1800s. Their work was almost unimaginably grueling. Consider this fact: they would regularly walk their goods to market ... in Boston.

The goods they were transporting were animals, and in the fall, that often meant turkeys. Flocks containing hundreds or even thousands of them were destined to end up as the main course for Thanksgiving (a day that was celebrated, though not yet as an official national holiday) or Christmas.

The most amazing thing about the stressful effort of getting the birds to market alive is that some farmers made the trek repeatedly. They had to; they were that hard up. As impractical as they may sound today, turkey drives were a commonsense solution to a major problem: how to get the surplus of farm-raised turkeys in Vermont to the mass market of Boston. In the days before trains, slaughtering them and shipping them on ice wasn't an option. So, the turkeys had to arrive alive at the market. The only way to get them there en masse was to make them walk.

The number of people going on each farm's excursion may have ranged from several to several dozen, depending on how many birds were

DRIVING TURKEYS TO THE PICKING-HOUSE.

WIKIMEDIA COMMONS

available to take to market. The various jobs, however, remained the same. The drovers, as the name suggests, drove the turkeys, using a prod to urge them along. Sometimes, they would sprinkle feed on the ground to coax the birds forward. The drovers occasionally tied a bell around the neck of a dominant turkey, making the others more likely to follow.

Other workers would take up the rear, watching for strays (turkeys had a tendency to wander off and join a different flock when they passed another turkey farm). Workers also watched for predators that might view the flock as an easy meal and even for people who might claim a stray turkey as their own. The drovers relied on others to drive a supply wagon that carried their food and tents, as well as enough corn to help the birds maintain their weight during the trip.

Where each day would end was largely up to the birds. The whole contingent hit the road as early as it could and then walked until nightfall. As dark approached, one of the lead birds would flap its way into a tree, and that was it. The day was over. The other birds would immediately find their own places to roost and nod off.

Charles Morrow Wilson wrote of the problems drovers faced in his 1964 novel *The Great Turkey Drive*. Though a work of fiction, Wilson's book was informed by the oral tradition about the drives. He wrote that drovers faced trouble when they tried to cross covered bridges. Apparently, the birds often mistook the bridges' darkness with nightfall and fell asleep partway across, choking off the bridge. The solution that Wilson's drovers found was to carry hundreds of birds, one at a time, across the bridge and into the sunlight. Sometimes, the drovers carried lanterns, to try to trick the birds into walking a few extra minutes each day.

Turkeys were, in fact, ill-suited physically for the long walks. Farmers found that they had to tar the birds' feet to protect them. The awkward caravan could make about ten or twelve miles a day across fields and along the crude roads of the time, so the entire trip could take as long as three weeks.

Often, farmers took the treks on pure speculation. They had no guaranteed buyer at the other end. And if birds died en route – typically about 10 percent were lost to predation, disease, and straying – farmers had to do what they could to recoup the loss. Sometimes, they would augment their flock by buying additional birds at farms they passed.

As they arrived in the city, the Vermont farmers fattened up their birds just before selling them. They made their sales and then returned with cash or finished goods that were unavailable in Vermont.

These journeys were undertaken in the fall. At that time of year, the traveling farmers could find leftover grain in the fields for the birds to eat. Of course, it didn't hurt sales that Bostonians were looking for something special to put on their tables for the holidays. An 1830s cookbook notes that Bostonians were sure to find turkeys most plentiful each November and December.

Today, the old turkey drives are remembered in stories and songs. Musical historian Margaret MacArthur helped a group of fifth graders from Newbury, Vermont, learn about their local history by composing a song (at right) celebrating the drives. —*Mark Bushnell*

Long ago there was no money

In the town we live in now.

They sent flocks and herds to Boston

Of turkey, geese, sheep and cows

To get turkeys into Boston,

They had to travel far

So farmers spread upon their feet

Heavy coats of tar

Across the Bedell Bridge

A drover boy named Murphy

Drove on foot to Boston

One hundred fifty turkey

Along the Coos turnpike,

many went astray,

'til he sprinkled corn and gathered

many more along the way.

—*Margaret MacArthur*

INDUSTRY

Meat Production in Vermont

Until recently, I was farming part time and working full time with livestock farmers through UVM Extension's Center for Sustainable Agriculture. But this year, I swapped roles, and now I work part time with Extension and farm full time. In both roles, I've had plenty of opportunity to talk with other livestock farmers in Vermont about the challenges they face and the opportunities they see.

When I hear people outside the industry talk about meat production in Vermont, the discussion often goes right to limitations in processing capacity within the state because they hear stories about how hard it is to find a butcher. That is true in some ways, but definite progress has been made in the last decade or so.

For starters, we have new large (in Vermont terms) meat processing operations: Vermont Packinghouse in North Springfield (in a former Ben & Jerry's plant) and Northeast Kingdom Processing in St. Johnsbury both opened seven or eight years ago, and that has helped a lot. There are also smaller facilities that have opened across the state in just the last couple of years.

At the same time, the way that farmers have adjusted their methods has also made it possible to process more meat in Vermont. First, some farmers have changed their entire livestock systems, which has made a huge difference by spreading out demand for limited space at processing facilities. Historically, farmers have followed the traditional seasonal calendar for grazed animals: have calves or lambs or piglets in the spring, then ship them in the fall. For pigs and lambs, that would mean six to eight months; for calves, that would mean shipping in the following fall. This makes sense because animals grow so much better in the summer, when they don't

Vermont Packinghouse operates in a former Ben & Jerry's ice cream plant in North Springfield.

have to fight the calorie loss that comes with staying warm. Raising animals in the winter also costs more because the livestock require additional calories. But when everyone follows that schedule, it creates a huge processing logjam in the fall.

I worked for many years on the Vermont Farm to Plate Meat Processing Task Force, and the butchers would always tell us, "We have eight months of the year when we could process more animals, and we have to keep people on our payroll all that time."

I've been farming since 2000 on a fairly small scale: we started on a homestead level, but five years ago, we were able to purchase a larger property for Howling Wolf Farm in Randolph. More space has allowed us to follow a different vision. We have about 70 sheep, and we're raising about 40 pigs a year. Our hope in the next couple of years is to double the number of pigs. I switched my own schedule for pig processing.

GLENN RUSSELL

Instead of the classic system of buying piglets in the spring and then sending them to the butcher in the fall, I began buying piglets in November, raising them over the winter, and shipping them for processing in the spring. That was about 10 years ago, and at the time, I could call the butcher in the spring and get on their schedule in about two weeks. It was so much easier than trying to get on their schedule in the fall.

Now, I've shifted again: in 2021, I bought piglets in late summer and shipped them in late December. You can finish animals on good-quality hay, and we do that. With sheep, I have switched to having lambs that are born in May or June getting shipped the following July, at about 13 months' age. I think I'm fairly representative, as I've talked with other farmers who have switched their systems in order to get into butchers' schedules, too. You have to be creative, and you can't be afraid of change.

COVID BUMP CONTINUES

Demand for local agricultural products skyrocketed during Covid, and that includes locally produced meats. Livestock farmers found new ways to bring sales directly onto their farms. One farm might have poultry and raw milk, so they might form a partnership with another farm that has beef, pork, and lamb. This has happened all over the state, and I don't think that piece is going to go away. As farms expand their offerings at farm stands, it demonstrates

Howling Wolf Farm's ground lamb,
processed at The Royal Butcher in Braintree.

the power of the local farmer to provide food for the community.

Of course, this growth in demand brings us back to the issue of limited processing capacity. In early August 2021, when I was picking up lamb that had been processed at The Royal Butcher in Braintree, I asked them if things had calmed down a bit. They said they were still operating at maximum capacity. And that was at a time of the year that, in the past, would have been a slow period.

It's reasonable to think that the industry will figure this out. Vermont has water – too much water, at least in July of this year! But I have no complaints because it made the pastures regrow beautifully. I think that our climate will mean more animals coming here – being grown here – simply because we have water, and other parts of the country don't. I think that's an important component to think about when we consider the industry's capacity to grow.

When we think of the future of farm-raised meat in Vermont, it's also important to think beyond smaller direct-to-sale farms. Larger livestock operations often raise their animals in Vermont, but for logistical reasons, they send the animals out of state for processing. With additional capacity, there's so much potential in the next five years to capture some of those animals and get them processed in state. And then the meat could be packaged and shipped to markets out of state. Every farmer struggles with the question of how to capture value. When you send a live animal out of state, you may not be capturing the added value of the Vermont name or the savings to local consumers who purchase that Vermont-grown meat.

For example, Farmers to You, an online market based in Barre that connects small scale farmers with customers, has seen tremendous growth. They do home delivery in the Boston area – meats, vegetables, all different kinds of Vermont products – and they had to stop taking on new customers last year because there was so much demand. That's a sign of how much potential there is, but that doesn't involve shipping a live animal out of state: that's getting an animal processed here and then delivering it. That's how you really capture the value.

I'm eternally optimistic, but then, I think you have to be to be a farmer. —*Jenn Colby*

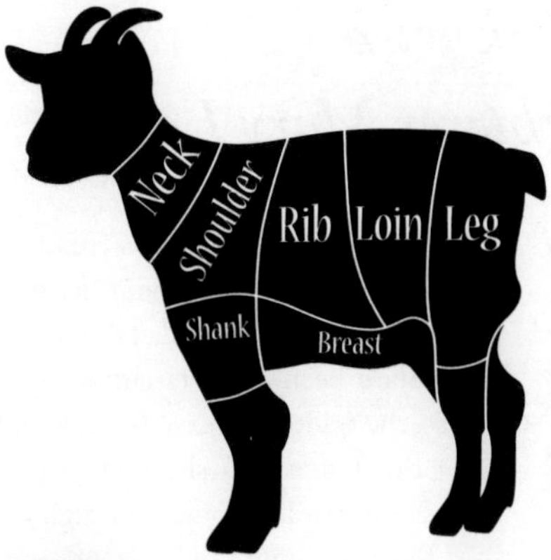

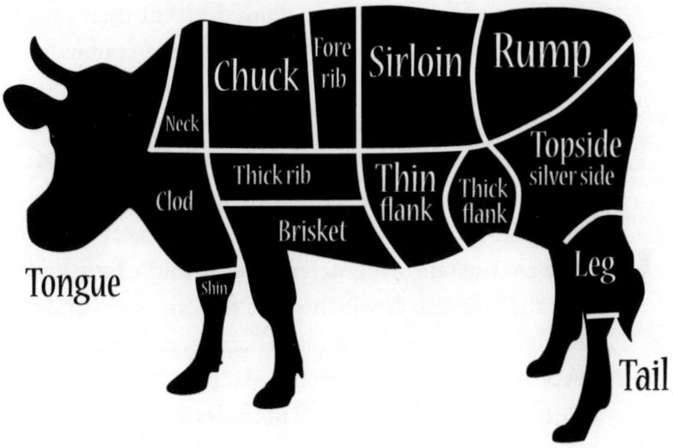

Neck Shoulder Rib Loin Leg

Shank Breast

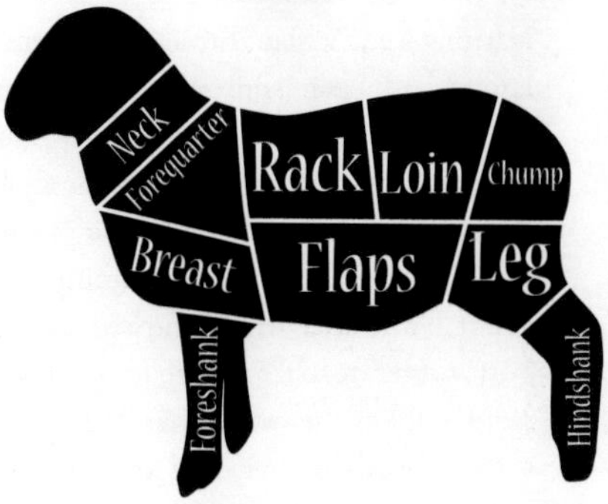

Neck Forequarter Rack Loin Chump

Breast Flaps Leg

Foreshank Hindshank

Loin

Spare Ribs Blade Leg

Head Leg Belly Tail

Hock

Chuck Fore rib Sirloin Rump

Neck Topside silver side

Thick rib Thin flank Thick flank

Clod Brisket

Tongue Shin Leg

Tail

Things to Think About if You're New to This

So, you've raised a few pigs or lambs in your side yard, and now you want them cut and wrapped. How to find a butcher? The first thing to know is that butchering is not glamorous, highly paid work, and if the butcher is making any kind of money at all, it's from their larger customers with standardized orders. So don't expect any butcher to bend over backwards for your one pig or three lambs, especially if you're a first-time customer.

The second thing to keep in mind is that, from the butcher's perspective, knife work is hard and saw work is easy. Nice big bone-in roasts? Easy peasey. A few passes through the band saw, some quick knife trimming and, voilá, that whole lamb shoulder is ready for wrapping. Butterflied legs, boneless shoulders, Frenched chops? Expect to pay more, or even offer to pay more. You want the whole thing ground into burger or trimmed for sausage? Definitely pay more, or the butcher might not return your calls down the line. You're asking her to skip the saw altogether and bone out the entire carcass with a knife.

This isn't to say you can't get what you want, just that you should understand the implications of what you're asking for. Three pigs with three different cut sheets, each highly specified with unusual cuts? Pretty fun if your butcher likes a challenge and lives to do a crown roast; less fun if your butcher is super busy. Consider sending your three pigs with the same cut sheet.

Finally, if you can arrange to have your animals butchered in a month that doesn't end in "-ber," you'll be a neighborhood hero. We're all trying to get our animals into the freezer at the same time, exactly when the grass runs out. If you can hold yours for an extra few months, you might find that your butcher is hungry for work instead of slamming down the phone. Might even be the time to ask about that crown roast. —*Chuck Wooster*

At Work with
Itinerant Slaughterer Mary Lake

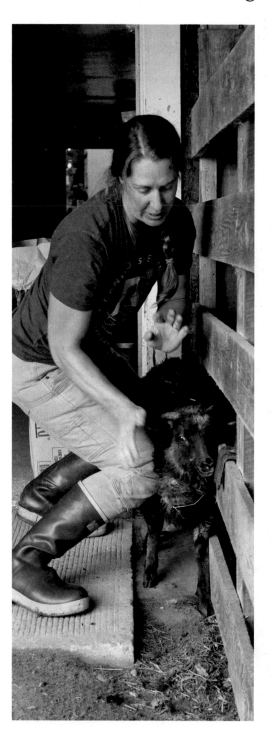

"People in my life were really confused," said Mary Lake about her decision to become an itinerant slaughterer.

She'd been a vegetarian in high school, for one. Also, the trade's not exactly female-dominated.

"But I liked it," she said. "And I kept doing it because it felt like something right."

Lake got into this line of work in 2010 after learning that a slaughterhouse where she'd sent 10 lambs had been shut down for inhumane animal treatment. She wanted to learn more about the process firsthand, so she asked for a job at The Royal Butcher in Braintree. She had to prove herself before she was allowed to shoot an animal – first by doing grunt work as a trimmer, then as a skinner and a gutter. Her teacher wanted to know that she was serious about the work. Then she had to spend weeks sawing heads in half and tracking the kill shot to learn the angles. Different animals – different breeds of the same animal – have different sized skulls and different sized brains, so there's an art to making quick, clean kills. Even after she was allowed to start shooting, she needed to spend evenings skinning the skulls of the animals she'd killed, fact-checking her work. She became part of the team and stayed for five years before leaving to start a family.

She's now a freelancer, and the slaughter work, along with sheep shepherding and sheep shearing, allows her to have a career in agriculture.

The phrase "itinerant slaughterer" seems like it comes out of the Middle Ages, but it's a contemporary legal term. Farmers aren't allowed to kill their own animals and sell them – it's considered a conflict of interest. (Ironically, Mary Lake herself hires someone to kill her own lambs that she wants to sell.) So farmers have two choices: they can truck the animals to a Vermont- or USDA-approved slaughterhouse like The Royal Butcher for processing, or they can hire an itinerant slaughterer to come to the farm and kill the animals, at which point the carcasses can be brought to a local meat cutter for processing. (In the eyes of the bureaucracy, the slaughterer and meat cutter are working on behalf of the buyer, which keeps the farmer in her "All-I-do-is-raise-the-animal" box.)

There's a pool of people, too, who are raising meat non-commercially, just for their own table, who hire out the slaughter work because they don't want to kill the animals themselves.

Lots of people are attracted to the idea of home slaughter for animal welfare reasons, and Mary's services certainly apply. She comes to them, so the animals don't travel and can maintain their routine. As she prepares to kill a sheep, she exerts gentle pressure with her legs and hips. This is based on the work of Temple Grandin, who has shown that animals are comforted by such pressure. Mary uses a penetrating captive bolt gun for the killing – it's a cylindrical tool that kind of looks like a lightsaber hilt from Star Wars. It's placed directly on the skull at the proper angle, and when fired, a bolt extends, then retracts. It's an elegant method compared to the .22 Long bullet-from-a-distance technique that many of us have seen

go terribly wrong.

Problems arise when the animals' owners don't think through the day properly. An animal should be confined before the slaughterer arrives, which means using a pen, not an acre-sized pasture. The site needs to be clean. Feeding the animal a last meal before Mary arrives makes her work harder (and gross), but some hobby farmers can't resist.

Mary handles all of this with great tact. She talks about the act of killing with unemotional, to-the-point bluntness but talks about the context of the killing in a thoughtful, expressive way. In these photos, she's conducting a slaughter workshop with the group Rural Vermont, sharing her craft with a group that included some people who had never seen an animal killed before.

"How many animals have you killed?" one asked.

"Thousands," she said.

"Does it wear on you?"

"In the beginning, I would count animals for my record-keeping," Mary said. "And around Thanksgiving, I would start to get really sad. Now, I count farms and think of all the people I've helped feed – think of all the good food that's nourishing our communities. I like being a part of practices from a simpler time, when growing your own food was more than just having a vegetable garden. That feels good."

—*Dave Mance III*

Pig Personalities

In the winter, all our work is confined to the barn's walls. It can be pretty boring for our tenants – especially the pigs. Sheep seem pretty content. Chickens are the masters of the barn and can go wherever they please, so they are thrilled. Pigs, on the other hand, become very needy.

Because of this, it takes twice as long to shovel the pigpens. The early risers are super eager to come and chat. I am quite familiar with pig noises, and can easily distinguish their communication. They make specific sounds to say, *I am hungry; I cannot believe you fed him before me; I am in pain; You are bothering me; I am going to eat you; I am scared.* Moms also say, *Lunch is served! Follow me.* And of course: *If you touch my child, you are meatloaf!*

It truly becomes a full-on conversation. Sometimes, I wonder if they are telling me their dreams, because if you bend over and look them in the eye, they go on and on and on. Some of them have very long dreams and take forever. Much longer than you have time for, especially if it is cold and the only thing that can keep you warm is shoveling. But yes, some pigs come over and want to chat – they are bored. And of course, we chat back in Pigish. My partner Stefano is the best at the farm in pig language. I am fluent at understanding but only intermediate in speaking. I can communicate, *I am afraid,* and, *I am going to eat you,* but the rest is pretty hard. The pigs have also learned to understand some Italian: they know "Go," "Go away," and "Stop that."

After they are done talking, they want to be scratched, and do not *dare* forget that this one likes the belly but hates the head – or vice versa. If you forget, they will let you know. There's no chance of ignoring them to shovel, because they know how to position themselves perfectly so that you have no alternative but to scratch them. As soon as you are done with petting one, another one gets up and wants his share – it never ends!

Some pigs care less about chatting or being petted and look for other types of entertainment to help with the boredom. Giuseppina, one of the sows, loves sticks. I have found her a few nice, sturdy wooden sticks over winter that she really likes. At first, I found her some thin, dry burdock stalks, and she was almost offended by my choice: she picked them up and put them right on top of the manure pile I was shoveling out of her pen. The sticks she likes, she will carry around. Sometimes, in the morning, she brings them to me if I am working in her pen. She does not want me to take them from her, but if she puts a stick down and I move it, she will pick it up and put it back in the same spot. Other times, she spends quite a bit of time pushing the stick through the fences to the group of pigs next door. It is a long stick, so it does require some concerted effort from pigs on both sides.

Some of the neat pigs organize all their troughs in a pile. (Yes, some pigs are very clean and neat, and others are filthy – just like with humans!) I have no idea how long it takes them and how they do it. I've never witnessed anyone in the act. For a while, I'd believed it was the farm assistants.

Other pigs find endless entertainment dumping their water on the floor. Probably because they have figured out that this leads to a flurry of activity and slipping and loud noises and foreign words from the farmers – these are the situations when our farm assistants learn Italian. What follows, of course,

is an effort to modify the trough design to make it impossible to flip. The pigs take it as a challenge. I have started to believe this is a sort of pig version of chess. So far, we are ahead of the game in most pens, but there's one grandmaster tending a perpetual ice-skating rink in front of their pen.

My favorite type of pig entertainment activity is what you can see in the pen of the *Giocondi*. "*Gioco*" means "game" in Italian, so "*Giocondi*" are "playful ones." They absolutely love hay, and every time you give them some, it is the *very best* day in their lives. They pick it up with their mouths and shake their heads as hard as they can; they move the hay from one corner to another and then back again; they roll in it; they make little 360-degree jumps that make the hay fly everywhere; they burrow into it. It is just the best thing ever. It reminds me of the way life was simpler when I was a kid, when the best things on Christmas Day were the boxes and the ribbons around the presents. I can't help but smile seeing our pigs going through that excitement every single time.
—*Alessandra Rellini*

MICHAEL ROACH

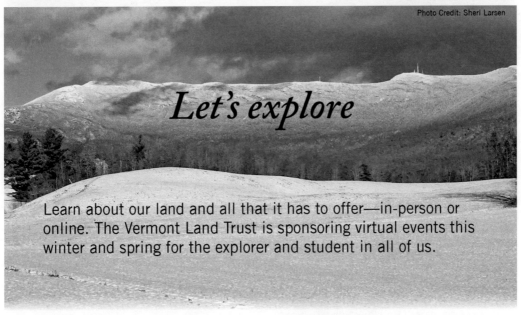

JANUARY

January

My wife and I were bushwhacking on a most glacial day; near noon, it was still ten or twelve below, and the sun, though flagrant, could warm nothing, even if it did illumine the diamond-bright flakes of frost that hovered in air like minuscule sprites you might meet in a dream.

Well north of our property, my wife spotted an odd-looking lump some fifty feet back in the brush. With mittened hands and a windfall branch, we managed to excavate a pair of deer skulls, nose to nose. Rodents had gnawed the tines to nubs, but enough remained intact that we could easily recreate the scene. Two rutting bucks had locked antlers.

We shook our heads at how slow and gruesome the animals' deaths must have been. If not for random misfortune, the larger one would have run the other off in short order. But for some bruises and scrapes, both would have gone on living.

It struck me hard, the degree to which life can depend on simply dodging ill luck – and not always by way of our caution. We were both already feeling pretty lucky to have dodged the year's pervasive and lethal coronavirus, at least up to that point.

It was also a year of righteous rage in the nation's cities, indeed of strife all over the planet. And there were gushing glaciers, ruinous drought, ungovernable wildfire – these were not transient matters, however removed from them our chilly circumstance might seem. Not at all.

For my wits' sake, I tend half-consciously to repress the naked truth that, regardless of the historical moment, like the rest of humanity I confront forces far larger than I can conceive. I distract myself from them, as I suspect most do, by concentrating on the existences of those closest to me, and needless to say, on my own.

I thought of a moment in the past spring, for example. As I cleared our fire pond's standpipe of debris piled around it by beavers, I felt one especially rough stick. That turned out to be a snapping turtle's tail. What if I'd grabbed the other end? I wouldn't have died, but you see what I mean. I still shiver to think about it.

And I shiver more intensely when I recall how, on a day years back, one as frigid as the day of the enmeshed antlers, my wife was late to fetch one of our daughters from nursery school. A good thing too. They came around a curve on the way home and saw a crumpled car on its side. A great orange gash flashed from a wayside pine, torn by the dead boy in the wreckage. He'd struck the tree mere seconds before, having spun on black ice across the very road my wife and daughter were taking.

How different life would feel today if they'd been on time.

Our family's intact, and not caged somewhere, not trying to shelter from bombs, not in a makeshift cardboard shelter over a grate, quaking with cold. We're assured of food, and only because we are blessed, not cursed, by where we were born and in what condition. Luck.

I suppose the weaker whitetail died first, and for him, that was surely a version of good fortune too. Just think of how long the stronger one may have dragged his antagonist's corpse around until exhaustion undid him.

We carried the two blanched skulls back home, scrubbed them clean, and nailed them over the woodshed door as… Well, what on earth to call them?

Icons?

Perhaps, though I can't say of what. —*Sydney Lea*

Gradually Normative

An abnormally warm December left many parts of Vermont with bare ground to start the month of January. This is abnormal, especially over the mountains, where the snow typically piles up early and persists until the green grass pokes through in April.

In my December entry, I discussed how winter here often gets off to a notoriously cloudy start due to excess moisture advecting into New England from the unfrozen Great Lakes; by January there's typically a bit more sunshine as ice coverage increases on the Great Lakes to the west and expansive areas of arctic high pressure build overhead, providing the opportunity for clear, cold days. That was not the case in January 2021, as we experienced cloudier conditions than normal. The latter part of the month was

Little snow could be found in early January 2021. This meager build-up was gracefully sliding off the roof at Bread and Butter Farm in Shelburne on January 6.

BREAD AND BUTTER FARM

seasonably cold, though. While some northern, traditionally snowy areas like Saint Johnsbury were drier than normal, clipper systems brought snow on eight straight days to parts of southern Vermont.

Vermont lore often points to a pronounced January thaw sometime during this month; while it is a strong talking point with Vermonters, sifting through more than a century worth of data yields no hard conclusions about whether it is a reality. Nor is there agreement about whether a January warm-up is even preferable. Some like the thaw, as it provides a reprieve from the bone-chilling cold and a chance to clean up previously rock-solid snow in the dooryard or weighted down roof; others look down on the thaw, as it can melt away the snowpack during the height of winter and destroy the light and fluffy snow consistency that most people prefer.

In January 2021, we saw just a quick stretch of above-freezing temperatures right in the middle of the month, but any thought of a prolonged thaw was erased as the end of the month brought bitterly cold temperatures, which dropped well into the teens below zero on January 31. —*Christopher Kurdek, Fairbanks Museum and Planetarium*

NATURE NOTES

CANDLEMAS DAY, which is February 2, is considered to be roughly the middle of the heating season. The good news is that half of the cold weather is behind us, although a more pessimistic old adage reminds us that we need to still have half our wood and half our hay on this date.

Walking in Circles

These odd, circular tracks were made by a meadow vole that had neurological problems that could have been caused by a brain parasite, brain tumor, inner ear infection, or a stroke. While the exact nature of an affected vole's neurological impairment cannot be confirmed without the vole in hand, it is highly likely that a common brain parasite, *Toxoplasma gondii,* is responsible.

The snow-covered corn field where these tracks were located was just down the road from a dairy farm, where it's likely cats could be found. This is relevant because cats pass this particular parasite on to rodents (and birds) that eat the cats' feces. The parasite goes to work on the brains of animals that have eaten cat feces, causing them to become disoriented (to the point where they lose their fear of cats). Cats then eat the fearless rodents and the cycle continues. When infected and disoriented, the rodents will often run in circles – hence, the unusual track pattern in the snow.

T. gondii can infect humans, too, through consumption of under-cooked foods, contaminated drinking water, and through contact with cat feces. This is why pregnant women are discouraged from tending kitty litter boxes, as the parasite can infect their unborn children. —*Mary Holland*

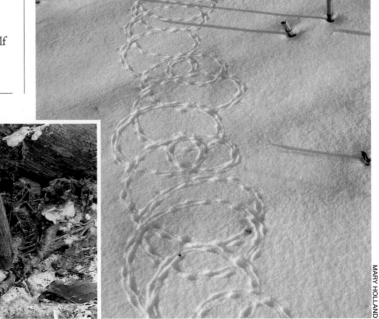

MARY HOLLAND

MARY HOLLAND

SNOWY OWLS have recently been seen in Vermont. We've all heard that they leave their arctic home when food there is scarce but another reason for these erratic irruptions might instead be that they occur following an unusually successful breeding season – successful because of an abundance of prey.

Hope for Moose

Moose were common in Vermont before Europeans got here, but land clearing and unregulated hunting led to their elimination in the 1900s. Regrowth of forests brought them back, and they especially flourished in the Northeast Kingdom in the wake of the big spruce budworm outbreak and associated heavy logging in the early 1990s, which was followed by abundant regeneration that led to a ready food supply. But this led to such a high moose population that they were soon creaming the forest.

A large number of moose hunting permits were issued to reduce moose numbers in the early 2000s, but then came a plague of winter ticks, which became a major cause of moose death in Vermont. Populations plummeted and a moratorium was put on hunting. Now moose hunting permits are available again, but in very limited numbers and only in the far northeastern corner of the state. Winter ticks benefit from higher moose density, so the goal is a targeted tick reduction through a targeted moose reduction.

Unlike most ticks, winter ticks (*Dermacentor albipictus*) live for just one year and only have one host. Other large ungulates, such as deer, are also susceptible, but they don't suffer as much as moose, which are literally plagued by these itchy ticks, often carrying 75,000 of them. When moose attempt to scrape them off, large hairless patches are created; overall health suffers and severe infestations cause anemia and death.

Entomologists at UVM have been working with a naturally occurring fungus, *Metarhizium anisopliae*, which has many different strains and is widespread in the soil. Ticks can fall victim to numerous strains of fungi in the wild, and in the lab this strain kills just about all of them. Cheryl Frank Sullivan, a former Ph.D. student in UVM's Entomology Research Lab, imagines the day when it can be cultured and spread in moose habitat. She believes that "boosting the fungal components that are already in the ecosystem" could make a big difference. Figuring out how to apply it may be a challenge, but as anyone who's ever seen the suffering of a tick-covered moose can attest, it's certainly worth a try. —*Virginia Barlow*

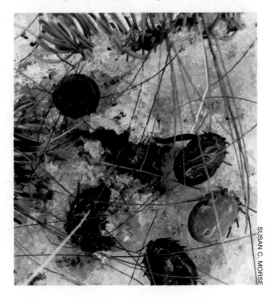

SUSAN C. MORSE

AT HOME

❧

Know Your Birch Bark

Winter Tree ID 101 involves recognizing "white birch," which we're sure readers of *Vermont Almanac* have long since mastered. But can you distinguish between the three different species of tree that people call "white birch" in Vermont? Here are some tips:

GRAY BIRCH 1
(Betula populifolia) has black triangle shapes where the branches meet the trunk, and the bark rarely peels. The bark sometimes leaves a residue on your hand. It has single, elongated male catkins and slender, bumpy twigs with a lot of white resin. The fruiting female catkins are relatively short.

PAPER BIRCH 2
(B. papyrifera) has inverted Vs where the branches meet the trunk. The bark readily peels and leaves no residue in your hand.

HEART-LEAVED BIRCH 3
(B. cordifolia) also peels, but it can have bronze or pinkish inner bark – a tell. At maturity, the bark can seem silver. The seeds have large, frilly wings and long stigmas; they look like tiny moths.

We didn't include leaf information, as the trees are bare in January. But if we had, it might not have helped distinguish between birches. There are general distinctions between the leaves – gray birch is triangular, paper comparatively rounded, heart-leafed vaguely heart shaped at the base – but

even experts can't reliably tell them apart. Botanist Jerry Jenkins has published an extensive photo-feature on the subject at northernforestatlas. org. He explains that everything gets messed up by the fact that gray birch and heart-leaved birch can hybridize, while paper birch is a notoriously variable species. Jenkins concludes, "Some birches are identifiable, some are not. Leaves, by themselves, are often indecisive. The more characters you have, the better off you are." He adds, "Any genus that produces plants that can't be named is worth getting to know."
—*Dave Mance III*

Ice Safety

Most everybody knows someone who has fallen through the ice. Sometimes, cautious and otherwise sensible people (not just children) have managed to do this, and there's not always a happy ending.

Though the surface of ice on a lake or pond may appear to be smooth and flat, the underside can be altogether different. Currents may leave thin spots where you'd least expect them. Thin ice is most encountered near tributaries or at a lake's outflow, but it can occur anywhere in a lake or pond where a current wells up. Even just a few inches of fluffy snow are enough to prevent cold air from thickening the ice below. Clear ice is stronger than cloudy ice, but assume that no ice is safe.

The best practice is to explore using a spud – a long, sharp-pointed metal bar. Jabbing it into the ice in front of you every couple of steps will provide a good early warning. If the spud punches through with just one firm jab, the ice is unsafe.

When exploring unknown ice, wearing a vest-style personal flotation device can both keep you warm on a cold day and save your life should you fall through. Venturing out onto frozen lakes is best done with a buddy, and at least one of you should have a coil of rope to aid in a rescue if necessary. Many styles of ice cleats are available to strap onto your boots to

A life jacket on your back and a pair of ice picks hung around your neck can save your life on winter ice outings.

prevent falls and to provide the traction needed to pull a companion out of the water.

But if you mess up, it's possible that not all is lost. The first step is to avoid panic. Rest your arms on the ice's surface and catch your breath. You have at least 15 minutes before hypothermia becomes severe. Best would be to have handheld ice picks staged in your jacket sleeves. These can simply be stout nails bedded into a wood handle or commercially made plastic handles with metal spikes concealed within retractable guards. Ice picks are used to claw yourself back up onto the hard, slippery surface in case you fall through the ice. If you don't have picks, kick your legs up to bring your body parallel to the surface and wriggle up onto the ice. Just be sure to go back to shore the way you came, even if it's not the shortest route.

Early-winter thin-ice conditions account for most accidental immersions, but the strong spring sun can weaken otherwise thick ice to the point that it will not support a person. Swollen spring brooks can undermine lake ice a surprising distance from the mouth of a tributary, and a sudden stiff breeze can break up a lake rapidly as wave action on open water eats away at the ice around it. —*Mike Scott*

It's all Downhill

The winters of my single-digit years contained copious amounts of snow. But just as the last falling flakes of a storm mysteriously taper off, so did the perceived depth of the snow as I aged, like an opened bottle of soda pop losing its fizz over time.

We had many ways to slide down the snow-covered hills. Flying saucers were always fun. We had a couple of steel-runner sleds, too. There was a big ol' toboggan that we'd pile a bunch of kids onto and take off hooting down the hill. The first rider in front usually got a face full of snow; the last kid in back stood up dogsled-style. The toboggan's biggest drawback was that it was heavier than a dead preacher to draw back up the slope.

My Old Man, a thrifty Yankee, combined recycling with recreation to save money and allow his kids to have a blast to boot. As boss of a bus garage, he had first refusal on stuff headed for the dump. When a bus's front or rear bumper had to be replaced, he would bring home any usable end-pieces with the curve where the bumper wraps around the corners of

JERRY KING

the bus. That curve was perfect for the front of a sled. They were made of quarter-inch-thick aluminum alloy, and they were tough enough to kill a bear. He'd drill a couple holes in the front to attach a pull rope, and we had us a silver sledding rocket.

The width of the bumper varied based on the model of the bus. And as they varied, so did the width of a kid's backside. It was mix and match between butt cheeks and bus bumper. And nothing was worse than squeezing an oversized butt into an undersized bumper. You'd go fleecing down the hill, get some air on a bump, and pop out of the sled and land on the upturned edge of the rocket. You could also end up with the worst wedgie – snow pants and long johns. Their extraction could require a pry-pole and a fulcrum.

These full-metal-jacket sleds went down the hill like a bullet shot from a greased barrel, and they were, themselves, bulletproof. Although we often gave them our best shot, akin to kid-sized crash-test dummies.

There was a sledding hill across the road from our house. We used it for pasture, as it was too steep for haying. It had a group of trees midway up the hill around an old well with a hand pump and bathtub where I would water the cows in the summer. The hill got even steeper where it met the woods.

One Saturday brought my cousin Donny, who was visiting to do some sledding. We soon discovered that he had forgotten his hat. I lent him a blue tuque with a big pompom on the top that I'd gotten for Christmas. I wore my favorite tattered Moriarty.

After a couple runs with our bus bumpers, we hit on the bright idea of stomping a trail through the woods up to the summit. It would double the length of our ride! We figured if we survived running the gauntlet of trees, it would be smooth sailing. To add to our enjoyment, at the bottom, there was a two-strand barbed-wire fence, then the four-foot-deep roadside ditch on Route 117. I didn't consider this a problem. Being the safety-conscious sledder that I was, I knew I had the failsafe system of the "bailout." This technique was used so often that it was hard to tell the difference between a scheduled safety bailout and an out-of-control annihilation.

We climbed to the top and took a gander down our nosedive of a trail. I recall distinctly that there was some debate as to who would go first. Donny claimed that because he was inexperienced with a bus bumper, and because he was the visitor, it was my duty as host

to pack down the new trail for him. So I was elected to go first, though I insisted the election was rigged and, therefore, fraudulent. This claim started a trend that was slow to catch on in the mainstream but would come back to bite us all in the butt in the fall of 2020.

I pointed my bus bumper down the slot in the snow we'd trudged up and plopped down into it. I laid the pull rope on my lap so I could use my hands to steer, peered down the hill, and thought twice about it. Newton's first law of motion states that an object's velocity will not change unless it is acted on by an outside force, which can be calculated as "Force equals mass times acceleration." With math not being his strong suit, my dumbass cousin gave me a shove. To say that I was moving when I came blistering out into the pasture would be more than accurate.

I soon realized there was no way in hell that I was going to stop before the fence and roadside ditch. Time to deploy the emergency bailout. I laid back and rolled off the bus bumper into a wonderful white explosion of snow and boy. My bus bumper shot between the two-strand barbed-wire fence, jumped over the roadside ditch, darted across Route 117, zipped between the cars parked in our driveway, and stopped just shy of our front porch. It was impressive.

I stood up and was brushing the snow off me when I heard what sounded like a damaged fire siren. Donny came screaming out of the woods at warp speed. He had made the rookie mistake of hanging onto the pull rope like reins and I think he was yelling, "Whoa!"

Without any means to steer, he left the trail, and like a wood-seeking missile, he headed for the group of trees surrounding the water pump. He selected the largest tree and center-punched it with a bell-ringing note from the bus bumper that pealed splendidly in the frosty air. Donny's bell got rung, too. He was pitched out of the bus bumper, thumped his cranium on the tree, and bounced back into the sled.

I traipsed over to where he was lying dazed on his bus bumper. It didn't get a scratch.

"Donny, you was supposed to use your hands to steer. You ain't riding a freakin' horse. I see it right off."

He made a crude hand gesture that I thought was uncalled for. Especially since it was my tuque that saved him. That big pompom on top cushioned the blow and prevented severe injury.

I still have that hat and wear it quite often.

—*Bill Torrey*

A LOOK BACK

A Line in the Sky

Oftentimes the past is reflected subtly in nature: like a stand of chestnut oak where there had once been a forest fire, or old stone walls where there had once been a hill farm.

But sometimes the past requires no imagination at all to picture, as is the case with the gloriously decrepit abandoned Cold War radar station that sits on top of East Mountain in Vermont's Northeast Kingdom.

"The summit of East Mountain could have been plucked from a scene of a post-apocalyptic movie about life after a nuclear holocaust" began one story about the site by author Wilson Ring.

The complex, which towers above the treeline, has been beckoning trespassers since it was abandoned in the early 1960s. The buildings are just carcasses, but the floors and walls of the four boxlike towers are a foot thick, the steel still strong. In their day, they were

covered with white, inflatable domes that housed radar equipment that scanned the sky day and night, looking for Soviet bombers.

About a mile below the summit, but still in the wilderness, is the old Lyndonville Air Force cantonment that once housed almost 200 people: barracks full of bunk beds and a huge mess hall and a machine shop and a post office and a bowling alley and basketball court. The beds and tables are gone, the hardwood floor has been ripped out of the basketball court, but the husks of everything are still there. Again, this complex is three-quarters of the way up a mountain, miles from the nearest maintained road. According to an old news clipping, many urban airmen looked at a stint at the base as they might have looked at a stint in Siberia. (When they were stationed there, in the late 1950s to early 1960s, the nearby towns of Victory and Granby still didn't have electricity.) One entire wall of the mess hall contained a mural of Chicago's Lake Shore Drive – an artistic nod to the civilized world.

The whole thing serves as a testament to America's can-do spirit and penchant for excess. The entire complex was built in 1956, which, considering the harsh conditions and lack of local infrastructure, is doubly hard to believe. And then it was promptly abandoned only seven years later. —*Dave Mance III*

Judging a Dairy Cow

Every Ag fair in Vermont has a dairy cow show, and you can often identify the people in the crowd who weren't in 4-H by the confused looks on their faces when the judges speak. It's sort of its own language. Here's a quotation pulled straight from a 2021 contest at the Vermont State Fair in Rutland; we asked judge Megan Hill to walk us through the quote, line by line:

"Two really nice cows, but the first has an advantage of being another month fresh[1]. I love how hard she is over the top, so much spring and depth in the rib[2]; she's also dairy-er, carrying that back to a nice attached fore-udder, high, wide rear-udder[3]. I will grant that the second place cow tracks out on a better set of feet and legs[4]."

1 A cow is considered "fresh" when she starts nursing; this fullness enhances her characteristics and gives an advantage over a dry cow.

2 "Hard over the top" means there's no fat anywhere on the top line of the animal, which is good. "Spring of rib" positively describes the width of the animal's ribcage in its front quarter. It's an indication of good heart and lung capacity. Think of the bulky chest musculature on a professional swimmer – that would be the human equivalent.

3 Dairy cows are supposed to be lean and angular, to the point that some laypeople worry they're underfed. From the back they should look wedge shaped. The word "dairy-er" refers to this angularity as well as other distinctive dairy cow features that stand in contrast to rounder, meatier beef cow features. A nicely attached fore-udder refers to how the udder attaches to the body wall and indicates that the cow will be more productive. High, wide rear-udder attachment is good for the same reason. Some udders have low attachments, or are tucked inward, which limits the cow's milk capacity. Ideal udder shape includes four evenly spaced and sized teats that hang straight down from the same height in the horizontal plane. This geometry is important because the suction cups on a milking machine need to slightly pull down on the teat to work effectively. If one teat is higher than the others, it might not "milk out" at the same rate, which may lead to under-milking on one quarter or over-milking on the others. This can lead to mastitis and may make it difficult for a farmer to keep the cow healthy and productive over her lifetime.

4 Feet and legs are hugely important to a cow, since they carry so much weight. Judging here is somewhat intuitive – legs should be wide and balanced. Feet should be well rounded with deep heels and good toe spacing. There's a proper hoof angle that judges look for that best distributes the cow's bulk.

PHOTOS BY DAVE MANCE III

*Judge Megan Hill at work. Hill grew up on Four Hills Farm in Bristol and
refined her judging skills at the University of Minnesota.*

The Power of Dairy Farms

Food and energy. They're probably the two most critical components for human survival. And now they're both being produced at Goodrich Farm in Salisbury. The third-generation dairy farm has long been in the food business – Wilbur Goodrich began milking cows there in 1956. Today, his grandchildren, Chase and Danielle Goodrich, own the farm and they see energy production as an essential part of its future.

The brother and sister duo began exploring the possibility of producing energy on the farm when they took it over in 2009. Back then, the Great Recession had further squeezed already struggling dairy farms like theirs and they wanted to diversify their income. They spoke with nearby Middlebury College about the possibility of installing an anaerobic digester on the farm to produce energy that could help power the college. It took nearly a decade of discussion and research before Goodrich Farm partnered with Vanguard Renewables, a Massachusetts-based company that specializes in the development of "organics-to-renewable energy" projects.

Producing energy from cow manure isn't a new concept. A number of larger dairy farms in the state have been using digesters to produce electricity (the methane from the manure fuels an engine that runs an electrical generator) for more than a decade now. The heat generated by the process reduces heating fuel expenses for the farm and the electricity can be sold onto the grid, notably through Green Mountain Power's "Cow Power" program. This program allows utility customers – individuals as well as businesses – who choose to take part pay farmers for the electricity plus a small surcharge for its renewable benefits. Some 12 Vermont dairy farms, representing approximately 10,000 cows, are part of the Cow Power program, which

The anaerobic digester tanks and accompanying infrastructure to produce renewable natural gas from food waste and manure at Goodrich Farm in Salisbury.

PHOTOS COURTESY VANGUARD RENEWABLES

produces roughly 16 million kilowatt hours per year, enough to completely power about 2,200 Vermont homes.

What makes the project at Goodrich Farm so unusual is that they're not producing electricity, but rather natural gas. Renewable natural gas (RNG), to be specific. From an energy standpoint, that's more efficient than converting the methane to electricity. And the Goodrich Farm digester won't be filled with just manure, but also food waste from Middlebury College as well as other large food waste sources in the area, providing a welcome outlet in light of the recently enacted Vermont law banning food waste from landfills.

Goodrich Dairy Farm is large, at least by Vermont standards. There are 900 dairy cows and they grow 1,750 acres of hay and another 650 acres of corn. This gives the farm the space and the scale to produce natural gas in quantities that justify the infrastructure needed for a project like this, which is

Brother and sister Danielle and Chase Goodrich are third-generation dairy farmers and first-generation energy producers.

significant. Two separate one-million-gallon anaerobic digester tanks "cook" the manure and food waste for approximately 30 days, and have the capacity to accept 100 tons of manure and 80 tons of food waste every day.

The resulting RNG is moved in a Vermont Gas Systems' pipeline from the farm to Middlebury College's main power plant, where it will satisfy approximately 40 percent of the campus's thermal heating needs. The college signed a 20-year agreement to purchase about 55 percent of the gas produced at Goodrich Farm, the rest will be sold to Vermont Gas customers.

After the gas leaves via the pipeline, the remaining material moves on to a 250,000-gallon pretreatment center. Phosphorus is removed onsite, so the waste product makes an environmentally friendly fertilizer (some 17 million gallons a year of it) that

can be reapplied to fields. The phosphorus is sold to farms where the nutrient is lacking in soil and where it can be applied without running off into water sources.

Vanguard Renewables touts that Goodrich Farm's anaerobic digester is now the largest east of the Mississippi River, and notes that the benefits extend beyond the creation of renewable, non-fossil fuel heat: "The project features an extensive phosphorus removal system to protect the Otter Creek Watershed which feeds into Lake Champlain. Additionally, the facility will generate high quality, low-carbon liquid fertilizer that will reduce the farm's reliance on synthetic, chemical fertilizers. The farm will also benefit with reduced greenhouse gas emissions, animal bedding, and an annual lease payment for hosting the anaerobic digester facility."
—*Patrick White*

The Grazier's Grin

May 2021, as Vermonters yearn for an end to Covid confinement, dairy cows on the Franklin Farm in Guilford aim to spring forward. Bedded in the barn and shut in the yard all winter, they've watched the fields greening; watched John and David, son and father, ride out on four-wheelers to fix fences for the first paddocks in the pasture, which straddles the Massachusetts border. Sixty-five girls line up at the gate, set to gallop.

Mary Ellen Franklin, John's mother, has participated in this liberation caper since 1989. "Our good friends call it 'Independence Day.' That's true for all of us. Chores change. Less to do in the barn. Cows are feeding themselves. Spreading their own manure. Lower overhead. From now on into the fall, we'll be wearing our graziers' grins. I think our cows will, too." She gazes at the herd – Holsteins, Jerseys, HoJo crosses, faces to the field – and laughs, "Time for dessert!"

From her first close encounter with dairy cows,

Mary Ellen was smitten. Visiting a college roommate's family farm, she spent the weekend communing in the barn and never looked back. "I had to convince my first farmer, O. J. Manning, to hire me with no experience. I was about 20. His herdsperson was a woman who mentored me." Mary Ellen gathered skills on each farm: raising calves, maneuvering heavy equipment, weighing out and delivering custom rations to every cow six days a week. In her spare time, she read dairy magazines. Later, she learned to milk and manage a herd. Her travels brought her across borders to Vermont.

1988, sap running: Mary Ellen was milking for the last time on The Bunker Farm in Dummerston. The cows were up for auction. David Franklin, easygoing, soft-spoken, appeared in the parlor. "Like all struggling farmers, he was looking for an experienced milker. He offered me a job." She'd seen him before; heard about the farm's annual pig roast for family and

Mary Ellen and David Franklin

friends who helped out. The farm seemed like a lively place. Mary Ellen agreed to consider it. A few weeks later, she showed up to work.

For the redheaded milkmaid and the leap-year farmer, the arrangement was brilliant. "Soon, we were 'twitterpated,'" like the rabbits in Bambi. As the season heated up, the two were making more than hay. Besotted yet solid, the couple was wedded the following March. "Coming back from our honeymoon, through Leyden, Mass., the northern lights shimmered and guided us home. It seemed like a great omen."

David's uncle Russell Franklin still owned the farm at that point. Russell wanted David to invest in "a real farm" somewhere flat, not this hill farm, which relied on rented and borrowed fields. But David was an eighth-generation Guilford farmer. Mary Ellen said, "This farm seemed like a good place. The guy and cows I loved were here." The herd thrived. Their firstborn, John, arrived, followed by twins, Paul and Neil.

As young parents, the Franklins stopped using noxious chemicals. They began moving toward organic practices in the mid-1990s. A course in holistic management from the University of Vermont Extension shifted their perspective. Willie Gibson, their visionary facilitator, describes himself on LinkedIn as "a Certified Crop Advisor agronomist engaged in life-long [sic] learning about the science and mysteries of this world, and the human quest to be exceptional Stewards of Creation and One Another."

BIRTHDAY ODE

Mary Ellen, mentor, farm wife, mom,
And grand, you chose our hills for
Raising grazing herds, then sons.
Years flow, you follow. Sugaring

Each spring, you keep the recipe for
Lois Cutting's heirloom maple cream.
Living with a vision, the health of
Earth is under hoof. Walk about with
Novices. Note how pastures teach.

Frisky through the sixties, you're
Ready to call and coax home
Ambling horses, and horse around with
Nimble Maeve, sharing all you
Know of wisdom, craft, or cookery.
Love thrives side by side, on a sofa,
In a paddock. Let's celebrate your
Nature: Laughter before Labor.

—Verandah Porche

Mary Ellen explained, "Holistic management took farming back to solar, water, and mineral harvesting: turning sunshine into grass, and soil fertility and water and minerals into something cows could eat. We came to consider all of the resources of our farm beyond pounds of milk – maple, sawlogs, the forest, firewood." Stewarding their vision, they pulled their plan together: it would be diversified, sustainable, organic, and community minded. "Through the course, we all became such good friends. We shared pasture walks, monitoring what was growing there, how we moved the cows around at certain intervals, how fast the grass was coming back." In winters, they held potlucks with topics to tackle. The women formed their own group, part of the Women's Agricultural Network.

John and David run the farm now, so Mary Ellen has time to roam. Always an equal partner and an innovator on the farm, she's pleased to see more women in leadership. Since 2018, she has traveled statewide to match experienced grassland farmers with aspiring novices. As education coordinator for the Vermont Dairy Grazing Apprenticeship Program, she provides hands-on, foot-powered support to each partnership. "We pass knowledge on to the next generation, teaching in two years what took us twenty years to learn. You don't have to keep reinventing the wheel alone."

Currently, there are 22 approved mentors in Vermont, all on grazing dairies. Four already have apprentices on their farms. The program is growing and evolving. Recently, the board voted unanimously to replace the term "master grazer" with "mentor grazer." Mary Ellen says, "I've never met a farmer who was comfortable with the term 'master grazer.' No master's degree, no mastering the land – we're partners, all learners."

Dairy Grazing Apprenticeship is the only accredited apprenticeship for farming in the country. Its mission is to provide a guided pathway to independent farm ownership, to develop grazing careers, and to strengthen the economic and environmental well-being of rural communities and the dairy industry.

The apprenticeship is an "earn while you learn" opportunity. It is composed of 4,000 hours of paid employment and training over two years. Of those hours, 3,712 are on the farm under the guidance of an approved mentor grazier. The other 288 hours are spent taking courses on farm and pasture management, herd health, milk quality, soils, and holistic management, complemented by peer discussion groups, pasture walks, farming conferences, and networking opportunities.

Mary Ellen says, "Apprentices have that fire in the belly for dairy. They know the drill – how to recognize and treat health problems in the herd." While working with mentors, apprentices have stepped in for some farmers in emergencies and given others unexpected respite. She adds, "I wish this program had been around when I was getting started. Being brought along by someone who really cared, I would have had more confidence."

For Mary Ellen Franklin, lifelong learner, steward of the land and her community, the science and the mysteries matter. "From my first day in the barn, it was like fireworks – lightning. It's kept me lucky for so, so long. Five nights out of seven, I still have farming dreams."

—*Verandah Porche*

A Big Loss

The financial challenges for dairy farming in Vermont have been well chronicled in recent decades. In general, farms have followed one of two paths to success (or at least survival): get bigger or go organic. More cows means being able to take advantage of economies of scale (though in Vermont the scale is still tiny compared to megafarms elsewhere), while organic milk means being able to charge a premium in the marketplace.

Some farms that fall into the latter category got a jolt in August 2021 when Horizon Organic, a major buyer of organic milk in Vermont, notified their partner farms that they would no longer be purchasing milk from them. Horizon is based in Colorado and is part of Danone, the international conglomerate that owns Dannon yogurt and Silk milk, among other brands. The company plans to source its organic milk from larger farms in Texas and California in an effort to reduce shipping costs. Basically it's cheaper to pick up milk from a few large dairies than it is to run trucks to many small dairies every day.

Another factor: Some small-scale farmers say that the National Organic Program has become lax with its certification in terms of how cows are fed and raised, and this has allowed truly large-scale dairy operations in other states to sell their milk as organic, which was once the domain of just small farms. This gives these big farms the best of both competitive advantages: large scale and the organic premium.

Horizon's decision left 28 Vermont dairy farms reeling and without a primary purchaser for their milk (in total, 88 farms in the Northeast were affected). The company provided about one year's notice that the contracts would be ending, so these farms can sell to Horizon until August 2022. There are concerns, though, that it will be difficult to find markets for all the milk after that. There are other large buyers of organic milk in Vermont, including Stonyfield Organic, Organic Valley, and Upstate Niagara Cooperative, but early indications were that their demand wouldn't be nearly enough to compensate for the loss of Horizon.

The Vermont Agency of Agriculture, the Northeast Organic Farming Association of Vermont (NOFA-VT), and organic dairy farmers quickly began meeting to make plans for a new path forward. Some good news came on October 14 when New Hampshire-based Stonyfield Organic announced it would buy as much milk as possible from affected farms. Stonyfield said its goal was to help save these family farms.

When the Horizon news first hit, Randolph dairy farmer Abbie Corse, a NOFA-VT board member who sells her milk to Organic Valley and not Horizon, told *VTDigger* that the strain from Horizon's announcement has been real. "These aren't just jobs. These aren't just pieces of the economy. These are entire lives that are tied up in a farm," Corse said. "Even having to go through a process of receiving a letter like this is something that – I just don't think the average person understands what that means for these folks."

NOFA-VT reports that the number of dairy farms in the state has decreased 37 percent over the last year; in that same time, the number of organic dairies has dropped by 8 percent, making organic a (relatively) bright spot. There were 181 organic dairy farms in the state in 2020. The hope is that finding new markets for that milk will keep organic dairying a viable and vibrant part of Vermont agriculture. —*Patrick White*

JL DAMON

FEBRUARY

February

This February, people are out and about. Nearly every day, our local sledding spot in Underhill is packed with children and their huge tubes. At the base of the hill, the rec department has groomed a ski track that is being used by everyone from the high school Nordic team to the Mansfield Nordic Club, whose members range in age from 5 to 78. So many have been coming to the hill to play and exercise that the town has opened an auxiliary parking lot, an unheard-of measure in this village of 3,000.

A little way around the bend, the town has set up a skating rink on the center green, where little rippers in hockey gear are zooming around their parents, who glide and chat with neighbors. Thanks to the pandemic, everyone is masked up or covered in a scarf, but there is an ease in people's movements that I haven't seen in a year. In the past, this rink has been hit or miss, suffering from warm weather, indifference, or both.

In the 21 years I have lived here, our public spaces have never been this full of picture-perfect winter merriment. It looks very much like the Vermont of Hallmark Christmas movies, which are rarely, if ever, actually filmed in Vermont. This year, our community has embraced the extraordinary resources we have, and driving through town, the scene is downright idyllic. On a day with bluebird skies, laughing children, and pristine snow, all I can think to myself is, cue the meet-cute between the handsome woodworker and the workaholic city girl.

I'm aware that the image of Vermont in the rest of the country's imagination is of snowy knolls, rosy-cheeked children pulling sleds, and burly men in red buffalo check, but it's not always like this. The truth is that climate change has made our weather unpredictable, and our kids are as likely as any others to sit inside, in front of screens for as long as they can get away with it. (The part about the guys in red flannel is true.)

One of the reasons for the flurry of activity this year is the excellent snow we've received. Though we are only 30 miles from the Canadian border, good coverage is not a given in this region anymore. While many winters are decent, some have been absolutely dreary. I have pictures of my children in 2016 geared up in boots and skis, standing on dirt, next to a single band of snow that was manufactured by the ski resort. This year, it is fluffy, deep perfection.

The other reason that people are outside is the same as everyone else's on the planet: boredom and isolation caused by the Covid pandemic. It's clear that many parents headed into their basements or garages to dust off whatever gear could get them and their children out of the house. That's when the rinks and hills started to fill up. It's not that we weren't outdoorsy types before; I just don't recall ever witnessing it with such volume and exuberance.

To be absolutely clear, I am not glad about the pandemic. We lost a beloved member of our community early on, before lockdown even started. The isolation has also taken a toll on our youth, causing an upheaval not just in their schooling but also in their mental well-being. There have been at least two teen suicides in adjacent towns since last March that I am aware of. More broadly speaking, the national statistics of death, unemployment and ongoing sickness give daily heartbreak. But the fact that it took a pandemic to get the whole community outside and past our location apathy is a morsel of good in a year that was truly bad.

Who knows if we will be able to recreate this year of outdoor wonderment? It partly depends on good snow, which only the weather gods can control. But our enthusiasm about the resources that are right here is up to us. In the meantime, please tell Hallmark to bring up their cameras, give those poor actors some legit, cold-weather clothing, and we'll show them how a bucolic winter scene is done. —*Laura Sorkin*

Winter Heads South

Much of Vermont is as close as you can get to the mid-way point between the tropical equator and arid north pole. And big snowstorms – or a lack of them – in February are determined by which air mass influences us. Moisture during this time of year often comes from the south or streams across the nation from the Pacific Ocean. Cold, dry air is a reflection of a northern jet stream.

Although Vermont is known for its snow, the right ingredients need to be in place for lots of it to fall. A Nor'easter is a great example, as it is a coastal system that draws a moist air mass northward and interacts with the cold air sinking from the north. If the cold and dry air slips too far south, the Mid-Atlantic states are left with Vermont's white gold, which is often unwanted and just a nuisance over those areas. If the warmer and moist air moves too far north, this can lead to "liquid precipitation" in the Green Mountains – a place where the "R-word" is unwelcome during the winter months.

The stars never aligned for any particularly big snow dumps this February, which was

Slow tapping in deep snow on February 21.

Snowfall departure from average (in inches), February 2021

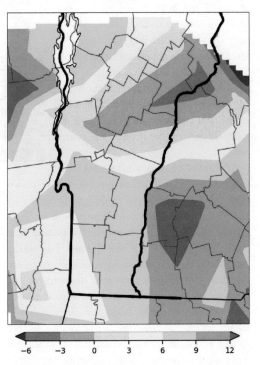

especially evident in the northern mountains. The Mount Mansfield snow stake was around 50 percent below normal much of the month. But multi-day, light snow events led to significant accumulations in parts of the state. This orographic precipitation is influenced by topography and makes it hard to forecast the weather in Vermont or make sweeping generalizations about snowfall totals. In parts of Bennington and Windham Counties – sometimes dismissively referred to as the Banana Belt – snow fell on more than half of the days in February, which led to knee-deep accumulations in the valleys and thigh- to waist-deep accumulations at higher elevations that lingered well into March. —*Christopher Kurdek, Fairbanks Museum and Planetarium*

NATURE NOTES

Drop Hunting

11/09/2018   09:16PM   CAMERA1

Late winter is a lean time for hunting magazine editors, as pretty much all the hunting seasons are over until May. So one of their go-to, how-to stories involves shed hunting. Deer and moose lose their antlers over the winter. Since it's exciting to find an antler, it's only natural to build content around "the hunt." My favorite tip from one shed-hunting story I read in *Outdoor News* is, "Above all else, look down – that is where the antlers will be."

It's hard to argue with that tip, but some of the others you read in these types of stories – drawn from a sort of conventional wisdom that's sprung up around the practice – are a little more dubious. Take, for example, the idea that mature bucks shed first, in late December or very early January. I think the extrapolation here is that since vigorous deer in captivity shed later than their non-vigorous counterparts, and since age and stress often correlate with decreased vigor, and since mature bucks are older and "run themselves ragged" during the rut, their antlers will fall first. Of course, there's a great deal of vigor baked into a rack buck's 200-pound body as compared to that of a 100-pound weakling forkhorn. And nutrition, which is both site specific and year specific, has a lot to say about vigor. Also genetics. And there are wildcards to consider, like coyotes, or dogs, or shed hunters, who can push and stress deer – or not – in the winter. There are

actually shed-hunting seasons in some western states to protect the animals from the stress caused by shed hunters; there are no laws regarding the practice here, but we'd be wise to self-regulate and stay away from where the animals congregate until the snow retreats and they get their health back.

This nice mature drop I found recently is an example that runs counter to the "mature-bucks-drop-first" thinking. I wasn't looking for it; I found it in the sugarbush at the base of one of the trees I was tapping. It was in a buck's bed, and I could see from the tracks that it was dropped during the last week of February. It was a particularly rewarding find because I know this buck – I'll include a picture of him in the flesh from hunting season, 2018. It's almost certainly the same deer because of his abnormally long brow tines. —*Dave Mance III*

CACHED EAR-CORN in a fold of maple bark, at least three-quarters of a mile from the nearest possible source of corn. Could be a nuthatch, which has a habit of caching seeds in crevices then hacking them open.

JERRY HIAM

FEBRUARY 1, 2021. 7:05 a.m. Sunrise one minute earlier than yesterday. 2 degrees; wind NW 1 mph, on the cusp of a Nor'easter. Sky: pot-bellied moon in the west – the tarnished remnant of a bright disc. Long clouds, gray-blue, trimmed in pink. Between them, the blue light of sunrise. Mink tracks reduced to a trace, the evanescent thread of an itinerant hunter, to be erased tonight. Wetlands: archipelagos of sweet gale, brown islands glazed by frost. Tiny crystals of frost outline alder limbs and coat sausage-shaped catkins. The haunting drumroll of pileated woodpeckers, secure in a fortress of pine. Pond: the illusion of invariability. Fools me again and again.

A tufted titmouse whistles an abridged song: two loud notes, *Peter, Peter.* Less musical – more robust – than a chickadee, who sings nearby. Birds seemingly in sync with the Gregorian calendar. High in the west, croaking beneath the weight of barometric changes, a raven lampoons the sunny morning … and anything to do with calendars. He *feels* the pressure of what moves up the coast.

FEBRUARY 14, 2021. 6:48 a.m.
Sunrise two minutes earlier than yesterday. 19 degrees (a veritable heat wave); wind NW 1 mph. Sky: grayish light, flat and untextured, an absence of warm color, a heavenly malaise unsuitable for Valentine's Day. No new mink sign or openings or snow, an aching flow dampened by recent weather's weight. Wetlands: sleepy marsh under a listless sky… then, suddenly, the bald eagles appear, conjured out of the east. A pair high above the reeds, heading north, love-struck. Courtship: airborne gymnasts above a lonely marsh. The female rolls over. Flies upside down. Touches the male's talons, the ultimate *high-five* (actually a high-four). And for me, for the moment, transitory bliss. Slow, rhythmic wingbeats, effortless flight, each wing slightly bent at the wrist – both birds cackle, chicken-voiced raptors. I watch the eagles disappear beyond the pines, the wind dissolving their discordant titters. Unmuzzled, the morning becomes rich with possibility.

On the road back home, red crossbills in the pines, their chatter slightly softer than the eagles'. Even though it's 24 degrees warmer than yesterday morning, chickadees refrain from singing. Perhaps stymied by cloud cover. Pileated laughs, the insanity of a woodpecker, then nothing – no drumming either by pileated or hairy. February sunshine: lodestone that triggers good thoughts, as well as bird music.

2020, Year of the Pandemic: 37 bald eagles nested in Vermont, fledged 64 chicks. A modern-day record. Extirpated as a breeder in the 1940s; returned in 2008. Hopefully here to stay. It's a rare trip down the interstate when I don't see one. —*Ted Levin*

Ted Levin's observations were taken from his Homeboy at Home During Coronavirus *blog, posted on Substack, which detailed his daily walks and ran for 450 straight days during the pandemic. In spring 2021, he sold his place at Coyote Hollow in Thetford and moved to Hurricane Hill on the ridgeline between the White River and Ottauquechee. We hope he keeps writing.*

JERRY HIAM

AT HOME

❦

Usnea Near You

With Covid still dominating the news and Vermont in a state of emergency, I hightailed it for the woods. For many years, there was a stash of usnea tincture in the root cellar awaiting a sniffle or a cold. When my boys were young, I believed it best to save antibiotics for things like Lyme disease and strep, so I would just have them drink a shot of usnea if they weren't feeling well. But I'd been lazy, and with this scary new virus changing the world, I realized I had hardly any left.

And so began the hunt around my hilltop. Pronounced "ooze-nee-ah" and better known as old man's beard, the long and light-green lichen tendrils grow from tree trunks and branches in Vermont forests and in many other places around the globe. In the Near and Far East it's considered to be a super effective natural medicinal, botanists use it as an excellent gauge of environmental pollution, and some refer to it as an indicator of true north. But, as was the case with Covid when this whole thing started, most people have never even heard of it.

I took up the old hunt with many purposeful walks off the porch and into the woods. Usnea prefers old or dead conifers in a moist forest, and we have plenty of such habitat in our surroundings. The singular focus on finding usnea rekindled my earlier fascination. Usnea is a combination of two organisms – a fungus and an alga. The fungus provides the core, the green alga sheath gathers energy from the sun, and two completely different life forms come together to create a new structure.

Some other lichens resemble usnea, and often, they are even found intertwined. The way to distinguish Usnea is to hold a lacy strand in your fingers and gently tug on either end. The outer green sheath will split, revealing a white inner pith that will stretch

before snapping. Usnea is elastic; other lichens aren't.

Usnea has been used therapeutically for over 3,000 years to treat bacterial and fungal infections. Native Americans used it as an expectorant, a dermatological aid for boils, and an absorbent emergency dressing for backwoods wounds. Today, it is still prescribed by Asian and Russian herbalists to treat pulmonary tuberculosis, scrofula, bronchitis, infected wounds, and external ulcers. Contemporary proponents of alternative medicine claim Usnea is useful for treating the common cold, sore throats, and coughs, and some studies suggest that it has anti-cancer and antiviral properties.

Given the right conditions – not too dry and sunny – usnea grows worldwide. Once, I was in Uruguay and saw miles upon miles of wooden post fencing draped with the beautiful tendrils. But even though I have seen huge clumps hanging from the trees below ski lifts in Switzerland, it is becoming less common to see it in western Europe. Apparently, lichens are on the decline there because of pollution and the depletion of suitable forest habitat.

Most interesting is how usnea can serve as an extremely sensitive filter, and therefore an ideal indicator for fossil fuel pollution. Heavy metals accumulate in usnea, and sulfur dioxide and acid rain will kill it. So if you decide to harvest some for its botanical properties, try to stay away from busy roadsides and heavily populated areas where pollution is heaviest. On the bright side, however, if you come across a forest with lots of healthy usnea, you may assume you're in a relatively clean environment.

Finally, if you're lost in the woods and remember that you once heard that usnea could show you where true north lies, do be careful. It grows on the moist sides of trees; in an open deciduous forest that can be the shady north side, hence the old-timey trick. But a denser, closed-canopy forest that holds moisture uniformly creates an usnea free-for-all on all sides of the trees. Throw steep hillsides and different shade angles into the equation, and your compass needle is swinging out of control. It's probably best to stick with gauging direction using the sun.

I can't quite walk my hilltop with my eyes closed, but I certainly can navigate the well-worn paths at night with a headlamp. So I paid no attention whatsoever to compass points as I greedily plucked the wispy fronds and stuffed my pockets to restock the shelves. Judging by the quantities available, it was a nice counterpoint to believe the woods were still healthy and unchangeable in a world that doesn't feel as if it will stop changing. —*Tania Aebi*

I AM A GOD TO THE BIRDS

I am a God to the birds
flocking to my feeder in winter.
A forgiving God who,
when winter winds bite
and summer's bounty is frozen,
miraculously provides fishes and loaves,
sunflower seeds and suet,
in exchange for their beauty,
their bickering, their blessing.
They cannot know how I praise them
through the glass, astounded
that they can fly and I cannot,
that for them fear is so ordinary,
so transcendent, that they proclaim
the glory.

When the winter of my soul chills,
when the fruits of summer are exhausted,
I turn to holy books to peck at their words
for seeds of truth, for sustenance, for exaltation.
I revel in the mystery, the prayer that a God
behind the window loves me enough
to feed my soul.

JACK MAYER

A LOOK BACK

Winter Hibernation

Elbert Stevens made a startling discovery one day in 1939. Sorting through possessions of his late mother, Hannah, Stevens happened upon a yellowing newspaper clipping.

That this story caught Hannah's eye, and later Elbert's, is understandable: it told of how in one poor Vermont family the elderly and infirm were put into a sort of hibernation so that others would not have to care for them during winter. The tale was so fantastical that it had to be some sort of joke. But the newspaper story gave no hint that it was.

Adding to the mystery was the fact that Hannah, who was a compulsive newspaper clipper, had neglected to note when or where the story had been published.

Elbert, who lived in Bridgewater Corners, took the mysterious story to the *Rutland Herald*, which published a report, including a complete transcript of the clipping, in May 1939. The *Boston Globe*, *Yankee Magazine*, and the *Old Farmer's Almanac* followed up with their own accounts. No one knew quite what to make of the tale, though some reputable big-city researchers wondered whether this folk medicine from the hills of Vermont might someday help cure cancer and heart disease.

The author of the original story, who was identified only as "A.M.," had begun his story by declaring, "I am an old man and have seen some strange sights in the course of a roving life in foreign lands as well as in this country, but none so strange as one found recorded in an old diary, kept by my Uncle William," which A.M. had inherited.

According to the diary, one January day in a poor town about 20 miles from Montpelier, William saw that "[s]ix persons, four men and two women, one of the men a cripple about thirty-years-old, the other five past the age of usefulness, lay on the earthy floor of the cabin, drugged into insensibility."

The men and women were then stripped down to a single garment and carried outside into the snow. William watched as the bodies began to lose their color. When he reentered the cabin, he was shocked to find his hosts engaged in everyday conversation, as if something strange and ghastly weren't happening just outside.

"[S]eated on a single block, [I] passed the dreary night, terror-stricken by the horrible sights I had witnessed," William wrote.

The next morning, he watched as his hosts lay the frozen figures, with a cloth over each face and a layer of straw over the entire body, in stacks inside a wooden crate, which was intended to protect them from animals.

Then, using a sled, the townspeople dragged the crate to the foot of a ledge, where during the winter it would be buried by a 20-foot-deep snowdrift.

"I left the mountaineers, living and frozen, to their fate, and returned to my home in Boston, where it was weeks before I was fairly myself, as my thoughts would return to that mountain with its awful sepulcher," William wrote.

Reading through his uncle's diary, A.M. learned that William had returned to the town the following May, when he watched as townspeople removed the bodies from the crate and immersed them in lukewarm water in troughs fashioned from hemlock trunks.

Nearby, cauldrons of water, tinged red by steeping hemlock boughs, boiled over a fire. This water was then used to raise the temperature of the water in the troughs. As the color began to return to the bodies, townspeople kneeled and tried to rub the life back into them.

"[S]light twitching of the muscles of the face and limbs, followed by audible gasps showed that life was not quenched," William wrote, "and that vitality was returning."

The once-frozen people were given shots of liquor and gradually they began to mumble, then talk, and finally sit up in their troughs. They were then led to a nearby house for a springtime feast. To William, they appeared no worse the wear for their winter's hibernation.

The press accounts about the mysterious clipping were too much to ignore for Roland Wells Robbins, an archaeologist. Robbins, with the help of Vermont State Library staff, figured out that the clipping came from an 1887 edition of the *Argus & Patriot*, a newspaper in Montpelier. Oddly, Robbins noted, the bizarre story hadn't elicited any letters to the editor in the weeks that followed its publication. And Robbins still didn't know who A.M. was or why he or she had written the story.

Robbins wrote what he did know in a 1949 article for *Vermont Life*. That article drew at least one important letter from a reader. A Mabel Hynes, writing from Florida, managed to fill in major gaps in the story. She explained that A.M. had been her grandfather, Allen Morse. Though Morse had once told the story, he had nothing to do with having it published.

Morse's daughter, Alice, had asked him to write down the tale, but hadn't told him why. Alice, who worked for the *Argus & Patriot*, arranged to have it published as a surprise 52nd birthday gift to her father. The newspaper editor's only condition had been that Alice set the type herself.

Perhaps Alice signed the piece with the initials A.M., because she shared them with her father. Or perhaps she realized that signing the article with her father's name would tip off many readers that the story was a hoax, because Allen Morse was a well-known teller of tall tales. If *Argus & Patriot* readers understood that this was just a wild yarn, then that would explain the lack of letters to the editor. Allen Morse originally spun this story at a family reunion at Curtis Pond in Calais, where he lived. Legend has it that Allen hadn't planned to tell the story that day, but decided to do so after the dramatic entrance of his cousin at the reunion. Benjamin Morse and his wife had arrived with an amazing story to tell. As the couple was riding north from Montpelier to the reunion, they had glanced over at a cemetery they were passing and seen a blue flame burst from one of the graves.

People surrounded Benjamin, barraging him with questions. This was more than Allen could stand. "That took the attention off him, and he had to do him one better," said Robert Morse, a distant relative of Allen, who grew up as part of the well-known Morse family of the Montpelier area. "Allen was supposed to be the storyteller in the family."

—*Mark Bushnell*

Adapting to the Future of Ash in Vermont

Anyone who spends time in Vermont's forests knows that change is a constant, whether it takes the form of seasonal shifts in the hues of the canopy or decades-long changes in tree cover and stem size following a disturbance. Nevertheless, some of the changes we are now dealing with just don't feel the same. Muddy winters, sweltering summers, and a proliferation of alien invaders all point to changing forest conditions with no historic analog. How Vermont forests will change over the coming decades in response to this multitude of factors is highly uncertain, but it's clear that novel conditions are likely to become the norm.

The detection of the invasive emerald ash borer (EAB) in Orange County on February 20, 2018, was a stark example of the new challenges facing Vermont's forests. First introduced to southeastern Michigan in the 1990s from Asia, this insect has now spread to 35 states and 5 Canadian provinces. It has caused significant mortality to several ash species, including the species native to Vermont: black, green, and white ash. Unfortunately, examples of ash trees' surviving an invasion of these metallic green tree killers are rare, generating a general sense of dread regarding what the future might hold for the over 150 million ash trees in Vermont.

One of the greatest effects will be cultural, as black ash has been central to the traditions and lifeways of the Abenaki people and many other First Nations tribes across the tree's range for millennia. In particular, its wood has long been prized for basket making. Efforts are underway both to protect individual trees with stem-injected insecticides and to collect black ash seed. This will provide future opportunities to restore ash trees once this invasive insect is under control.

Green ash, although the least abundant ash species in the state (approximately two percent), makes up a significant component of plantings along boulevards and greenspaces in many cities and towns. As a result, concerns surrounding EAB have focused on how the insect might change urban and residential canopy cover. The protection of select high-value trees with insecticides and preemptive ash removals followed by the planting of replacement tree species have been common strategies. The costs associated with

Dartmouth College Woodlands Forester Kevin Evans, Assistant Forester Riley Patry, and several forestry graduate students from the University of Vermont examine white ash sawlogs harvested from experimental treatments at the Clement Woodlot in Corinth, Vermont.

implementing these treatments across a municipality, like the over 1,200 ash trees lining streets and other public areas in Burlington, are not trivial. However, they are diminished when weighed against the myriad human wellness and ecological benefits urban and residential trees provide.

There's a reason white ash is the topic of most discussions about EAB in Vermont. A common component of northern hardwood forests, white ash constitutes 70 percent of the ash trees in the state. It is particularly abundant in rich soil. Referred to as a "gap-obligate" species, it establishes itself in large canopy openings created by disturbances and can quickly outgrow common associates, like sugar maple, which tend to bide their time in the shade. As a result, white ash is often one of the largest trees in our forests. Coupled with its desirable wood properties, this makes it one of the most valued timber species in the state. The arrival of EAB certainly motivated some to preemptively harvest white ash. Nevertheless, many foresters and ecologists, aware of the historical consequences of this type of selective cutting, are urging people to retain ash trees that are either too big or too small to harvest; these trees would serve as both a seed source and a reservoir of genetic diversity for a future forest. This alternative thinking is best encapsulated by Mike Snyder, Commissioner of Vermont Forests, Parks, and Recreation (FPR), who warns, "Don't be rash about your ash."

The forestry and broader conservation community has been connecting at workshops and meetings since EAB's arrival to share an understanding of the role ash plays in our forest and to puzzle through what adaptation strategies might best address the threat. An outgrowth is a recent large experiment at Dartmouth College's Clement Woodlot in Corinth, Vermont. The 180-acre site is a beautiful northern hardwood forest of over 40 percent white ash located just a few miles from where EAB was first found in Vermont. Foresters, ecologists, and scientists from Vermont FPR, the Vermont Land Trust, Redstart Natural Resource Management, Vermont Fish and Wildlife, Dartmouth College, and the University of Vermont are collaborating on a variety of treatments that build on principles of ecological forestry and sound forest stewardship.

The goal is to increase forest structure and complexity by creating different harvest gap sizes and retaining large living and dead trees. Greater forest complexity will provide multiple ways for the forest to respond to an EAB invasion or other future stressors. Keeping white ash a part of the future forest is also a long-term objective, so treatments include retaining some mature white ash and creating regeneration environments suitable for white ash seedlings. Management strategies also aim to increase the abundance of species adapted to future climate conditions by planting warm-adapted species like red oak and bitternut hickory in experimental harvest gaps. Unmanaged controls are also a key component of this work, and long-term monitoring plots are wired with environmental sensors to provide baselines for observing the role of white ash in our forests. This will allow for the documentation of how these unmanaged areas change once EAB passes. The full picture of how EAB will affect Vermont's forests is unclear. The goal is to make sure our response to this threat is anything but rash. —*Tony D'Amato*

The seedlings in this harvest gap are warm-adapted tree species.

TONY D'AMATO

February 19, 2021, Logging camp, Edward Legacy Logging, Shaftsbury

20 Years of Log Prices

$ per thousand board feet	2001	2011	2021
Ash	250	350	650
Yellow Birch	325	475	525
Cherry	550	425	500
Hard Maple	600	525	1000
Soft Maple	200	300	575
Red Oak	525	450	600

It's getting to the point in winter when you start really missing baseball games on the radio. Those of us in the western part of the state are likely to have Yankees games on local FM stations, and if we listen we hear announcer John Sterling say over and over again "Baseball: it's not like the other sports" before making an obvious point about how the best players fail 7 times out of 10 or how there are 162 games in a season or whatever other quirky-to-baseball thing comes to his mind.

Timber's not like the other agricultural crops in the state. Foresters and landowners talk about growing it, but it's almost never planted – when they say that they mean they make a few inputs in their lifetime that hopefully steer things towards a desired outcome, but otherwise they just watch it grow. And what they're watching grow defies easy categorization. Because they're working with nature, there's little room for specialization. When it is time to harvest, they take what the land gives them and then sell it into a decentralized marketplace that's constantly morphing.

The economics of a timber sale are just as hard to wrap your mind around as the rest of it, and part of the trouble is the time scale and the cloaking nature of inflation. Word on the street around here is that hardwood log prices are up, which is true compared to last year. But last winter's Covid-shocked prices are a pretty low bar.

We've been watching wood grow down here in southern Vermont for decades, so I went back and found some receipts from hardwood timber sales in 2001 and 2011 and compared them to a price sheet from this February, 2021. I focused on #1 sawlogs – that's a middle-of-the-road log. Three points of comparison is a pretty modest sample, but it is enough to give an illustrative snapshot of how things have changed.

What we see is that ash and soft maple have done well over time, which is heartening in the case of soft maple and bittersweet in the case of ash since the emerald ash borer, an invasive insect which was brought to the US on a container ships from Asia, is likely to kill it all soon. Part of the ash price is buoyed around here by the Ames Mill in Wallingford which buys a lot and forces other buyers to stay competitive; part is because the Chinese want it. I asked one industry insider if he was worried the Chinese might learn that the emerald ash borer is killing all the ash and use that as leverage to lower prices, and his take was that they already knew and wanted it precisely because it was going to be rare. Don't think too hard about that last line and the idea of global commerce causing a species-destroying plague and then cashing in on it, as it's kind of crushing.

Yellow birch and hard maple held their value, and in hard maple's case, it appreciated a bit. That's good.

Red oak and cherry were the dogs. When we adjust the 2001 numbers for inflation, we see that #1 cherry lost about 40 percent of its value over those 20 years; red oak lost around 25 percent. —*Dave Mance III*

Grading Logs with Dan Wood

It was a February afternoon at the Allard Lumber yard in Pawlet; one of those perfect bluebird winter days when the sky's high and the air bites. A month of cold had been good for woods work – loggers want the ground hard so the logs and machines don't sink in the mud – and the yard was filling up.

Dan Wood and Justin Davenport were grading. Jeff Twitchell was driving the loader. A load of wood from Washington County, New York, rolled in. The driver parked the truck and then got out to stretch his legs. The loader started picking logs off the truck, twirling them in mid-air so the graders could see both ends. They were looking at heart-size – if large, the mineral stain in the center of a log is considered to be bad. And they looked for signs of rot, compression, and spiral grain that makes boards twist when the log's opened up. The ends are windows into the inside of the log. On the ground they measured length and width of logs and scanned the boles for bird peck and other wounds, branch stubs, bark inclusions, signs of human damage, then wrote specs and their grading

decisions in code on the end of the log in crayon.

One of the things you hear all the time from foresters and non-profits who serve as the mouthpiece for foresters is that it pays to let good wood grow – it's like a commandment in Christian religious traditions. The economic argument is that a log nearly doubles in volume as it grows from 16 inches to 22 inches, so by waiting an extra cycle before you cut it, you'll double your money.

But at the yard, where logs are pure commodity, the message can be quite different.

"Foresters are always telling me that you need to let wood grow, and loggers are always telling me the wood's too big and gone by. Who's right?"

"The loggers," said Wood.

His whole job is to see lost value. The heartwood in a tree expands with age, so if he's lowering the grade on a 24-inch maple for having a large heart, he's thinking that at 20 inches it might have made veneer. There might not have been the bird peck in the cherry log that he downgraded for if it were cut last cycle. There were several examples he pointed out where value was lost because the logger didn't cut to length properly. "See this log," he said, pointing to a big, ugly red maple in the pallet log pile. "If they cut it at 16 feet, we could have made a mat log with it. By bucking it in the wrong place they lost money."

The challenges in the log business are substantial and he rattles some off. "Less and less loggers; less truckers; less wood being offered."

Fickle export markets are perplexing, and Wood points out that export markets for raw materials are, in general, a double-edged sword. Sure, it's nice to have an outlet. "But how many countries that aren't third-world send their raw materials overseas to have the value added?" he asks rhetorically. He was born and raised in the area, has been in the timber industry since 1978, and remembers the furniture mills, and dowel mills, and little random boutique mills that made things vertically integrated in the Vermont wood economy years ago.

Log graders have always had to walk a tightrope – if you grade too easy, the loggers and landowners are happy but you lose your employer money. Grade too hard and the loggers and landowners won't want to sell to you, which will lose your employer money.

Dan Wood at the Allard Lumber yard in Pawlet.

Technology has helped in this regard, as each log gets stickered and scanned, and the mill tabulates data on what each log eventually yielded. This effectively grades the grader. If you're off, they can let you know by exactly how much.

The logs were still coming off the truck when the next one showed up. It amazed me how fast the crew worked.

"How long does it take someone to get good at this," I asked.

"A smart guy can pick up 80 percent of this in a couple days," said Wood. "The other 20 percent takes years." —*Dave Mance III*

From Logs to Lumber

Most of us buy lumber from hardware stores and building suppliers and give little thought to where the wood grew or where it was milled. Even though timber from Vermont forests was a foundation of the regional economy – and remains an essential commodity today – many small and mid-sized sawmills in the Northeast had folded by the late 1990s. Wood from our region is increasingly trucked to industrial-scale sawmills as far away as Canada. Meanwhile, quality hardwood logs are exported directly to China for that country's burgeoning furniture industry. As I write this in spring 2021, a recent building boom in the US, coupled with shortages of home-grown timber, have us importing softwood.

But there are some who buck the growing tide of globalization and our disconnected relationship with wood. In Thetford Center, about a mile from where a water-powered mill once ran on the Ompompanoosuc River, Ellis Paige still operates a private sawmill and transforms trees he harvests from his own land into valuable lumber. —*Li Shen*

PHOTOS BY LI SHEN

Ellis Paige and Pete LaPierre maneuver a log towards the carriage on the left.

A 1945 International tractor motor runs the sawmill. The PTO-shaft of the tractor connects to the saw via a series of pulleys and belts that Ellis adapted from an old corn chopper. The pulleys reduce the motor speed of 1,100 rpm to the blade rotational speed of 700 rpm. Below: Dimensions are carefully set by moving the carriage sideways. The red line is the beam from a laser leveler that shows exactly where the saw blade will make the cut.

The log is secured on the carriage, which glides forward on steel tracks and feeds the log through the saw at the pull of the lever. The lever also controls its return. The hanging piece of plexiglass shields Ellis from flying woodchips.

Pete loads a finished post
onto the forklift.

The men communicate
with hand signs.
It's too noisy to hear
anyone speak.

MARCH

March

A dingy Frigidaire is March.

Our contents we despise in March.

Pandemic exile chills the heart.

Our longings crystallize in March.

Spring forward? Ha! we slide apart.

Smoke gets in your Ides of March.

A new regime, the open scars.

Will empathy thaw ICE in March?

What lies come loose in fits and starts?

May hoodlums testify in March.

A batter smirks: the fielders charge.

Fans wake to fantasize in March.

Shovel first then rake the yard.

Green spears our surprise in March.

Warm the seed bed by the hearth.

What faith we improvise in March!

November's bones. December's shards.

Beauty in Disguise is March.

Sap boils above the flaming arch.

Sweet with dreams we rise in March.

Inoculate my empty arm.

A viral prayer: Good-bye in March.

Verandah Porche

Fickle and Variable

Before I became a meteorologist I was a ski coach at Stowe through my 20s. If there is one group of people who follow the winter weather closely it is skiers and riders, as their sports heavily depend on it. Although they are often a very educated group when it comes to the weather, sometimes they can buy into common misperceptions. I often heard skiers excitedly claim that March is the snowiest month of the year; this isn't exactly false, but it does depend on the year.

A couple ways to describe the winter of 2020/2021 would be fickle and variable. January and February offered seasonally cold conditions, which helped to preserve the snow that was on the ground and any new that came along. But March 2021 was far from fruitful in the snow department, and many record-high temperatures were set throughout the month. The mean temperature in Burlington was around 4 degrees above normal, with precipitation more than an inch below normal. Only 1.4 inches of snow came over Vermont's biggest city, which is about a tenth of the typical snowfall for this month. Many other sites throughout the state offered the same dry and warm readings as well. At least five days offered record-breaking highs; there would have been more but for the epic warm spell of March 2012, which set some untouchable record highs in the upper 70s and 80s through the middle of the month.

Near the end of March 2021 a cold front swept a line of thunderstorms through the state. Although common during the summer months, thunderstorms are far less likely to be seen at the end of the winter. Rarer still are winter tornadoes, but that's just what occurred in Middlebury on the 26th, as an EF1 tornado provided hurricane-force winds of around 110 mph, resulting in some structure damage and two injuries reported. This event was likely the only twister to have ever come over the state in the month of March. There were reports of a March tornado back in the 1950s, but we now think that the event was actually downsloping winds rather than an actual tornado.

Just to reinforce the idea that the month was variable, accumulating snow made a return to parts of the state on the Friday after the Middlebury tornado. —*Christopher Kurdek, Fairbanks Museum and Planetarium*

NATIONAL WEATHER SERVICE

Painter Road, Middlebury, the morning after an EF1 tornado came through.

NATURE NOTES

BRYAN PFEIFFER

Shards of Sky

Idare you to name a more elegant songbird here in North America. The soft, rustling warble. The glow from its plumage. And the gentleness by which it goes about its business. The eastern bluebird scores 10s all around. Other bluebird species – mountain and western – tie for second by virtue of their big, wilder, less intimate habitats. Tufted titmouse, doe-eyed and plaintive in song, might come in third. Chickadees? Wonderful, of course, but more plucky than elegant. Waxwings and phainopela – yeah, they'll make you euphoric, but not like a bluebird. Certainly not at the end of winter here in Vermont, where the ice still locked up Shelburne Bay on Lake Champlain this past weekend. The bluebirds at the bay, however, were melting that ice (and given the chance could probably disable Ice Nine). Especially this male who sang for us and landed on this snag above for my pal Josh Lincoln and me to photograph. —*Bryan Pfeiffer*

AMARA DUNN / NYSIPM

THE STATE CONDUCTED its annual hemlock woolly adelgid survey this year on March 16, and found that 51 percent of the insects in the study block had died. (During the mild winter of 2020, only 39 percent succumbed to the cold.) This year's winter temperatures averaged only slightly colder than last year, but researchers hypothesize that the fluctuating temperatures in March, when we experienced periods of warming temperatures followed by successive days of deep freezes, probably accounted for the extra mortality. The spread of this invasive insect, which has decimated hemlock stands to the south of us, tracks closely with winter weather. During cold winters, they almost all die, which keeps outbreaks contained. During warm winters, they spread.

An Image 30 Years in the Making

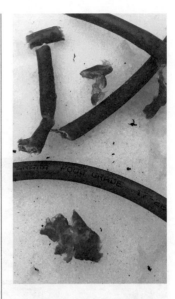

I grew up exploring the woods, lakes, and swamps in central Michigan. Skunk cabbage was a particular favorite, given its early and odiferous appearance and magnificent unfurling. Somewhere along the way I noticed the snow melted around the plant as it emerged and, years later, after I began a career teaching people to use thermal imaging cameras, I knew I had to get images that showed this unique phenomenon. Little did I know it would take 30 years.

My work with thermal imaging took me all over the world, mainly working with large electric utilities. But my heart was always seeing the natural world through these amazing cameras, which are capable of seeing temperature differences of a tenth of a degree or less. I was lucky enough to photograph cheetahs in Botswana; I delighted in seeing that juvenile elephants were much warmer than adults as their physiology began to regulate body temperature; I marveled that bees had to warm up in the early morning before they could fly, and that moths' wing muscles produced heat at night; I was invited to work with Dr. Bernd Heinrich to observe how ravens' bodies managed heat by shunting blood to their feet and head.

But always on my list was to look at the thermogenic skunk cabbage emerging from the frozen ground. Unlike my childhood territory, the plant did not grow near my Vermont home. Plus, with my busy travel schedule and Vermont's often unpredictable weather, being in the right place at the right time – infrared imager in hand – proved difficult.

Finally this spring I found myself in a large patch of the plant along the shores of Lake Champlain, snow still on the ground and that skunky smell in the air. There were the plants clearly melting their way into spring, so packed together I had trouble getting around without damaging them. Most of the plants showed a temperature rise of 5 to 10 degrees F but several were 30 degrees F or more warmer than their surroundings. Finally, I was in skunk cabbage heaven, smiling like a fool, happy to have seen this remarkable – one might even say impossible – piece of nature in this way after years of imagining what the image might look like. —*John Snell*

I FOUND THESE CHEWED bits of maple tubing in a coyote bed in my southern Vermont sugarbush. One of the intact bits still read "food grade" – perhaps the coyote read and misunderstood the phrase. Bad jokes aside, we're told that domestic dogs like chew toys because they strengthen their jaws, clean their teeth, and relieve boredom or anxiety. Certainly any of these ideas would translate to a coyote snowbound in the March forest. —*Dave Mance III*

AT HOME

❧

Apple Grafting

This spring, as the snow started to sag, I began to think of enlarging and diversifying the tiny orchard that I planted the previous spring. Not only was I interested in buying and planting more fruit trees, I was also thinking about creating my own trees and starting a new generation of the best wild trees around our property. To do this, I knew I would need to learn how to graft.

Grafting allows us to clone, and thus preserve, specific apple trees with desirable traits. If a seed is planted, it will grow into a new variety, not the same as the mother tree. Grafting has been an interest of mine for a few years now, and I was excited to finally try it out. I reached out to my good friend Virginia Barlow, and we set to work learning how to graft. In this article we will share what we have learned about this art in hopes of helping others get started. Notice! We are not professionals!

SCION WOOD

Scion wood is essentially a piece of the tree you wish to grow. It is typically gathered a couple weeks before leaf-out. The ideal scion has three to four small buds with one large terminal bud on top. Scions are sometimes short, that's okay. They will grow! Make sure to gather extra scions, as you may decide later that some aren't good enough for grafting. You can store scions wrapped in plastic in the fridge for several weeks.

ROOTSTOCK

Rootstock is simply the roots and about a foot of the trunk of a small sprout grown just for grafting – you attach the scion to it. Make sure to order your rootstock long before grafting season or rootstock will be sold out (we were just barely able to get rootstock this spring). Semi-dwarf rootstock is most common. Rootstocks are bred for hardiness, disease resistance, wind firmness, and vigor. No one rootstock is ideal for all these traits. We ordered our rootstock from Cummins. The other option is to find baby wild apple trees that can be used as rootstock, and later transplanted to a preferred location. This is what we had the best luck with on our first attempt.

GRAFTING

The idea of grafting is relatively simple: you align the cambium (the nutrient-carrying inner bark) of both the scion and the rootstock and hold it in place. If done correctly, the rootstock transfers the nutrients to the scion and the scion becomes the real tree. There are two common kinds of graft cuts: tongue-and-whip and cleft. We had best luck with the cleft graft, but, like I said, we were beginners. While grafting, make sure to keep all parts wet.

Cleft grafting is the simplest method. With a sharp knife, split the rootstock down the grain about an inch. On the scion, cut a slim wedge at the base end and wedge the scion into the slit in the rootstock. Make sure you align the two cambiums.

For tongue-and-whip, you start by cutting a diagonal bevel at the top of the rootstock and the bottom of the scion. Then, as shown in the picture, you cut about an eighth of an inch horizontally and then remove the wood on the top half down to the horizontal cut. Repeat this process on the rootstock and slide them together.

The final step is wrapping. This creates a moist environment for the graft, which enables the scion and the rootstock to grow together. To wrap the graft, you can use grafting tape, which can be ordered online. Another method is to use strips of plastic bags. We found no difference in results between the two methods but the tape was easier to use. Wrap the graft thoroughly, covering about an inch and a half on either side, and then, as a final layer of protection, wrap the graft in blue tape. You can plant the graftling in the garden for the summer, then in the fall, transplant to a more desirable location. —*Wendell Durham*

At left: The author with a grafted tree.

At right, from top:
Tongue-and-whip cuts before assembly
Cleft graft
Grafted seedlings in garden bed

A LOOK BACK

Vermont Life

EDITOR TOM SLAYTON REMEMBERS AND REFLECTS

For 72 years, *Vermont Life* magazine put Vermont's best foot forward.

It was founded by the State of Vermont for that purpose in 1946 – the thinking was that Vermont needed to promote itself more effectively to capture some of the post–World War II tourism business and attract new residents. Cars had become more reliable since the war years, and Americans were traveling more. Vermont wanted some of that.

The most popular publication in the US at that time was *Life* magazine, which practically invented photojournalism. And so a Green Mountain version of *Life* magazine, to tell Vermont's story and illustrate it with color photography, was conceived: *Vermont Life* was born.

In its earliest years, under founding editor Earl Newton, the magazine was frankly promotional. For example, an article titled "On Country Living" promised those who moved to Vermont "a more serene and normal lifestyle" than that found in big cities. Winter articles in those early years consistently referred to snow as "white gold" and assured readers, "Vermont winters aren't what they used to be." Although the magazine remained relentlessly positive over the years, later editors took a more objective journalistic stance.

The defining editor of the magazine, the man who established an identity for it that would endure for more than 50 years, was Walter Hard, Jr. He was editor from 1950 until 1972, and he crafted the balance of solid, in-depth stories and luscious color photos of Vermont that came to typify the magazine.

As the magazine matured in the 1960s and 1970s, it aimed to capture the essence of Vermont and to convince outsiders – and, to some extent, Vermonters themselves – that we were in "a special world." It became a record of the people, places, and ideas that make Vermont distinctive.

To be sure, the magazine made missteps. An early

one was the cover of the autumn 1947 issue: it consisted of a posed photograph that showed a diaphanously clad young woman holding an enormous palette and a big paintbrush with which she was "painting" the autumn leaves red and gold. Titled "Autumn Dryad," it wasn't innovative or delightful. It was ridiculous and cringeworthy.

As the magazine's editor, I made my share of mistakes. One such mistake was publishing a photograph of a workman wearing a baseball cap emblazoned with a cleverly disguised profanity. Another was the time I captioned a New Hampshire church steeple as being in Vermont, based on a photographer's labeling error. That one got me national publicity – the kind I didn't want!

But such kerfuffles passed quickly, and the magazine continued, four times a year, to promote the state in a subtle way that we, the editors, hoped would be intelligent.

Vermont Life's circulation quickly blossomed from a first issue of approximately 25,000 copies to a per-issue circulation of nearly 100,000 copies at the magazine's peak in the 1970s and 1980s. Out-of-state subscribers – the "Vermont diaspora" – were the largest portion of our subscribers, though in-state subscriptions and newsstand sales were healthy, too.

In my opinion, for many years, *Vermont Life* was remarkably successful in promoting both tourism and immigration. One study showed that the magazine provided a direct economic boost to the Vermont economy of $33.5 million every year. Nevertheless, publishing a four-color magazine is an expensive business, and consequently, Vermont's state-owned magazine had a complicated financial history.

For its first 20 years, *Vermont Life* received an annual subsidy from the state of Vermont to make up the difference between its expenses and its income. For many years, *Vermont Life* carried no advertising.

Then, in 1969, the magazine published "Vermont,

A Special World," which was the first coffee-table color photobook about Vermont. It became a best seller, and put the magazine in the black for several years. The magazine had already begun selling the *Vermont Life* wall calendar, which, I was told, was the best-selling wall calendar in New England for a time. That kept money flowing in and helped keep the magazine profitable even though it carried no ads.

That profitability lasted for another 20-plus years, through the 1980s and into the 1990s, when falling calendar sales and increased production and mailing costs for the magazine began causing deficits. That's when we decided to incorporate advertising, a move that put us back in the black for another 10 years.

As the Internet developed, maintaining print circulation numbers became increasingly difficult for magazines. *Vermont Life* had a paid circulation of about 90,000 when I became editor in 1985. By the time I retired in 2007, circulation had fallen to about 78,000. Eventually, competition from the Internet for ad revenue and the further waning of calendar sales pushed us into deficits again. By then, I'd had enough of the struggle to maintain profitability within the strictures of being, technically, a state agency, so I retired.

In the decade after I left, circulation continued to fall and deficits kept growing, and in May 2018, the state closed the magazine down.

Why was the state willing to fund deficits from the 1940s until the early 1960s but not in the 2010s?

The perception was that the magazine had outlived its usefulness. The state first attempted to sell *Vermont Life* to a private publisher. Though it received several offers, it declined them all, ostensibly because not enough money was offered for what, by then, was a financially struggling publication with minimal circulation. Officials said publicly that *Vermont Life* was just too valuable to privatize. And then a few weeks later, they pulled the plug and ceased publication. A 72-year tradition had come to an end.

During its lifetime, a series of seven editors oversaw the publication of *Vermont Life*. I was editor number six. Each editor brought a slightly different vision and aesthetic to the magazine.

My approach was to have, over the course of the four annual issues, something for everybody: for Vermont residents and the larger out-of-state readership; for young Vermonters and older Vermonters; articles on rural Vermont and articles on our lively village and urban cultures. I hoped that *Vermont Life* could help both Vermonters and visitors value, and ultimately protect, the Vermont that we know and love. Though small, it's still beautiful, unusual and valuable.

I used to refer to myself as "Keeper of the Sacred Myths," knowing that Vermont was and is much more complicated and diverse than any pastoral portrayal can convey while knowing also that myths can be deeply true – a pathway to our unstated understanding of ourselves and our place. —*Tom Slayton*

INDUSTRY

Researchers at the University of Vermont's Proctor Maple Research Center employ a small army of vacuum chambers in their maple research. The data that's collected supports a variety of work, including studies on optimal timing of tapping, influence of tree size on sap yield, spout design, even the question of whether sap yield is diminished if tap holes are drilled at an angle.

2021 Maple Season Review

According to USDA National Agricultural Statistics Service (NASS) data, Vermont sugarmakers put in 5.9 million taps in 2021 and produced just under 1.5 million gallons of syrup. While those numbers are impressive – Vermont made 45 percent of the entire US crop – production was off by 22 percent when compared to the 10-year average. The 2021 Vermont maple season was a reminder that despite new technologies and a steady increase in taps and syrup produced, maple production remains bound to the vagaries of late-winter temperatures.

Lower than average sap sugar content and less than ideal sugaring weather were common explanations for the drop in production. The 0.261 gallons of syrup per tap is the lowest average yield since 2012. Early March 2021 was too cold in many sugarbushes to allow for any meaningful sap runs. This stands in stark contrast to the previous year, when warmer weather allowed many sugarhouses to be boiling during the early season. The cold was followed by above-average high temperatures in late March and April. In 2020 – a year of near perfect sugaring weather – there were just 11 days in April that were recorded as above average. In 2021, there were 11 days with above-average high temperatures in just the first two weeks of the month.

Many sugarmakers who contribute to the University of Vermont Extension's "Vermont Maple Bulletin" blog shared that total sap production was on par with a good season but the low sugar concentration of the sap prevented them from hitting their syrup production goal. Three-quarters of respondents said sap sweetness was "below" or "significantly below" their long-term average. Many also compared the 2021 season to that of 2012, when an abnormally strong high-pressure ridge in the jet stream in March resulted in five days of temperatures in the high 70s or low 80s in many parts of Vermont. That extreme warmth was responsible for the production of off-flavored syrup and the premature end of the season. While not as extreme as 2012, the warmth in late March and early April in 2021 nonetheless set Vermont sugarmakers up for a short season.

When the hard work of any maple season is done, sugarmakers have decisions to make as to how to sell their crop. In 2020, 88 percent of the roughly 2 million-gallon Vermont maple syrup crop was sold as "bulk," meaning the syrup was sold to another business (commonly referred to as a "packer") where, along with syrup from many other sugaring operations, it's packed and then sold around the world. This represents a significant change in how Vermont syrup has been marketed over the past 20 years. Increased consumer interest in healthier foods and natural ingredients has fueled demand for pure maple syrup. While producers receive a higher price when selling syrup directly to the consumer, the demands of marketing and selling are too much for many maple farmers, who have instead chosen to focus on production.

Despite the growth of production in Vermont and elsewhere in the US in recent decades, the over 6,000 sugarmakers represented by Québec Maple Syrup Producers still produce more than 70 percent of the world's maple syrup. So their production has profound effects on the demand and pricing that Vermont producers experience. Production north of the border in 2021 was mixed, with some generally warmer locations faring poorly and colder areas seeing decent runs of sap. In total, Quebec producers made around 11.8 million gallons of syrup from 48.3 million taps.

The Covid pandemic affected both the 2020 and 2021 sugaring seasons. As most sugarmakers can attest, after the excitement of tapping has ended, much of sugaring involves long days of checking lines, making repairs in all types of weather, and boiling sometimes late into the night – by default, social distancing tends to be fairly easy during much of this work. But to the degree that the pandemic prevented visitors to Vermont sugarhouses, there were impacts for those sugarmakers who derive a significant amount of their sales from retail customers.

Thanks to Covid, there was a noticeable increase in backyard or hobby sugarmaking in Vermont and across the region. With more people working from home and children doing school remotely, there were plenty of opportunities to try sugaring on a small scale. Equipment manufacturers report strong demand from homeowners looking to experiment with making syrup for the first time. Some suppliers of buckets, spouts, and small evaporators had to turn customers away for lack of inventory. —*Mark Isselhardt*

GOLDEN DELICATE

The tap I hammered
into this hole drilled in the sapwood
offers the first
tap
on the bottom of the pail,
a second tap, and all that follow,
dripping sap sounding the pail's
hollow, a tapping that starts a season,
that stops me, hammer in hand
in the settling shadows, standing in the snow,
in the tapping, sap in the steel
spouts, drops from the fluted tip
tapping the metal pail, tap
after tap, as if keys striking the bare
platen of the bucket, letter by letter
at eternity's pace, news of the sap's weather
and our brief harvest of sweet ascent.

BILL DRISLANE

Sudbury, Vermont, 1948

DAVE MANCE III

A LIGHT IN THE DARKNESS

Dark maple syrup has always had its fans, but historically they've tended to be the woodchucks among us, not people with exquisite palates and wallets to match. Recently, studies have shown that maple syrup exhibits antioxidant activity and inhibits colorectal cancer cell growth. Curiously, the darker the syrup the more the antioxidant activity. That dark syrup, sometimes disparagingly compared to crankcase oil, may soon be available and preferred as a phytomedicine for treating gastrointestinal cancer. And, for some of us, it's always been the best tasting as well.
—*Virginia Barlow*

Last syrup of the year (left) contrasts with the first syrup of the year.

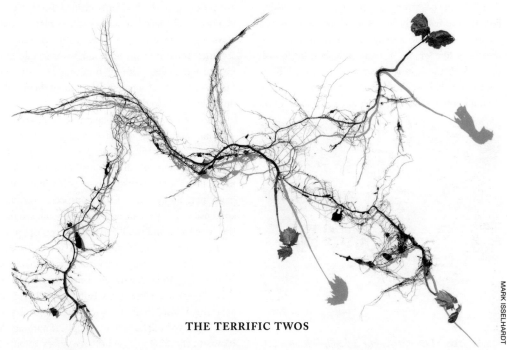

MARK ISSELHARDT

THE TERRIFIC TWOS

Even two-year-old sugar maple seedlings can develop an impressive root system. According to the USFS's Silvics of North America, sugar maple seedlings make the most of the early growing season before the upper canopy closes and sunlight is significantly more limited. Ninety percent of seasonal height growth occurs within the first 18 days. Sugar maple seedlings also exude chemicals that can inhibit yellow birch when root growth periods overlap. —*Mark Isselhardt*

Sugarhouse Certification

THIS IS HOW THINGS CHANGE

When sugaring operations started rapidly expanding a decade or so ago, a common worry among small producers was that the maple industry was going to become the dairy industry, where mega-farms increasingly dominate the landscape. That worry has been realized. According to our interpretation of numbers compiled by the *Maple News*, the 14 biggest maple producers in the state of Vermont (0.5 percent of the total) accounted for about 30 percent of the close to 6 million taps that were put out in 2020. In dairy, in 2020, the 34 farms in the state that milked more than 700 head housed about 39 percent of the cows (50,000 +/- out of 125,000 +/-).

It might be wrong to be against something just because it's really big. And in maple, we're not seeing the dramatic decline in small and mid-sized producers like we are in dairy. But we'd be foolish to overlook the history of agriculture since USDA Secretary Earl Butz's infamous dictum to "get big or get out," with all the sad stories about the dissolution of family farms and kindly land stewardship in favor of industrial ag that followed.

In dairy, we can look back and see that the adoption of refrigerated bulk tanks in the 1950s hastened the decline of small hill farmers who couldn't afford the tanks or didn't have the infrastructure to accommodate milk trucks, and it facilitated the rise of bigger farms on paved roads with access to capital. Today, maple may be approaching a similar inflection point with the push toward sugarhouse registration and regulation. Behind the scenes, regulators are pushing for food-safe facilities, because in the abstract who doesn't want safe food? The packers become the implementation mechanism for these regulations when they stop buying syrup from people who aren't certified. But the rub is you can't easily make the state's rustic sugarhouses and steaming wooden cupolas into state-of-the-art food factories. You can't really tell a small or even mid-sized producer that they need running hot tap water and flush toilets in their sugarhouse or a lot of them will go out of business. So there's tension.

The Vermont Maple Sugarmakers Association, working with packers and regulators, has created a sugarhouse certification program – the goal was something people on all sides could live with. At the moment it's a voluntary program – if you choose to participate and pay the fee, an inspector will come and ensure that your sugarhouse meets the standards they've created and you'll get a sticker you can put on your jug if your sugarhouse passes. You can see the standards on the group's website: vermontmaple.org. If you're a sugarmaker who sells everything retail, there may be no need for any of this. But if you sell in bulk to a packing house, there's a chance that in the relatively near future you might need to comply. If nothing else, it's worth checking things out to see what's potentially coming. Galvanized iron or steel, copper, and brass, for instance, are all disallowed in these new standards. And yet the sugaring supply catalogues are still full of pumps and pans that feature gleaming copper and brass pipes and fittings. Ⓥ

MAPLE NEWS

Sweet Tree LLC's state-of-the-art boiling facility in Island Pond, Vermont. The company is a subsidiary of Connecticut-based Wood Creek Capital Management, a $2 billion hedge fund that most notably owns music publishing rights to "Bust A Move," "Come On Get Happy," and the song catalog of Kenny G.

Sugarhouse Celebration

Dori Ross grew up on a farm in rural Canada, perhaps the only place in the world where maple is as big a part of the culture as it is here in Vermont. She moved to Vermont and started Tonewood Maple, a food products company that sourced its syrup from sugarmakers in the Mad River Valley, then moved back across the border to Quebec. In 2021, due to the Covid restrictions that forbade Canada/US border crossing, Tonewood was forced to stop operating. And so Dori put her energy into a new project that aims to identify, document, and help preserve Vermont's sugarhouses. They're currently reaching out to the maple community and assembling a publicly accessible list. The final outcome will be a photo book that showcases these architectural legacies. To learn more, visit www.sugarhousevermont.com

PHOTOS BY MIKE RIDDELL

Vasseur Sugarhouse, Fayston

Getting Together

IN AN ERA OF BIG MAPLE, CORY KRIEG IS HOPING A COLLECTIVE OF SMALL SUGARMAKERS CAN FIND STRENGTH IN NUMBERS.

About the only thing that's gotten smaller on the Vermont maple scene over the last decade or so has been the size of the spouts used to tap trees. Back in the days of buckets, a big maple operation might have been 1,000 taps. Now there are sugarmakers in Vermont putting in as many as *half a million taps* a year. This scaling up has led to bigger vacuum systems, monstrous RO machinery, enormous oil-fired evaporators and, in some cases, sugarhouses replaced with literal factory buildings to house it all.

While the mega producers have been grabbing headlines in recent years, it's the small-scale sugarmakers who still capture the imagination. Alone at night in the old sugar shack, loading wood into the fire box and evaluating syrup by sight and smell. While most small sugarmakers don't have any desire to emulate the big guys, they do have to compete with them. Syrup from big packing houses, dressed up in folksy "family farm" labels, trickles down into the boutique markets. And where it comes to bulk purchasing, large producers have leverage that small producers don't.

Cory Krieg is one of those small sugarmakers – he operates Maple Flower Farm in Bethel, which includes his wife Liz's cut flower operation. Krieg is also an engineer, so he set out to design a marketing solution to help small sugaring operations compete. Realizing that few small producers – farmers who sugar in the winter, part-timers like himself who have other jobs, traditionalists who simply wouldn't know what else to do with themselves from February to April – have the financial means or the expertise or the desire to develop a full-blown ecommerce website, Krieg saw an opportunity for strength through numbers. In 2020, he created Traditional Maple Farmers LLC, built a website, and designed an automated system for processing orders. His vision is for a collective made up of small sugarmakers who can all sell through this venue.

Cory Krieg with the new sugarhouse he built at Maple Flower Farm. Krieg created Maple Farmer as a way to help small-scale producers sell their syrup online to a national market.

In its first year (the 2021 maple season), a total of six small sugarmakers in Vermont (including Krieg's own farm) joined the collective. In a nutshell, the system works this way: Before the season, farmers in the collective all receive a supply of Maple Farmers glass bottles and the cardboard box/packaging needed to mail the syrup. (Krieg spent quite a bit of time researching the best packaging system in terms of preventing breakage while still allowing two packages to fit inside a flat-rate mailing box.) Members fill the bottles themselves with their own syrup and add a sticker on the back with their particular farm's name.

Each farm in the collective provides Krieg information about the grades of syrup they have available, and he lists that on the website (there's also a page with information about each farm). When a customer visits the website, they can either select the farm that they wish to purchase from or let the system automatically select it on a rotating basis. All syrup is sold in quarts.

Once an order comes in, Krieg sends the shipping information on to the individual farm. They put the bottle in the box, take it to the Post Office and ship it out directly to the customer. From the sugarmakers' perspective, all the behind-the-scenes work – the website, ordering packaging/supplies, placing online ads, order tracking, etc. – is all taken care of. And when Krieg sends them the customer shipping information, he includes a check for $12 a quart ($14 minus the $2 cost of the bottle), which is nearly double the current bulk price.

And being part of the Maple Farmers collective doesn't take away from a sugarmaker's ability to continue selling their syrup locally through retail stores or at farmer's markets or any other outlet they want. They also maintain control of their own syrup at all times. So there's really no downside for small sugarmakers who don't have their own online store and who can't sell all that they produce through local retail channels.

Krieg is hopeful that more farms will join the collective. "I think there's a huge potential for this," he says. "My goal would be to work with one hundred or two hundred small maple farmers." (If you're interested in learning more, contact information is available at maplefarmers.com.) As more farms join and the Maple Farmers website continues to grow, he's optimistic the whole enterprise can expand in a way that helps small sugarmakers compete in a marketplace increasingly dominated by big players, while also getting traditionally made Vermont syrup into the hands of eager customers. —*Patrick White*

Dispatch from the Sugarwoods

12:28 p.m., 1/28/21. This was the only peek of sunshine in the sugarbush on this particular day, and it only lasted a few seconds. But there was a peek of light.

Biologists maintain a winter severity index that allows them to quantify how hard a particular winter is on wildlife. Weather conditions are monitored, and points are accumulated when the temperature hits zero and when the snow depth is 18 inches or more. At the end they have a snapshot of how hard things were that they can compare to other years.

While reflecting on the sugaring season of 2021, it occurred to me that there should be a sugarmaking severity index. Records would start the day you started tapping and the tabulation would run through the end of production. Each day within that window when the snowpack was above 18 inches would earn a point, as line work and tapping is exponentially harder on snowshoes than on bare ground. Each day that the high temperature deviated from the norm by more than 10 degrees would earn a point. Each day that a business partner or employee failed to show up to work would earn a point. Minor mechanical issues that affected sap flow would earn a point, and major mechanical issues that profoundly affected something (you burned up the evaporator pans, say) would earn five points.

I didn't keep detailed enough notes this year to get an exact tabulation of our operation's score, but a back-of-the-envelope reckoning would put our snowpack points for the year at around 38, our temperature deviation points at around 22, and mechanical issue points at around 14. Because my father/business partner missed the whole season with a bum leg, I'd add 68 points in the "help didn't show up" category – that the number of total days I was a one-man show. I didn't tabulate days when friends or family chipped in. The grand total here is 142. As a point of comparison, I tabulated around 21 points in the great-weather, everyone-was-healthy season of 2020. So by this metric, my 2021 season was about 576 percent more difficult than the season before.

Even if the only point of this exercise is therapy, it still feels useful. When laypeople ask how the season went, I'll tell them we were off by a third. When other sugarmakers push for details, I'll say we averaged around 21 gallons of sap per tap, down from 30 the year before. But those figures don't give a sense of just how hard – just how off – this year was in our woods. Other sugarmakers who had or have had similar years – and they all have – will relate.

But it is what it is. One of the good things about

4:56 a.m., 3/26/21, salamander rescue.

getting older is that your perspective broadens. As a young man, I used to be happy with 12 gallons of sap per tap. Middle-aged me is balking that I even wrote that line, thinking that there was a lot less riding on a season when I was 20 years old. But young me is still in there somewhere, and immensely grateful that the trees gave so much.

Midway through the season, I just happened to look closely at the tongue that connects the trailer hitch to the pickup and noticed that it had cracked and was hanging on by a strip of twisted metal. Had the trailer broken free with a load of sap on it, it could have been a disaster. That didn't happen.

Near the end of the year I found a spotted salamander trapped in a bulk tank swimming in 1,600 gallons of sap. I pumped it down, climbed in and rescued the silly thing. Later, I told my 4-year-old about it, and the next day, I'm told, it was the talk of Evergreen Preschool. Nobody there would have even comprehended what 20 gallons of sap per tap means, but the fact that I rescued a salamander gave me Ryder-from-Paw-Patrol status.

We can't often change the circumstances that are in front of us, but we can change how we experience them. —*Dave Mance III, March 28, 2021*

Vermont Evaporator Company

The Sapling Evaporator burns wood in an enclosed barrel chamber, which boils sap in a stainless-steel pan. After sugaring season, the pan pops off to create a grill, smoker, or wood-fired bread and pizza oven.

Kate Whelley McCabe grew up in a log cabin in the woods of New Hampshire. Her husband, Justin McCabe, hails from a farm in South Dakota. It was their rural roots that drew them to Vermont and led them to try their hand sugaring on their 10-acre property. Quickly realizing the limitations of boiling in a pot over a propane grill, and finding nothing on the market designed for modest backyard operations, Justin began tinkering with his own wood-fired evaporator design. With financial buy-in from family and crowd-funding support, Vermont Evaporator Company was born in 2015.

Maple is big business these days in Vermont, but we asked Kate what she appreciates the most about sharing the art with hobbyists.

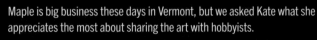

"We work hard at showing people how easy it is to make syrup in your backyard. Anyone with access to the trees can do it. And then we try to make the process even easier and more fun."

And Kate still marvels at how much there is to know about sugaring beyond the usual "how-to" focus: "We have a blog that we use to contextualize sugaring by writing about history, science, current events, nature, industry, climate, culinary arts, and literature."

Montpelier, Vermont • vermontevaporator.com

APRIL

April

There was a sense of timelessness about the view to the west, back when we move-ups bought the land on Salem Pond with our friend Bruce. We could sit outside on any clear evening and watch the sun sink down and disappear behind Owl's Head, fifteen miles away. In April, the rolling fields across the valley progressed from shades of brown to pale green. The other way, across the pond, we saw the blue mountain ridges of East Haven, and the moon rise over them at night. Yes, we had bought the best land, the best view, and we were filled with a certain pride.

Our land partner, Bruce, framed up a cabin on top of the knoll, with a porch on front and a good roof. The stove pipe had a jaunty little cap on top that rotated with the wind, so smoke would never blow back down into the tall cast iron heating stove inside, standing up as smartly as it could on its four stumpy legs. Homesteading, with no electricity and no running water, we became back-to-the landers.

For seven years we enjoyed that view we thought we owned. When an RV park went in on those rolling fields, trailers and Winnebagos became part of the view, along with a big fat laundromat building we could not un-see.

Bruce planted a row of trees: maple, birch, balsam fir, white pine, and spruce. If clipped to just the right height, there would be no RV park, but still plenty of sunset and Owl's Head.

In 1970, Bruce married, and put his dreams for the land on hold. He moved back to New Jersey to work. In 1972, Robert and I joined the commune craze; we too moved off the property.

Something happened to Bruce in New Jersey, perhaps a crisis of hope for which he had no remedy. He drove his car into his parents' garage and closed the door. His widow and two young sons came to the knoll with Bruce's ashes, which were buried under a white cross behind the cabin.

For 40 years, the row of trees on the west grew and grew, and all the little wild seedlings and saplings that had dotted our hillsides and the top of the knoll stretched high until the abandoned cabin was slowly pinned into place by run-away box elder, thick stands of prickly spruce, and impenetrable tangles of silver and brown blackberry canes. The cabin had been built on a bare hilltop; now it was moldering in the depths of a 40-year-old forest.

Squatters found it, both human and wild. Weather and rain worked their way in. The porch roof sagged, foundation timbers rotted and bowed towards earth, the stovepipe lost direction and fell, taking the weathered cross down with it. For fifty years, land taxes were the only thing that kept the two families connected.

When we sold the land last year, the buyer wanted to know, "What's that fallen cross?" Bruce's son answered: "My father's ashes are there, but not my father. It's not a place I care to visit. I have four beautiful children – in them I see my father every day."

Satisfied, the buyer remarked to no one in particular, "You know, I bet if we mow down a bunch of trees, we'll have some great views."

We had nothing left to say. —*Mary W. Mathias*

Best Mud Season in Years

Prior to working at the Fairbanks Museum, I was employed in Vermont's tourist industry. I interacted with many people from other states and countries during the winter and summer months. Guests to the state would be very envious of me when it came to living in this special place. Tourists, after all, usually come during the most beautiful and prime times of year: winter, when the snowpack is deep and brightens what would otherwise be a bleak and somewhat lifeless landscape; and summer, when warm sun and lush green forests and farms abound. Rarely are tourists around for Vermont's fifth season: mud season.

Other parts of the Northeast experience this phenomenon, but the abundance of dirt roads in our state amplify this rugged time of year. While "April showers bring May flowers" applies to most of the country, here April showers are often rain and snow showers, and mixed precipitation brings mud. And more mud. As well as a desire for spring to actually make an appearance.

Mud season 2021 was a bit different from the norm, as the combination of a light snow season and an early start to warm and dry conditions made for relatively tame conditions on backroads. It was the best mud season I can remember.

April Fool's Day saw most of the state pick up roughly 2 inches of snow, but what followed was mainly dry, windy, low-humidity conditions that sparked worry about (and several actual) wildfires. By April 8, temperatures, which had been in the teens just days earlier, soared into the 70s. April 9 saw Montpelier (72 degrees) and Burlington (76 degrees) set new daily records. Warm weather continuing into the weekend led to numerous reminders that, although air temperatures felt summerlike, water temperatures were still in the upper 30s and low 40s in Vermont lakes, and thus caution (and a lifejacket) was advised for any boating activities.

Even at the stake atop Mt. Mansfield there was little snowpack to be found this April. In fact, the 19 inches measured there on April 11 broke an all-time record for the lowest level on that date. (The mid-April average is about 50 inches.) Higher elevations did add a little snow during a stretch of active weather from April 18 to 22, but by the last week of the month temperatures were back into the 60s, before April ended the way it began, with rain and snow falling on the 30th. —*Christopher Kurdek, Fairbanks Museum and Planetarium*

JOHN LAZENBY

With warm, dry conditions prevailing in early April, road crews got a jump on grading. On April 7 in Montpelier (shown here), driving conditions looked much better than during most mud seasons.

NATURE NOTES

RED MAPLE FLOWERS were especially abundant this year, and the spent petals covered the ground at this log landing. Wild bees and honey bees will need to find pollen elsewhere, among the marsh marigolds, perhaps, or the sugar maples.

WINTER FIREFLIES *(Ellychnia corrusca)* are frequent visitors to sap buckets and spouts each season. As larvae, these insects feed on rotting wood and overwinter as adults in bark grooves. In early spring, adults emerge to feed on flowers and sap, often falling in sap buckets and becoming a nuisance to sugarmakers. Although not a significant stressor to the forest, this insect has historically been used as a predictor of the end of sugaring season.
—*Vermont Department of Forests, Parks, and Recreation*

JERRY HIAM

PERHAPS INSPIRED BY A YEAR OF SOCIAL DISTANCING, I took to studying the way that flocking birds space themselves. Robins in fields tend to stay four or five feet apart. Juncos, at a bit more than half the size of robins, keep about 18 inches apart. Does this suggest a feeding area that a given bird can expect to exploit? Or could it have to do with predators? Or basic bird hygiene? They all seem to know the rules.
—*Virginia Barlow*

APRIL 25, 2021: The year's first morel in the patch that grows near the wood ash pile outside the sugarhouse.

Reconsidering Check-Valve Spouts

When the weather gets warm in April, bacteria start to accumulate on the inside of maple tapholes and the sap stops flowing. For years, sugarmakers have been trying to figure out ways to keep their tapholes wet late in the season. In the mid-to-late 20th century, some did it with paraformaldehyde tablets. The chemical was subsequently banned when it turned out to be creating exaggerated dead zones in trees; there was also the PR problem of syrup containing traces of the same chemical that's used to embalm corpses. Starting around 2009 some sugarmakers started using check valve spouts, which in certain scenarios make the trees run longer. The principle here is that a ball valve in the spout keeps sap from backwashing into the taphole, which is where microbial contamination is introduced.

They kind of work – you

can see from the accompanying pictures that this tree was tapped on February 10 with a check valve spout, and on April 7 the tap was pulled and it was still wet. In the interim two months the weather had been warmer than normal – i.e. perfect conditions for the holes to gum up and stop running. We tapped some trees with check valves, and some with regular spouts. This was not a controlled experiment and there was some ambiguity in the results, but it did seem that the trees with check valves were, on average, wetter when all was said and done.

The problem was that because of the abnormally high temperatures this year, the sap went off flavor in our woods in late March. There wasn't any economic justification for boiling, so the sap kept coming and we just let it run on the ground. The check valve spouts cost twice what a normal spout

costs, which in our modest 3,500-tap operation amounts to an extra $800 annually. Certainly not money well spent this season.
—*Dave Mance III*

AT HOME

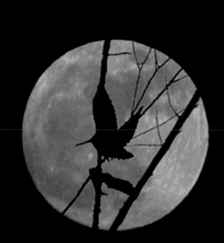

SPRING WOODCOCK

From a meadow along the road,
a male woodcock rises
in a twittering spiral
into the darkening sky.
We won't see her,
watching still as a stone
on the edge of a tangle of shrubs.

Her black bead of an eye
assesses his descent for virility,
while we,
a species incurably romantic,
feel our hearts in our throats
at the beauty of his panicky,
heart-breaking
song
as he tumbles
back
to earth.

JOAN WALTERMIRE

NANCY WHITEHEAD

Inoculating Shiitake Logs

The best time to inoculate logs for shiitake mushrooms in the Northeast is in April. Any earlier in the year and the new spawn might be subjected to extreme cold; any later and the logs are in danger of drying out. Ideally, you'll have cut the logs during the winter, in their dormant phase, and let them sit for a few weeks to rest. The standard size to use is 40 inches long and 4 to 8 inches in diameter. The best wood for growing shiitakes is oak, but maple, ironwood, and other hardwoods also work, so long as it is not a fruit wood, like apple, because these have natural anti-fungal properties.

To inoculate, you need a drill, a source of spawn, wax to cover the spawn, and a means of identifying the strain and year. There are numerous variations on all of these tools and materials, the choice of which comes down to how many logs you want to do and how much money you want to spend. The most low-key approach for a hobbyist is to buy "plug spawn," which is a wooden dowel that is already inoculated with the shiitake spawn. Drill a hole, hammer it in, cover it with wax to keep it from drying, put an aluminum ID tag on the log, and lay it in a shady spot for a year.

If you want to do more than 20 logs per year, upgrade to an angle-grinder (10,000 rpms vs. 500-2,000 rpms for a regular drill) and buy an adapter (chuck) with a sharp drill bit to blaze through the drilling process. Order the brass plunger tool and the sawdust spawn, which is much less expensive in larger quantities and is available in more varieties. Buy a cheap deep fryer to keep the melted wax at the ready; you'll be able to use this tool every year, though never for deep frying again. And invest in the 250-pack of aluminum tags, because once you are bitten with the mushroom-growing bug, you'll be all in.

No matter the specific equipment you select, the process is the same: drill, fill, wax, label. Once you are all finished, put the logs in a cool, shady spot in the forest, stacking them just off the ground. Keeping a high moisture level in the logs is the only thing you need to pay attention to for the rest of the year. They should get about an inch of water a week. If there's a period of heat and no rain, water the logs with a hose or soak them in a cool, clean creek. Make no mistake, you will feel foolish watering logs, but keeping them from drying out is the most important step. If you've done it right, you will see patches of white at the ends of the logs by late summer. Depending on the type of shiitake strain you chose, you will get mushrooms the following summer. —*Laura Sorkin*

Fencing the Garden

It's time to figure out a fence for a new garden plot I put in this year, and the options seem endless and imperfect. I'm going to want to keep cottontails, woodchucks, deer, and birds out, and so the logical solution is a 2,000-foot cage. Of course I also want an aesthetically pleasing place to spend time, so right away the practically perfect is the enemy of the good.

In past gardens I've used single-strand electric fence, three courses high. And it worked well for deer. I'd smear peanut butter on the wire to train them. Each fall the fence came down, and each spring a tractor could till, unimpeded. The downside was that it wasn't effective for cottontails or woodchucks, which could go right under. And it was a pain to weed-whack the perimeter, which is important because any grass growing up into the fence can short the electricity. Besides, I want to try to not use a tractor anymore,

so having a fence that's removable isn't as big a plus as it was.

I decided on a whole different approach and went the classic 2x4-welded-wire route. In theory this will thwart woodchucks and bunnies. [Editor's Note: As summer progressed, I learned that young-of-the-year bunnies can go in and out unimpeded, so take that into consideration as you scheme.] The structural qualities of this type of fence can also be nice, both as a means of growing plants vertically and as a way to help suspend bird netting over vulnerable crops. The downside, besides the fact that it's labor intensive to build and maintain, is that it still leaves you with a deer problem. Whitetails can jump eight feet high, so to really keep them out you'd have to run two courses of 4 foot wire and turn your pleasant garden plot into something that looks like a prison yard. I'm going to

Above: Make-shift fence puller. Right: Backfill your posts with gravel; don't use concrete.

Incomplete corner brace assembly. See following page.

try to get around this by putting 45 degree kickers on the corners – these will angle out and up, away from the fence – and running a single strand of wire between them. I'm hoping this will mess with the deers' depth perception and make them hesitant to jump.

Once the decision on fence style was made, it was time to source posts. Cedar makes good posts. Locust makes good posts. Unfortunately, I have neither of these species growing on the back 40. So I went online and found Ed Fox, a farmer in Pittsford who was selling freshly cut white cedar posts for $5.50 each. This seemed like a good deal to me. Plus I got to use Vermont wood and put the cash money right in his pocket instead of in a register at a big box store. After loading them on a trailer, he watched with amusement as I tried to tie them down. "If you get pulled over, just say you're a farmer and you've got enough problems," he said.

Once home, I dug 28 holes roughly 2 feet deep and about 8 feet apart. I backfilled each hole with gravel. I ran a course of wire down the long side of the rectangle, then I put a 12- to 16-inch strip of landscape fabric in between each post and under the wire, covering it with gravel. I don't want to have to fight weeds.

I reinforced the first corner – see the next page for an in-depth look at this. Then I stapled the wire onto the first fence post. At the other end, I cut a disposable 4-foot limb, stapled that to the wire, attached the limb to the tractor bucket with a chain, then used the tractor to apply tension to the wire. It worked fine for a home garden. No need for the fancy fence pullers that the professionals use. Four or five fence staples in each post completed the run. I strung the other three sides of the rectangle in the same manner. —*Dave Mance III*

❧

How to Build a Proper Fence Corner
with Brian Leach and Regen by Design

Whether you're putting up a 2x4 welded-wire fence around your garden, or a high-tensile fence around 100 acres of pasture, you're going to have the same challenge to contend with: How do you anchor fence wire to a rigid point in space?

The solution is to build a proper corner brace assembly.

"It's important to understand the way the forces work in a brace assembly," said Brian Leach, a mechanical engineer and farmer from Pawlet, Vermont. "The primary load is coming from the horizontal tension from your wire or wires. Without a brace post assembly, the fence post that's serving as the anchor will want to tip over. So the brace assembly takes that horizontal load on the end post,

transfers it through the brace pole to the top of the inside post, and then from there the wire assembly transfers that load back down to the lower portion of the end post. At that point, a large component of the horizontal load becomes a shear on the base of the end post rather than a torque. That's what makes that end post resistant to the horizontal load."

The images here are courtesy of Regen by Design (regenbydesign. org), a Vermont startup that produces educational content related to farming and food systems. The group worked with Leach on a series of six videos that covers all aspects of fencing.

The organization was co-founded by Philip Ackerman-Leist, who was a professor of Sustainable Agriculture & Food

Systems at Green Mountain College for two decades before that small, independent school closed in 2019. He worked next at Sterling College as Dean of Professional Studies, where he established the college's first online curricula despite once being skeptical of the idea of remote learning. "It turns out I was wrong about online education," he said. "I learned that when it's done well, it can be flexible, affordable, and cross-cultural; there's a richness that can be tapped."

Ackerman-Leist left Sterling last December, and after Zoom calls for two months trying to assess educational need and secure funding, he launched Regen by Design in February. Part of the premise is that a lean educational model, which

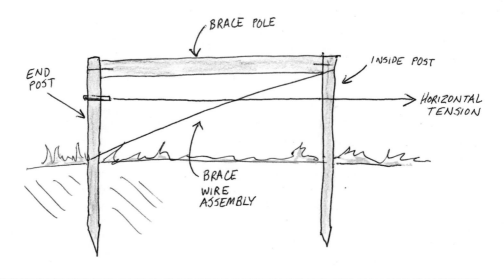

REGEN BY DESIGN

doesn't have brick and mortar to maintain and generations worth of debt and obligations, is free to respond to need instead of the demands of an institution. "Education, if anything, is about service," he said. "There's all this disaggregated knowledge out there, and institutional barriers, and cultural barriers, and paywalls. What we're creating is an online constellation of ideas – a knowledge ecosystem. In some cases we'll work with small organizations to create content for their audience. Some of our work is international and designed to facilitate ideas and conversations between cultures. We're trying to get beyond the traditional idea of courses, and instead work to facilitate a community of knowledge."

There's a sense of urgency to this work. "When Vermont looks at green jobs and strengthening a green economy, two of the best fits are agriculture and higher education," said Ackerman-Leist. "And right now we're letting both fail. [Since 2019, three small Vermont private colleges have gone out of business and another enfolded; meanwhile, the state college system was $12 million in the hole and teetering on the brink of financial collapse before a recent $88 million bailout.] Building out education, building out agriculture and local food systems, this helps all of us."

—*Dave Mance III*

"Current" Events

Credit Robert Frost with the proverb, "Good fences make good neighbors." This may actually be true. I would fine-tune it and add that good electric fences make good, cautious neighbors and can supply a fair amount of entertainment. This windfall of amusement was discovered upon the electrification of the fences around our farm when I was a kid.

My Old Man always worked under the assumption that if you were going to do something, then by all means, do it up proper. If a fence is going to be electrified, make sure it has enough juice to give a cow a realistic preview of what barbecuing is all about. This strategy also cuts down on the time spent keeping grass and weeds from touching the fence and grounding it out. Get the current hot enough, and any offending weeds will be cut off shortly after contact. There may be an occasional grass fire to battle, but this serves to supply yet another opportunity for entertainment and exercise.

The brand of electric fencer dad used was called "Weed Chopper." It just as aptly could have been named "Cow Stunner," "Crotch Burner," or "Kid Taser." I once saw one of our heifers make the poor choice of swishing her tail at flies whilst standing too close to the mega-charged fence. Her tail snagged on the top wire. She dropped to her knees with a moan, jumped up with a bellow, then lit out like she was running in the Preakness, leaving a clump of tail hair smoking on the fence.

Then there was the time My Old Man and our good farmer friend and neighbor, Garth Perkins, needed to enter one of our pastures to check on the health of a cow. Dad stood six-foot-two, and when he came to the two-strand electric barbed-wire fence, he easily threw one leg over, then pivoted a little on it as he swung the other leg over to cross it. Garth was only five-foot-eight, and he tried to imitate dad's maneuver. He came up shy of the necessary clearance. I'd never seen a man become so animated so quickly, nor viewed one outside of the theater who danced so well on his tip-toes while yodeling.

As owners of the fence, or "Keepers of the Flame," as Garth once referred to us after the coverall episode, it became my duty to warn friends and visitors of the stunning quality of our fence, should they be in the vicinity. If it was a dumb-ass cousin or a neighborhood nemesis, my warning could come a bit belatedly, if at all.

"Is that fence electric?" one of my many annoying turd cousins would ask.

"Yeah, but we only turn it on at night to save electricity. It ain't on now. Go ahead and touch it."

Being the low-wattage chumps most were, they'd take hold and get their batteries boosted.

"Yeeow! You said it was off!"

"Oops, sorry. Could've swore I shut it off this morning. My mistake."

I always made sure I could outrun whoever got jolted, or at least get a good head start while they were recovering their senses.

The most painful application of electricity to a singular body part that I ever witnessed occurred late one summer afternoon. Lute Bouchard, his younger brother Twitch, Dickey Hawley, and I were heading home from a jolly good time spent at the swinging tree in a ravine between our place and the Hawleys'. We all took turns going under the fence. As we gathered on the other side, Lute announced he had to "squeeze the weasel."

Of course, when one kid takes a whizz, others are free to join in, which is what his brother did. And as Twitch was squirting away, Lute came up from behind and grabbed him by the shoulders and pivoted him to change the direction of his flowage to intercept the fence wire. The result was reminiscent of the little piggy that went, *"Whee! Whee! Whee!"* all the way home. Though this did add credibility to Twitch's nickname, I'm happy to report that later in life, he was able to sire numerous children.

I still have nightmares about the unpleasant incident that may have stunted my growth enough to make me the second-shortest pupil in class throughout grade school. A bunch of us were playing hide-and-seek over at the Hawleys' one summer evening. Unnoticed by us, Mr. Hawley had extended his one-strand electric fence about 30 feet into the hay field to give his crow-bait horses something to eat: His regular pasture looked like a putting green. When whoever was "it" commenced counting, three of us took off running to hide in the deep grass of the hay field. We were trucking flat out in a skirmish line when we hit the fence. I was short enough that it caught me right in the throat. We ran into the fence so hard and fast that we stretched it out, like you'd see in a Road Runner cartoon, and we couldn't get away from it. By the time I got untangled, you could've lit a cigarette off my nose. I was spitting sparks for a week.

The days of the serious electric fencer are long gone. Used to be you could drive along the road past a farm with the car radio on and hear the pulsing static of a fire-spitting fence buzzing along to the beat of the music, a sizzling reminder that the farmer there had himself a proper fence that was respected by both man and beast. Now, they have solar powered fencers that barely make a chicken cackle. With the reliable old Weed Chopper, you could fry an egg – and the chicken that laid it. —*Bill Torrey*

JERRY KING

A LOOK BACK

A Ban on Billboards

The Vermont environmental movement owes a debt to Ted Riehle, which might seem a little odd given today's political landscape. Riehle was a Republican, which meant something different when he joined the Vermont House in the late 1960s. Riehle was also quite wealthy, owning a Lake Champlain island, complete with private landing strip.

Riehle might not fit our current image of an environmentalist, but when he joined the Legislature in 1965, he wanted to rid Vermont of what he regarded as a blight on the landscape: the hundreds of billboards that lined the state's roadsides. It was an ambitious undertaking, particularly for an inexperienced lawmaker. Perhaps Riehle was new enough to politics that he didn't realize the challenges he faced.

The debate over billboards wasn't new. During the early decades of the 20th century, as American culture became increasingly car-centric, businesses hit upon roadside advertisements as a way to connect with potential customers, particularly tourists. Writer Vrest Orton railed against the negative effects of Vermont's tourism boom. He took aim at "national advertisers, who have an urge to plaster all the roads retaining the least vestige of adjacent beauty with massive, gaudy and hideous sign-boards, so that it might truly be said, 'Behind the signboard lies Vermont.'"

By 1936, roughly 750 full-sized billboards and thousands of smaller advertising signs lined the state's roadsides. Seven of those billboards were in Springfield and drew the ire of a group of residents who fought to have them removed. Using petitions, posters, handbills, and threats of boycotts against advertisers, the group managed to have the billboards taken down.

The Springfield drive grew into a statewide effort known as the Vermont Association for Billboard Restriction. The Rotary Club, the Grange, and the Daughters of the American Revolution, some of the most influential social institutions of the era, protested what they saw as a commercial infringement on the public's right to view the landscape. They also argued that billboards were dangerous distractions for drivers.

Renowned journalist Dorothy Thompson, a part-time resident of Barnard, summarized the anti-billboard arguments in a letter to the *Rutland Herald* in 1937: "If aesthetic considerations do not move us, let us consider the matter from the standpoint of cold cash. Vermont has beauty to sell. Thousands and thousands of tourists come here every summer, for no other reason than that Vermont is lovely. They can see billboards from Connecticut to California. The absence of them is a positive asset."

The debate over billboards quickly became a question of natives versus out-of-staters, according to scholar Blake Harrison in his 2006 book, "The View From Vermont: Tourism and the Making of an American Rural Landscape." Opponents called out-of-state billboard companies parasites, arguing that they were destroying the beauty of the state for their own profit. Billboard supporters, mainly advertisers and billboard companies, noted that opponents also relied on out-of-state support, in this case coming from tourists and part-time residents, like Thompson. Weren't billboard opponents putting the interests of people who could afford to travel above the interests of Vermont businesspeople trying to make a living? Besides, billboards sometimes provided tourists with useful information, they argued. Without the signs, tourists wouldn't be able to find their destinations.

The Vermont Chamber of Commerce found itself stuck between competing business interests, but it ended up opposing billboards. Tourism in Vermont was unmistakably on the rise during the 1930s, and the chamber took the position that removing the billboards would benefit the state's economy, its residents, and its visitors.

The Legislature tried to find a compromise. Rep. Horace Brown, of Springfield, successfully championed a bill in 1939 that, while keeping billboards legal, limited their size and location. The closer to the road a sign was, the smaller it had to be. The law was challenged, but the Vermont Supreme Court found that property owners had no inherent right to place signs on land adjacent to public roadways.

After the law's passage, the number of roadside signs fell roughly 50 percent between 1938 and 1943, but hundreds of billboards still lined the state's roads. Legislative efforts to further curb billboards continued through the '40s, '50s, and '60s, but to no effect, until Ted Riehle took up the issue.

Riehle, who represented South Burlington, told state Senator Jim Jeffords that he planned to introduce a bill banning billboards. Jeffords replied that if Riehle could get the bill through the House, he would work to get it through the Senate. Riehle rallied support the old-fashioned way. This being an era when politicians and the press socialized freely, Riehle hosted parties at his Montpelier apartment for legislators and journalists, and may have won some over at these gatherings.

The billboard industry hired lobbyists to fight the proposed ban. But, as historian Michael Sherman writes in "Vermont State Government Since 1965," "The press dragged the lobbyists and, by implication, their legislative friends out of the comfortable, dark recesses of the State House and made them fair game for front-page exposure."

Billboard opponents found lighthearted ways to make their case. They popularized a poem riffing on a famous bit of verse by Ogden Nash:

"I think I shall never see,
A billboard as lovely as a tree.
Perhaps unless the billboards fall,
I shall never see a tree at all."

The issue remained hot during the 1968 session. Billboard companies and advertisers labeled efforts to ban the signs as communist. Who was going to compensate them for removing the signs and giving up this inexpensive means of advertising, they asked.

Riehle and other billboard opponents suggested a compromise. The bill would phase out off-premises billboards over the next five years and would strictly regulate the size, location, and lighting of on-premises signs, but the state would pay to post more discreet signs for local businesses. The bill passed both chambers with strong Republican support and was signed into law by Governor Phil Hoff, though many of his fellow Democrats refused to support the legislation.

Vermont became the first state in the continental United States to ban billboards. Hawaii prohibited the advertising signs back in the 1920s. Maine and Alaska are the only other states to outlaw billboards.
—*Mark Bushnell*

State leaders watch as a billboard is torn down following the 1968 passage of a law banning them in Vermont.

Jim Andrews and the
Vermont Reptile and Amphibian Atlas Project

itting in his office in Salisbury with color photographs of turtles, salamanders, snakes, and other Vermont reptiles and amphibians scrolling across the screen behind him, Jim Andrews recalled that when he was growing up in Middlebury, his mother was "the go-to snake lady in the neighborhood." Mostly children, but adults too, would show up at the door with snakes they had found (sometimes alive, sometimes dead), counting on her to identify them.

As coordinator of the Vermont Reptile and Amphibian Atlas Project since 1994, Jim Andrews has become the go-to herpetologist in the state. Through the website VtHerpAtlas.org, Andrews is in touch with citizen-scientists from every corner of Vermont, gathering data, disseminating information,

COURTESY OF JIM ANDREWS

Jim Andrews has dedicated his life to sharing information about – and fostering an appreciation for – Vermont's herps (reptiles and amphibians). Here, he's holding a common watersnake.

and identifying species from photographs and sound recordings. During the active season for reptiles and amphibians, Andrews said he receives five to ten "useful records" per day – that is, a sighting of a particular species confirmed with a photograph and a description of its location.

In addition to maintaining the website, Andrews and his colleagues publish an updated *Vermont Reptile and Amphibian Atlas* approximately every five years. The *Atlas*, like the website, provides a trove of information, notably a town-specific distribution map for each species, along with charts showing their relative abundance and details such as comparative carapace lengths of Vermont turtles. (In case you're wondering, the spotted turtle is the smallest, with an average carapace length of 4.8 inches, while the snapping turtle is the largest, with an average length of 15.6 inches.)

Starting as a project of The Vermont Reptile and Amphibian Scientific Advisory Group, the aim is to gather data throughout the state on the presence and distribution of the native salamanders, frogs, turtles, lizards, and snakes. In the introduction to its first published report, in April 1995, Mark DesMeules, the group's original chair, noted that the idea for the atlas could be traced back to 1853, with the publication of Zadock Thompson's *Natural History of Vermont*. Over the next 143 years, while amateur and professional herpetologists carried on field work, there was, DesMeules writes, "no attempt to consolidate Vermont herp knowledge in printed form until Charles Johnson published . . . *The Nature of Vermont* in 1980."

Since then, concerns about threatened and endangered species have galvanized efforts to not only gather useful data, but also involve more people in the project. In the most recent print version of the *Atlas*, the 2019 update, Andrews writes, "The goal … is to gather and disseminate data on local reptiles and amphibians in a way that involves and informs Vermont residents, landowners, and land managers so that they will become more effective stewards of wildlife and its habitat." Since 1995, Andrews notes, over 7,000 individuals have contributed more than 98,000 new records. Contributors include students from elementary school through graduate school, as well as amateur and professional naturalists.

As an environmental science major at the University of Vermont in the 1970s, Andrews may have felt he was carrying on a family tradition. Besides growing up with a mother who knew about snakes, Andrews said he often accompanied his father, "a country doctor who loved hunting and fishing," into the woods and along the streams. One of his grandfathers was a botanist; an aunt was a serious bird watcher. "I once saw a picture of my grandmother with a table full of snakes," Andrews added with a smile. He went on to explain that she had been teaching in India at the time, and was showing her students how to tell the difference between poisonous and non-poisonous snakes.

After college, Andrews taught junior high biology for ten years and did field work for the Nature Conservancy during the summers. He began to see that while a lot was known about Vermont's mammals and birds, there was little information available on reptiles and amphibians. And so, when he went on to get a master's degree in biology at Middlebury College, he specialized in ecology and herpetology. He has been involved in research and teaching ever since, first at Middlebury as a research herpetologist and research supervisor for several years. Currently, Andrews is a lecturer in the Rubenstein School of Environment and Natural Resources at the University of Vermont, teaching both herpetology and ornithology.

As part of his effort to engage more citizen-scientists, Andrews also teaches adult education courses at Hogback Community College in Bristol – classes that include Introduction to Birding, Tree Identification, and Vermont Reptiles and Amphibians. He is frequently invited to give presentations on particular species and their habitats by organizations such as The Nature Conservancy and The Audubon Society.

These outreach efforts are paying off handsomely, as the majority of reports Andrews receives each year come from citizens who are not professional scientists. The contributors' section of the *Atlas* contains hundreds of names of people who have made at least 20 reports, including nearly 200 names of those contributing a hundred or more. Anyone interested in getting involved can find tips for searching, identifying, and handling, as well as information for reporting species, on the website and in the print *Atlas*.

A comparison of distribution maps from 1995 and 2019 shows many examples of how the work of citizen-scientists has advanced the understanding of Vermont's herptile population. In April 1995, the red-backed salamander, for instance, had been documented in 24 Vermont towns. In the 2019 update, the presence of the red-backed salamander has been confirmed with a photo or specimen in all but 13 of the state's 255 towns. It is presumed to be present in those 13 as well, just waiting to be found.

The Atlas Project highlights species designated as threatened or endangered, according to the Vermont Endangered Species Law. The endangered category – defined as "in immediate danger of becoming extirpated in the state" – includes these five: Fowler's toad, boreal chorus frog, spotted turtle, five-lined skink (the state's only lizard), and the timber rattlesnake. Three others are classified as threatened; that is, having "a high possibility of becoming endangered in the near future": spiny softshell turtle, North American racer, and eastern ratsnake. Of Vermont's 40 species of reptiles and amphibians, eight others are listed as "of special concern" because they are rare.

Tracking sightings throughout the state gives scientists a better understanding of habitat loss and fragmentation and their effect on species that require specialized habitats. The North American racer, Andrews pointed out, once covered most of the Connecticut River valley in the Windsor area, but there has been no report of a racer in several years. "This is a snake that covers a lot of territory and likes a few miles of open territory for sunning," Andrews said. Such species are particularly vulnerable to habitat fragmentation, he noted.

Changing weather patterns also play a role in species survival. For the leopard frog and other species that lay their eggs in vernal pools or floodlands, drought is a big problem. The spring salamander, which, Andrews explained, "takes a few years in the larval stage," won't survive if its stream dries up. The mink frog appears to be starting a northward push, perhaps toward colder water.

Asked what he saw as the most important issues for species conservation, Andrews replied immediately, "We need worldwide stabilization of population. We need working ecosystems that sustain life. And we need to be more thoughtful about resource use per person." He paused, looking around his office, its shelves filled with years of reports. "Sooner or later we have to deal with it. Otherwise, we will continue to lose species."

One of the lost may be the boreal chorus frog. A lowland species, its breeding call has not been heard since 1999, Andrews said. Last documented in the northwest corner of the state, in the town of Alburgh, this tiny frog (average length 1.4 inches) might well be part of the historic record only, its remaining call a recording in the archives. —*Catherine Tudish*

Chicken Little

RAISING A SMALL FLOCK CAN BE A BIG ADVENTURE

How does an entire county sell out of chicken fencing? A pandemic, that's how. What a time, in the spring of 2020, driving from one store to the next looking for usually easy-to-find items! The one out-of-stock item that really put me in a bind was that fencing. We all understood the shortage of disinfectant wipes, but I never anticipated a fencing shortage. How foolish of me.

When it comes to self-sufficiency in homesteading, the ground floor is rearing a small flock of chickens. So that is what I intended to do: start from the bottom and work my way up. Sounds easy enough, right?

I did my research and decided to take the leap by ordering a dozen baby chicks from my local feed store. As soon as I dropped off the order form, my anxiety crept in. Or was it a nesting reflex? Because before I knew it, I was out fixing up an old coop in the barn on our property. I fixed

the doors, removed all the old bedding, and secured the floor with the last of the chicken wire I had left.

I worked on the coop a little at a time until I thought it was ready to go. I nearly scared myself

to death reading about all of the horrible things that could happen – predators, disease, mites – the list of wild possibilities was terrifying. But no matter: I was committed to building a foundation for our self-sufficiency, and I knew this was my journey to get there, barred rocky as it might be.

Chick Day. Time to become proud chicken parents! "This won't be so bad," I had convinced

myself. "They'll just require a bit of attention." Luckily for me, I had two great sons and my better half, with whom I was able to share the process. That morning at the breakfast table, it was all talk about the brooder. Have we controlled the draft? Do we have the temperature at 95 degrees? Will the chicks be safe there? If I didn't overthink an issue, then my six-year-old did. And if I hadn't considered it, then my sharp thirteen-year-old had. Of course, the lesson is that getting into chickens alone is possible, but having a team is way better.

We arrived at the feed store, put the truck in park, looked at each other, and all took a sigh. Like we were fathers in the maternity ward, knowing things were about to change. I remember marching into the store and walking out with a box of chicks

who were chirping up a storm. My goodness, they were the cutest things ever – but the chirping, chirping, chirping. That unsettling sound was a sign that the girls were not happy.

Now, the goal was to get these chicks comfortable, and that can take some time. We had chosen to set up the brooder in the garage because it was much warmer and more secure than the barn. After some time, we figured we were on the right track. The chicks stopped chirping so much. They started scratching and playing and flying. Yes, flying. Flying right out of the brooder. So then we made a roof, and everything was great. Until another problem arose, and then another. (Are you starting to see the pattern here?)

In all seriousness, it is such a privilege to be around the chickens. The connection that they help you to develop with your food is a powerful thing. It is not just chickens and eggs, either: raising chickens helps foster an understanding of the struggle that is food and nourishment. The cycle of life. One thing feeds another, which in turn provides for another, and so on. Any contamination at any point in the process is felt eventually, somewhere down the line. Raising food is hard, and it deserves to be appreciated. Either by doing the hard work yourself or by raising up the farmers who do it for you.

The chickens grew up. They got too big for the brooder, so I took my last piece of fence and made a pen outside for the daytime. It was easy to see that's where they belonged: they love to be outdoors, and they love to be in the grass. Unfortunately, chickens have no respect for your lawn. They will completely destroy all of it if given the chance. And your flower beds, gardens, driveway – nothing is off limits. Especially when you have no fencing because you decided to start raising chickens during a pandemic. I had always dreamed

of having free-range chickens until I learned what happens when you have truly free-range chickens. Now that I've learned, I'm more into selectively free-ranging my chickens.

For us, raising chickens has been an eye-opening and empowering experience. We started with 12 chickens in 2020, and a year later, we had 8 remaining. In the spring of

2021, we added 18 additional birds to our flock. We have made it through multiple foxes, one of which was run off by my son with a chicken in its mouth. It did drop the chicken, but it damaged her comb. We call her Floppy. Multiple bears passed by, fortunately without incident. And it turned out that one of the chickens we received in our initial flock was actually a mean rooster we named Hawk. I believe we have made out pretty well, aside from needing to replant some grass, reclaim our garden beds, and sacrifice some blueberries. We have given away countless eggs and learned that egg yolks are not yellow.

So we arrive at the question, "Is it worth it?" I certainly found that it was. If you earnestly want to understand where your food comes from, you have to raise it. Since I began raising chickens for eggs and for meat, I appreciate them now more than ever.
—*Aaron Carroll*

This Farm is for the Birds

POULTRY – BOTH EGGS AND MEAT – TOPS THE MENU AT MAPLE WIND FARM

It was chickens that brought Beth Whiting and Bruce Hennessey to their 192-acre farm in Richmond. The husband-and-wife team actually started Maple Wind Farm in 1999 at their home on 136 acres in Huntington. "It was a hilltop farm, with hardly a flat place on it," says Whiting. It worked for pigs and cows, and the pastures were amazing, "but when our pasture poultry operation started ramping up, there was nowhere to put the small (roughly 10 x 14-foot) chicken tractors we were using at the time," Whiting recalls.

In looking for a more suitable (i.e. flatter) farm, they found their current site along Route 2 just east of Richmond and began renting it. That allowed them to expand their poultry operation, and even open a USDA-certified processing facility. The move also led to them starting an 18-acre vegetable CSA that's since been discontinued. "There's such a thing as being too diversified," says Whiting.

In 2013, the Richmond property came up for sale, and Whiting and Hennessey decided to sell the development rights to their home property in Huntington to be able to afford the purchase. The Vermont Land Trust also purchased the development rights to their new property at the same time. Not long after, though, a fire razed the 18,000-square-foot

Layers in the grass at Maple Wind Farm.

historic barn on the property. "It burned to the ground in about two-and-a-half hours," says Whiting. "That was a big hurdle to get over; we had to sit down and consider whether farming was still in our future." She said it was the incredible outpouring from neighbors and fellow farmers in the state that got them through and convinced them to rebuild.

One of the few pieces of equipment that survived the fire was the metal chicken processing building (think large shipping container) that sat alongside the old barn. It now sits alongside a new barn: one that has modern features like a loading dock and large walk-in coolers/freezers. "That led us to scale up our chicken business even more," says Whiting.

Elsa and Orion watch over the flock of layers in the pasture.

Poultry – both chickens and turkeys – are the heart of Maple Wind Farm, but they also raise pigs – 125 to 150 a year – and cows, which they buy when they're 700 to 800 pounds and then finish on high-quality pasture.

"Everybody is on pasture during the pasture season," says Whiting. "One of our big tenets is movement, so most of the animals – other than the pigs – get moved every day."

LAYER HENS

Walk into the Maple Wind Farm barn and you'll see large stacks of egg flats sitting beside an egg washing machine. Their egg operation has about 1,800 laying hens at any time; they're "production reds" that lay brown eggs. A new batch arrives every April and goes directly out onto pasture. Once they begin laying (it takes about one month after they arrive), the prior year's hens are sold to another farm out of state that has a market for stewing hens.

Eggs are collected daily and washed twice a week; it takes three staff members to run the egg wash machine. "The eggs pretty much move to our customers within the week," says Whiting. Customers purchase the farm's products in a variety of ways, notably at City Market in Burlington, Pete's Greens, local restaurants/bakeries, and the Burlington Farmer's Market, and there's an option to order online and pick up at the farm. "We don't have a farm stand here, so people go online, order and pay, and then everything is packaged for them for pick-up at the farm, or we also have a New England shipping program," she explains. This online system was around long before Covid, but she says having it in place helped tremendously during the pandemic. "Also, we were already doing home deliveries," Whiting adds, "so we were set up for increased demand."

During the summer months, the layers move through a 30-acre parcel on an 85-acre farm in nearby Bolton that Maple Wind rents from the state. "It's a great piece of land, and we're now in our second 10-year lease," says Whiting. There, the hens have two large, covered structures (with water, food, and nest boxes) that they can come in and out of. They're protected from predation by livestock guardian dogs that live with the birds. Currently, it's a team of two Great Pyrenees.

In December, when the last of the meat birds are gone for the winter and the water lines out in the pastures freeze, the layer hens are brought back up the road to Richmond and spend the cold months in the structures that serve as the chicken brooders during the summer. (Picture large greenhouses covered in plastic fabric.) They get bales of hay to forage on during the months when the pastures are white.

With 1,800 hens, you monitor the condition of the flock largely by tracking egg production, explains Whiting. The number of eggs collected is tallied each day. "If we see a drop in production, we know something is wrong," she says. Maybe there's something that needs to be addressed about the flock health.

BROILERS

The chicks come from Moyer's Chicks, a hatchery in Pennsylvania. Each new flock arrives at just one day old in a climate-controlled truck; Maple Wind gets 1,000 new chicks each week during the non-winter season, totaling about 23,000 chickens each year. Once at the farm, the new chicks are settled into the covered structures where they have access to water dispensers and automated feed lines and heated "Ohio brooders."

Inside the brooders, peat moss is used as the bedding material. The peat moss is much more absorbent than wood shavings, which removes the odor of ammonia in the chicken waste. And if the chickens consume a small amount of peat moss when eating their food, it's not a problem; wood shavings, on the other hand, can create digestive issues. "We've seen a much lower younger-stage mortality rate using the peat moss," reports Whiting. A new, thin layer of the bedding material is sprinkled daily in any areas that have become soiled, and the entire accumulation is scraped out at the end of each season and composted. For a farm that sees more than 20,000 chickens a year pass through, waste management is a remarkably small issue.

After about two-and-a-half to three weeks the birds have grown their white feathers and are ready to move out onto grass. At about eight weeks old they are ready for processing. Maple Wind Farm is unusual in that it operates its own USDA-certified processing facility, which can process 200 birds per hour. It takes ten crew members to run it, and they're the same people who also work in the field. Whiting says that a diversified farm means diversified roles; for some new hires expecting field work, the processing end of the equation can be difficult to adjust to. "But this is part of the food system," says Whiting. "Some people embrace it; some people decide it's not for them."

Slaughtering is done on Mondays (Maple Wind Farm's own birds) and Wednesdays (when it processes for other chicken farms — a service that is in high demand). Maple Wind works closely with three partner farms that raise collectively over 10,000 additional birds under their same protocol. Maple

Chicks arrive and are housed in brooders.
In a few weeks, they're ready to move outdoors onto grass.
At about eight weeks, they are processed for meat
at the farm's USDA-certified facility.

Wind buys the birds by the finished weight and then sells them to their customers. Partner farms get the income and the fertility and don't have to market and sell the product themselves, which is a symbiotic arrangement. Following slaughter, the chickens get air chilled overnight, and Tuesdays and Thursdays the crews are packaging the previous day's chickens. A motorized system to move chickens along the line during the parting process and a double-chamber cryovac machine have been added to boost efficiency.

Once packaging is complete, the meat is moved into huge walk-in coolers and freezers and organized so that it can be directed to the correct customer. "FIFO (first in, first out) is very important to us," says Whiting. The goal is to be sure that all the inventory continually turns over rather than just grabbing whatever is at the front of the freezer. Between the agricultural aspect of caring for the animals and the logistical aspect of USDA processing, storing, handling, boxing, marketing, selling, and delivering the products, Whiting says the latter is the more challenging part of the business.

Just as the chicken waste in the fields is used for fertility, all of the unused chicken parts – the feathers, the offal, even the "pink (bloody) water" – from processing are buried and composted and spread later on the fields.

TURKEYS

The farm also raises and processes about 1,200 turkeys a year. They also arrive very young, and require special care. "Turkeys are very fragile, so we have to keep them in a brooder a little longer. They're more skittish

Maple Wind Farm's turkeys

Bruce Hennessey and Beth Whiting

than chickens, and they tend to pile up more. We just want them to be a little hardier before we move them out to a pasture," explains Whiting.

Turkeys begin arriving in May; processing begins in late September. Understandably, the lead-up to Thanksgiving creates a major rush on turkeys, so processing must begin early and not all birds are delivered fresh. One large customer in the Boston area, for example, orders 600 turkeys and those are processed ahead of time and frozen. The processing work is more physical than [for] chickens, too. "We spread out the processing dates – turkeys are just bigger and heavier, so we can only do about 150 a day," says Whiting. And not all turkeys are sold whole; the farm holds back turkeys for cutting into breasts and making ground turkey. (That's a winter project, when the Maple Wind crew has more time to debone and part them out.)

ON THE FARM

Interested in visiting a farm that raises chickens on a large (at least for Vermont) scale? Maple Wind Farm hosts a number of events during the year. These include a popular series of fried chicken dinners monthly from June to October. And the farm has introduced a series of on-farm chicken cutting workshops, and other pork workshops are in the works for the winter. —*Patrick White*

JL DAMON

MAY

May

I grew up in Wyoming and that background nearly ruined me for hiking in Vermont. At lower elevations the natural vegetation was bunchgrass and yucca and I could walk or ride horseback for miles with panoramic views in all directions. The creek bottoms supported a thread of scrubby cottonwoods and box elders, but the rest was an expanse of wind and water carved geology – wide draws, sweeping benchlands, rock outcrops. If I went to the high country, timberline was around 9,000 feet. Above that lay another 3,000 feet of elevation. So I was a vista snob.

In 1979, fresh out of college, I moved to Vermont. Of course I wanted to go hiking. Who wouldn't? I asked around about good places to go, and then, in the usual manner of recreational day-hikers, I would pack a picnic and set off for whichever mountaintop or waterfall had been recommended.

My disillusionment was swift. Time after time, I hiked for miles through the woods with nary a vista to be found. In every direction, I saw the same thing: trees. Trees and more trees and not a hope of seeing beyond them. If I was headed for a summit, the trail usually made a beeline straight up. If trail stewards created switchbacks, eager hikers cut across them. The stewards did not have the help of 10,000-foot elevations to make air-starved hikers grateful for every switchback.

If I was lucky, I would emerge from the trees onto a space of bare rock. If I was less lucky, I would find a fire-tower to climb. And what was the view? In most cases an expanse of nondescript humps and hollows covered in (surprise) trees. If I was hiking with a companion, we might spend some time debating the identity of this or that higher bump. Is that Ascutney? Moosilauke? Hunger Mountain? They were all roundish lumps with a small bald spot on top.

After a few years in Vermont, I started farming and that put an end to my hiking. In good weather, some task always demanded my attention. In bad weather, I wasn't inclined to hike. I didn't feel great regret. Hiking wild land in the Northeast had proved to be a disappointment. Instead I grew attached to the farmed landscape, the rolling fields I traversed on my tractor.

Decades passed. I retired and moved off the farm. On sunny days, I could do whatever I wanted. But not long after that, the pandemic arrived. Not only could I not fly out West to go hiking, I was discouraged from leaving my immediate neighborhood. But I had time and a dog, so I started walking.

Most of the trails near my home didn't go anywhere. They made a few loops through the woods and returned me to my car. There were no vistas. Just the same miles of trees I had scorned thirty-five years earlier. But in walking those trails, I made a discovery: I had been looking with the wrong eyes. Craving the western panorama, I had seen the trees as a wall blocking my view. Heading for a destination, I had seen the trail as a way to get there. Now I was on trails with no destination, and instead of squinting ahead to see around the next bend, I started looking at where I was.

I have always been near-sighted, so it should have been second nature to look at things within feet of me rather than miles away. Oh, well. Now I was looking, and what came into focus was an intricate landscape that is every bit as spectacular as the carved rock formations of the west. Just much smaller. (And buggier.) The vault of branches over my head sheltered an infinitely various world. The velvet green; moss on a rotting log set aglow by a shaft of sunlight. The multiplicity of shapes and veinings in a glade of ferns. A fleeting cap of snow on a shelf fungus.

I have a terrible memory for plant names. Each spring I return to my flower guide to re-identify the small blue flower I see in the woods near my house. Mertensia. Each time I think, "This time I will remember," and then in the eleven months before its next blooming, I forget. But it doesn't matter. I am grateful to the people with the gifts to make the book. But my own pleasure in the close-up landscape is not analyzing or cataloguing. My pleasure is simply in noticing how beautiful it is.
—*Edith Forbes*

Variable and Changeable

Spring weather in Vermont is always unpredictable. It's never too late to keep those extra layers on stand-by or too early to get out your summer swimming gear. Either way, you're likely to be over- or under-prepared for the weather at some point this month. Winter still has a light grip, especially over the higher terrain, but the northern jet stream continues to retreat north allowing for temperatures to increase throughout the month.

May 2021 opened cold and snowy in some parts of the state – turkey hunters were "tracking" toms on a few inches of fresh snow on opening morning. But in the high elevations, where there's often still a solid snowpack, things were stingy. Less than 20 inches of snow was on top of Mount Mansfield on May 1, with the average for the start of May being around 50 inches. May spring skiing conditions were marginal, for those who still had the skiing bug left in them.

The month was, on average, warm and dry. The US Drought Monitor listed 75 percent of Vermont as being in a moderate drought starting on May 4, with the remainder of the state being listed as abnormally dry. There was some rain in the middle of the month, but by the end of the month half the state was listed as abnormally dry, with the eastern part of the state being listed as moderate drought. Only the southwestern part of the state got typical amounts of rain.

Thanks to warm conditions through much of the month, the waters of Lake Champlain saw their earliest reading of 63 degrees or above on May 21 – breaking a record that dates back to the early 1970s. Record breaking temperatures in the lower 90s over the Champlain Valley on the same day surely helped to further speed the warming of the lake waters. Montpelier tied the record high temperature for the day on May 27 as the mercury hit a balmy 87 degrees.

Record-breaking heat did not last long, as a cold and dreary Memorial Day weekend followed. Sub-freezing temperatures were recorded over the valleys, with higher-elevation snow over the southern Green Mountains. Yes, snow on the unofficial start of summer. The snow did not mix down to the valleys, but it has before on a few Memorial Day weekends. —*Christopher Kurdek, Fairbanks Museum and Planetarium*

Snow was around to begin (the view here is from May 1 in southern Vermont) and end the month, but in between was mostly warm and dry.

The irrigation pond at Sweetland Farm in Norwich was nearly dry during the summer of 2020 –
a scene that has become all too familiar around the state the last few years.

Drowning in Drought

Burlington received a total of only 1.42 inches of rain in May 2021, a month that averages nearly 4 inches. Montpelier saw just 1.1 inches of rain in June – 3.11 inches less than normal. This was a continuation of dry conditions that began a year earlier. The National Integrated Drought Information System reports that "Since 2000, the longest duration of drought in Vermont lasted 60 weeks beginning on June 23, 2020, and ending on August 10, 2021."

We asked Dr. Lesley-Ann Dupigny-Giroux, Vermont state climatologist, for context when looking at recent stretches of dry weather in the state.

Drought occurs in every climate and can include all the types of droughts that we have been experiencing recently: meteorological (dry weather conditions), agricultural (a lack of water for crops), and hydrological (a lack of water in waterways and in the ground). Drought depends on multiple factors, including high temperature, high winds, low atmospheric humidity, low soil moisture, and depleted groundwater supplies. The 2020-2021 drought was particularly severe from a hydrological perspective, with record-setting low values in our waterways and USGS wells last fall and up until late July 2021. The rains that we received in July and August 2021 helped tremendously.

The 2020-2021 drought was not an anomaly. Drought can occur at any time of the year in Vermont, and the timing, length, and severity determine which communities and sectors are most affected. Snow droughts affect recreation and tourism differently in the winter than do agricultural or soil moisture droughts in the summer. Similarly, if drought persists from one year to the next, the impacts are widespread and particularly noticeable in our backyards, lakes, streams, groundwater wells, municipal supplies, and leaf-peeping in the fall.

Recently, droughts have been observed in Vermont in 1998-1999, 2006-2007, 2010, 2011, 2012, 2016, 2018, and 2020-2021. Historically, the 1960s were a cold and dry decade when multi-year droughts were prevalent not just in the state, but across the Northeast. Similarly, severe and long-lasting droughts were observed in the 1910s and 1930s.

I am concerned about all types of drought across Vermont and the larger Northeast. Regional droughts tend to be more severe and longer lasting. Drought has been described as a "creeping phenomenon," with a slow onset and slow recovery. Over the last few years, we have seen more instances of what are called "flash droughts," where the combination of the lack of precipitation plus high daytime temperatures leads to drought impacts that are observed on the timescale of weeks rather than months. In flash droughts, the effects are noticed relatively quickly and they include signs such as plants burning to a crisp or long stretches of sunny, dry days at times of the year when some type of precipitation is usually received. —*Lesley-Ann L. Dupigny-Giroux, Ph.D.*

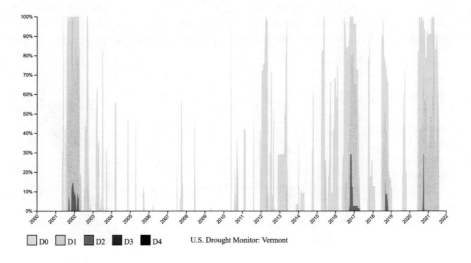

DO DI D2 D3 D4   U.S. Drought Monitor: Vermont

NATURE NOTES

BLUEBERRY CELLOPHANE BEE *(Colletes validus)*
Size ½ inch

If there is sand near blueberries, chances are these bees are nesting there, in holes, waiting for warmer weather.

DAISY HEBB

HEMLOCK POLLEN was prolific in May, coating every nearby surface with a lemon-lime-colored film.

Common lowbush blueberry *(Vaccinium angustifolium)* is native to the Northeast. It grows in sun to part-shade in acid soils, less than 6.8 pH, moist to droughty.

SUGAR MAPLE TREES are monitored for the timing of budbreak and leaf out each spring at the Proctor Maple Research Center in Underhill. This year, the buds broke on April 12 – the earliest in their 30-years of recordkeeping and about 21 days earlier than the long-term average. But then cool weather in April and early May slowed things down. Full leaf out came on May 15, only four days earlier than the long-term average.

Trees, including sugar maple, have two types of buds: vegetative and flower. Vegetative buds contain immature leaves that, following bud break, develop leaves and produce new woody twigs, whereas flower buds contain immature flowers, many of which will become maple seeds.

MARK ISSELHARDT

MAY 27, 2021 – Where are all the red-eyed vireos? (I thought I'd *never* say that.) Every spring is different. Water levels are high some years, frog choruses deafening. Other years, water levels are low, choruses politely quiet. One spring, a moose. Another, a northbound golden eagle. But this spring (so far), a *silence of the vireos*. During May 2020 pandemic birding, I'd walk through a tunnel of red-eyed vireo songs, small overlapping territories, one after another. Woodland elevator music. A gradation of vireos, the most abundant songbird in The Hollow, the most abundant songbird in eastern North America. But this year, for the moment, the valley belongs to ovenbirds, emphatically screaming out of mosquito-infested shadows. —*Ted Levin*

Red-eyed vireo

IF, BY CHANCE, you found a baby barred owl hatchling in the grass beneath a nest that was 30 feet up in a dead white pine – way too high to climb – you might find a nearby tree cavity and stow the little one in there. Feed it freshly trapped, chopped-up mice. Wait for the parents to locate it and take over the feeding themselves.

AT HOME

✿

Precise Picking

Foraging season has begun, and the holy trinity of springtime edibles – fiddleheads, ramps, morels – take center stage.

If you're wondering how many **FIDDLEHEADS** you can pick without harming the plant, Vermont Fish and Wildlife Botanist Bob Popp says: "Studies indicate that limiting harvest to less than 50 percent of the fronds limits impacts and does not reduce availability the following year." But in our observations of mature ostrich fern plants that hadn't been harvested, we were surprised by how varied the plants were. Some had four fronds, some five, some six, some eight. Whether this is a reflection of maturity and vigor, or if it's from some other cause, we're not sure. But knowing about this variability, why not just pick two from each clump? That'll almost always keep you under 50 percent.

As for **WILD LEEKS** (also known as ramps), they mostly reproduce vegetatively by sending out underground runners, and only the larger, older bulbs are capable of this. Common sense comes into play: if you're the only one picking, and you're only picking a handful of bulbs each year from an acre-sized patch, it's hard to argue you're not picking sustainably. If you're in an area

with only a smattering of plants, though, or picking a shared resource on public land, harvest only the leaves and leave the bulbs in the ground.

MORELS are mysterious, so the answer to how-many-should-I-pick? is ambiguous. One school of thought holds that mushrooms are like apples: the caps you pick are like the fruit, the below-ground mycelium is like the tree. Following this logic, clean picking is fine. After all, it doesn't hurt an apple tree if you take all its fruit. The more conservative school of thought holds that we ought to

be leaving spores in the woods to make new flushes, so leaving one-third to one-half of all the caps you find in any given flush is best practice. There's an extensive US Forest Service report online that reinforces this ambiguity. "We simply do not know what impact [intensive harvesting] might have on morel reproduction, populations, or diversity," the researchers write. "There might be negative impacts, or, for all we know, morel harvesters might be spreading more morel spores further on their boots than would be spread by the wind." Ⓥ

Pruning Blueberry Bushes

I do 90 percent of the maintenance on my blueberry bushes in April and May. By then, the snow has melted and the soil is soft, which is an ideal time to pull perennial weeds that have snuck in during the previous summer. And with bare branches you can see the form of the bush clearly, which makes it easier to prune.

I start by cutting out anything that is obviously dead or diseased. Then I'll cut branches that are drooping into the walking rows so they don't cause problems for the mower later in the summer. Some of the bushes are 20 years old and need the older branches pruned out. A blueberry branch reaches its maximum productivity at around eight years old, after which it declines in fruit. Pruning these old canes can be a painful exercise because they are often robust stems that are plainly still healthy. It is important to keep the bush producing new stems, however, and taking out the old ones lets light into the center where new growth starts. You will need very sharp tree pruning cutters for this and should cut as close to the base as you can manage.

My acidic soil is already ideal for growing blueberries. In fact, when I first planted the small whips, the soil was so acidic (pH = 4.2) that I had to add compost and lime to get it up to a more reasonable 4.8-ish. Soil that is too alkaline inhibits the plant from taking up nitrogen and they will sit there looking yellow and sad. If your soil pH is above 5.5, add sulfur and mulch with pine needles, if possible, to bring it back down. Fertilize with a slow-release, granular fertilizer meant for acid-loving plants, like Pro-Holly or Holly-Tone.

Lastly, mulch the patch with two inches of wood chips or sawdust. Blueberry bushes are pretty hardy, but if you want good fruit and a pleasant picking experience, you might as well pamper the shrub and yourself and keep it weed-free. —*Laura Sorkin*

Before and after pruning

White ash male flowers

MARY HOLLAND

SEXING ASH TREES

Ash trees are dioecious, which means that male and female flowers appear on different trees. In field studies, foresters have noted that in many places there are more male ash trees than female ash trees – one theory is that there's a greater reproductive cost for female flowers. Since emerald ash borers are likely to kill most of the ash in Vermont over the next 20 years, and proactive woodlot owners are looking to thin ash now, it makes sense to spare female trees where we can. Female trees make seeds, and male pollen is windborne and can travel considerable distances.

Late May is a good time to identify a tree's gender. Male flowers are bulbous and have a reddish-tinge – they're much easier to see than female flowers. If you miss the spring window, come back in late summer and look for seeds on the female trees. Flag them, so that when you make harvesting decisions, you'll know.

PHOTOS BY LAURA SORKIN

A LOOK BACK

Angling Memories

May is the month I get excited about fishing. The weather and the waters warm up and the fish are hungry. It is time to grab my rod and head for one of the many small brooks in and around Bradford for a few hours of solitude and a chance for a meal of fresh brook trout, or square tails as I learned to call them.

A few six-inch trout rolled in corn muffin mix and cooked in virgin olive oil make a meal fit for the gods. Add a side of morels cooked in butter, homemade rolls, and a glass of wine and it doesn't get any better. The satisfaction of having worked for the meal makes it all the more enjoyable.

This time of year my thoughts often turn to the past and memories of fishing in my youth. Some of the best memories I have of growing up involve fishing with Dad and Mom and my school buddies. One of the earliest memories I have of opening day involves Dad taking me to the little brook that enters Lake Morey after flowing by Lanakila. Although it was over 60 years ago, I can still vividly recall the

cold mist rising soon after daylight as we fished the brook, managing to catch a few trout. The number or size didn't matter to me, what was important was spending opening morning with Dad.

A year or two later I knew I had come of age when Dad took me north to Ferdinand and the "Madison Camp." I had listened intently to Dad, Uncle Bud, Uncle Merritt, Paul Nye, Jim Hodge, and Walt Osgood talk about such places as Ferdinand Bog, South America Pond, Madison Brook, Paul Stream and Unknown Pond. Suddenly Dad had decided I was old enough to make my first trip to that revered region to which the men would occasionally retreat.

My mother also liked to fish, but with five children, her recreational time was very limited. Mostly she would fish with us when we took our annual camping vacations to places like Maidstone State Park, or in later years after Mom and Dad built a camp on Nelson Pond. Mom had the patience of a saint, and would spend most of her time helping untangle the lines of the children she was trying to teach how to fish.

I grew up near the height of land on Fairground Road in Bradford, and Roaring Brook was less than a mile away. I had an old metal telescoping rod that Dad had given me and it served me well, catching a lot of fish and withstanding terrible abuse. I carried my worms in a Prince Albert tobacco tin and had a canvas creel in which to put my trout.

The six-inch regulation was in effect in those days so we all had marks on our rods to indicate what fish we could keep. I will admit we tried to stretch a few fish on occasion.

Neighbor and classmate, Francis Stockman was most apt to be my

Dad at the Madison camp in 1968 or '69. The area is now part of the West Mountain Wildlife Management Area.

My father, Harlie, and two younger brothers, Randy and Rick. Dad died in 1995.

fishing companion on the upper stretches of Roaring Brook and on the many streams in West and South Newbury. Our means of transportation was generally a Ford 9N tractor. It may not have compared to one of today's expensive SUVs, but it served us well, getting us to places with ease that would have taken a lot of time and effort had we been riding our bikes.

It is time to go fishing. I now live in the woods that were once part of our farm, so I think I will try one of the brooks I fished some 60 years ago. Now I get to choose between many expensive rods and reels, something that was not a problem when I was young and owned only one. I doubt I will catch more fish than I did then. —*Gary W. Moore*

INDUSTRY

Grains in Vermont

There are so many different stories to tell about grain in Vermont, from history to present day, of those growing grains at different scales, of Vermonters using different types of grains in different ways.

Grains have been a vital crop in Vermont for centuries. Corn was used, and still is, to make many traditional Abenaki dishes, as just one example. And according to the Northern Grain Growers Association, there were 40,000 acres of wheat growing in Vermont back in 1830.

But things changed dramatically, and Vermont hasn't grown much grain, really, since the 1800s. Once the Erie Canal was built and agricultural products could start moving around easily, the industry came to be dominated by farms out west. We don't have the space here for large-scale production and our climate is a bit too wet. We were more suited to a livestock type of agricultural system.

When I first came to UVM Extension in 2003, the focus was on feed grains for livestock. But about that time the localvore movement was getting started, and there was renewed interest in food that was grown within a 50- to 100-mile radius. People started to realize that they needed to eat more than tomatoes, and they began searching to see if it was possible to get staples within the state of Vermont. It was at that time, probably about 15 years ago, that consumer demand for locally grown grains really began to explode.

Consumers started going to bakeries, like Red Hen Bakery in Middlesex and O Bread Bakery in Shelburne, to buy bread that was made with locally grown wheat.

It remains true today that growing grains is easier to do practically and financially on large acreage. The return per acre is in the hundreds of dollars, while the return per acre with tomatoes is in the thousands. Since the value is so low with grains, you need a good number of acres to make it viable. Places out west can grow more for less, so their scales of efficiency are so much better.

But as the demand for locally grown grains has

increased, people have started to realize, "Oh, maybe we *can* grow grains here." That demand is the reason for the resurgence we're seeing: we can't grow grains on a large scale and compete with non-local products, but we can grow grains to satisfy the demand for high quality, local products. The resurgence is not huge, but it's real. And the growing supply is still not at the same level as the number of bakeries or beer producers here, so there's room for expansion, which is exciting.

WHAT GRAINS ARE GROWING HERE?

The low-hanging fruit is wheat that can be milled into flour. That's been the easiest to accomplish in Vermont.

Oats are another grain that grows really well here. But they require a lot of processing to get them into a food-grade market. With wheat, when it's harvested, you get the actual seed through a process called free-threshing, which means that when it goes through a combine, what gets dropped into the bucket is a ready-to-grind seed. Barley, on the other hand, has a husk on it, which is good for malting. But if you wanted to make pearled barley or rolled barley, you have to get that husk off. That's also true with oats. And that process requires special equipment, which doesn't exist in Vermont. There's no place in the state right now making rolled oats or oatmeal.

Without that processing infrastructure in place, oats really are only being grown for animal feed rather than human consumption in Vermont. There are varieties of hulless oats and hulless barley; I'm not aware of any farmers in Vermont growing those types yet, but that certainly is an opportunity.

Corn, obviously, is being grown in Vermont, and its use as a grain is increasing in popularity. We now have two tortillerias in the state – Vermont Tortilla Company (in Shelburne) and All Souls Tortilleria (Warren) – that are buying locally grown corn to make tortillas and chips.

There are also "ancient grains" – things like emmer and einkorn; you see these listed on products at the grocery store, but I'm not aware of anyone growing them commercially in Vermont. The hulling process is a challenge with them, and they tend to yield low, so you would want to have a ready market if you were going to try to grow those.

One grain that has gained a lot of popularity is spelt, and we do have a few farmers in the state growing that. It's a grain related to wheat that's primarily used in flour; it also has a different type of gluten in it, which some people can digest better than the gluten in wheat. That's what has sort of driven a small market for that.

A few people are growing rice in Vermont on a smaller scale, but Boundbrook Farm in Vergennes is the only one I know about that's doing it on a larger scale. Erik and Erica Andrus are running an integrated duck and rice farm there. They grow 5 to 10 acres of paddy rice that they imported from Japan; the paddies are flooded and the ducks are used to control weeds and pests.

THE FUTURE OF GRAINS IN VERMONT

One of the things I'm working on is figuring out how farmers who are already growing grains as a cover crop can tap into these new markets. There are about 30,000 acres of cereal rye planted in Vermont as a cover crop, so why not use some of it as grain? Rye seed has advantages: it's relatively cheap seed; it establishes later in the season than most other grains; it doesn't mind heavy or low-pH soil; and it's very well adapted to our climate. Other grains also work as cover crops, and farmers are planting them anyway. What if we could move even a fraction of that acreage into a value-added market, whether it's for flour or beer or spirits?

Different grains might work well for different farms. For example, there are both spring grains and winter grains. Winter grains include winter rye, winter wheat, and winter barley (the latter is not well adapted to the Vermont climate as it doesn't over-winter well). Spring-seeded grains include spring wheat, spring barley, and oats. Farmers in the Champlain Valley like to grow winter grains because they're on heavy clay soils. Spring grains need to be seeded in April, so if you're up in the Northeast Kingdom on better-drained soils, farmers there tend to plant grains in early spring.

Currently, grains make up only a small portion of Vermont's agricultural acreage. But there are plenty of opportunities for expansion. The biggest challenge for growers is that we're missing the infrastructure: the equipment to handle, store, and process (in some cases even to dry) the grain. I think those will come into place if there's a market; if there's a really good market, farmers will take care of that on their own. Right now we don't even have a flour mill in Vermont, so we're limited in that regard; however, many farms and bakers are milling their own flour onsite to be able to enter the marketplace. *—Heather Darby*

Brewing up (and Distilling Down) Demand for Grains

Barley is one of the main ingredients in beer, and certainly we have a ton of microbreweries in Vermont. And now we have one malthouse in the state [Peterson Quality Malt was founded in 2014 at what used to be the old Nordic Dairy Farm in Charlotte; in 2021, the property was purchased by entrepreneur Will Raap, who envisions creating a "grain-based agricultural hub" at the site with the addition of a tasting room for Whistle Pig Whisky, demonstration gardens, and other business and agricultural education components]. A malthouse takes barley and makes malt out of it, which can then be used to brew beer. That's really exciting, because while brewers sometimes use unmalted grains, they use a lot of malted grains. So having a malthouse is really key to being able to use Vermont-grown grains for brewing.

There are a good number of distilleries in Vermont, as well. Winter rye is a grain that we primarily see dotting the landscape as a cover crop, but if you take it to seed, that's what's used to make whisky. For example, Whistle Pig is a distillery that sits on a 500-acre farm in Shoreham where it is growing rye. And rye is a crop with a lot of potential in Vermont. For instance, Caledonia Spirits, now based in Montpelier, purchases its rye from local farms (it also uses a large amount of raw honey, much of it produced in Vermont). In fact, the company was started by Todd Hardie, who was very invested in buying local grains. He ended up selling the company and now he operates Thornhill Farm in Greensboro Bend, growing the rye for Caledonia Spirits.

—*Heather Darby*

Left: Rye is transferred from the combine to a gravity wagon at Thornhill Farm in Greensboro Bend.

Grains in the Home Garden

There are few crops we can grow in our home gardens that are as enchanting as grains. Among the oldest of our cultivated food crops, they connect us back through at least 10,000 years of agriculture, and therefore to every generation of farmers in the intervening millennia who grew, tended, harvested, and selected for the best qualities. Grains form a bridge to the earliest incorporation of wild plants into our domesticated foods. There is archaeological evidence of some ancestor of bread baked with wild wheat and barley in the Black Desert of Jordan some 14,000 years ago.

Today, grains are still among the most widely grown food crops worldwide and provide the greatest proportion of our nutrition. As a believer in the powerful potential of our home gardens, an advocate for building a strong local year-round food supply, and a seed saver of over 25 years, I've explored the full range of what's possible to grow in Vermont.

Grains entered my consciousness about 19 years ago. At a Northeast Organic Farmers Association conference, I saw huge bundled sheaves of wheat, their plump, nodding heads full of promise. I was instantly hooked. Today, winter wheats, and more specifically landrace varieties – those that have been farmer-selected in specific regions, have large genepools, and are capable of adaptation – hold particular fascination for me.

Wheat, barley, rye, and oats are obvious choices for us in Vermont, but many of the so-called pseudograins, such as sorghum, amaranth, and millet, also thrive here and offer variety on our tables. Turns out upland rice, a thoroughly unlikely crop for Vermont, grows really well here. All express beauty, flavor, nutritional value, and utility that is unparalleled.

In recent years interest has grown in einkorn,

emmer, and spelt, three ancestors of modern wheat, for their flavor and digestibility. Beyond those, the number of species and varieties still available to us is stunning. Yet, varieties that are not preserved now may be lost forever, including their hidden qualities that might make them important as we contend with climate change.

Grains are surprisingly undemanding to grow. They want only average fertility and too much can cause the ripening stems to lodge, or fall over. They are low maintenance, since the winter grains especially will produce enough leaf growth to shade out weeds. And each variety has a distinct personality, reminding us daily to appreciate these nuances.

Sourcing seed is a big part of the adventure. The USDA genebank, for one, has thousands of accessions, drawn from all over the world, many of which beg to be rediscovered and brought back into cultivation. Half the fun is looking for varieties that have the potential to thrive in Vermont. To that end, search for those coming from a similar latitude or climate, or length of growing season, or that have been cultivated for a specific end use. Examples include the Rouge d'Écosse (Red of Scotland) winter wheat, originating in a cool, wet climate, Tibetan barley with its huge grains and adaptation to a short growing season, and Pfälzer Dinkel spelt, a German variety used primarily for making pretzels.

There are other qualities that make grains irresistible. *Historical importance*: Surprise, a spring wheat developed by Cyrus Pringle, a Vermont breeder from the 19th century. *Sheer beauty*: Rothenburger Rotkorn spelt, whose stems range in color from green through purple to gold as the grain ripens. *Rarity*: Val Peccia rye, originating in the hindmost village of a valley in Italian Switzerland. *End use*: the Swiss variety Poppeliweizen, with stems so long – three feet between last node and head – that it was a preferred variety for straw weaving, and Maris Widgeon, an English variety prized for thatching. And finally, *mystery*: A nameless possible cross between an emmer and a rye, given to me by a friend and growing in my garden now, with its gorgeous blue-gray foliage and enormous heads. We are not sure exactly what it is!

My grain plots average 3x5 feet, small enough to permit trials of several varieties in one season. All are then exposed to the same conditions, making it possible to observe important differences in how each responds. Grains most want moisture at the beginning of the

season, when they are getting established and putting out first growth, but dry conditions later. In 2021 we had exactly the opposite: hot, dry weather early on, then steady rain right at ripening. A microburst on June 30 included strong winds and pelting downpours, followed by many consecutive days of rain – a worst-case scenario for grains nearing maturity.

Many heritage grains are much taller than modern wheats, making them susceptible to heavy winds. Moisture will cause mold and increased incidence of disease on the heads. This year I was able to observe which varieties were least affected by the adversity. One in particular, Breisgauer Begrannter Roter Land, a German landrace, was a standout. Even at five feet tall it was not affected by the winds. It showed all the desirable qualities of sturdy stems, plump heads, no evidence of mold, uniformity of height, and ease of threshing. There were several others that exceeded expectations, providing an invaluable indication of which varieties might be best suited to climate changeability.

All grains except rye are self-pollinated, which means we can grow many varieties at a time in our home garden. This is immensely satisfying work and fills a gap in the agricultural loop. Small farmers already struggling to make a living simply cannot afford to devote small plots of land to trials, or take the time required for tending the crops. We, on the other hand, who may start with only the 5 grams of seed the USDA provides, can make accurate observations over a season and increase the seed to a scale that becomes feasible for the farmer to grow.

If you choose to grow grains on a small scale, know that growing enough for a loaf of bread will be challenging. According to Gene Logsdon in his charming book, *Small-Scale Grain Raising*, it takes a plot about 10x109 feet to grow a bushel of wheat. Be advised, you will need to find ways to keep chipmunks and birds away from ripening grains. Still, dedicating your practices to the preservation of diversity, to the discovery of adaptable, flavorful, endangered varieties suitable for reintroduction into cultivation, is important work and a worthy and sufficient mission.
—*Sylvia Davatz*

At right, from the top:
Winter Durum (Kandur 2262)
Emmer (Blau-Emmer)
Hulless Barley (Excelsior Purple)

Ingredients for Success:
Vermont-grown Grains and Vermont-made Mills

Where would one start to examine Vermont's current synergism between farmers, millers, and bakers – with the bread in the store or the grain in the field? Let's start with Blair Marvin and Andrew Heyn at Elmore Mountain Bread, because all the grain they use is Vermont-grown, they mill it themselves, they made the mill they mill it in, and they sell their bread in local stores in the Northeast Kingdom.

Marvin grew up in Johnson and had no special interest in baking. She went west for college and met Heyn when she was a culinary student in Seattle. When they returned together to Vermont, Marvin began working at a restaurant in Morrisville, and the baker who was supplying their bread came in one day and asked whether she might know anyone who would want to buy a house in Elmore on 10 acres of land with a wood-fired bakery. She said she

didn't, but asked if she could come to see what it was all about. That was 17 years ago.

The family soon got into commercial baking, but the oven turned out to be too small and inconvenient. A second oven succumbed to a structural defect, but the third and current oven has been a marvel. It heats reliably (30 cords a year in thinnings from a nearby sugarbush), loads and unloads easily with a home-built loader, holds just the right amount of steam for perfect crust formation, and produces 600 loaves a day, running two days a week. The sourdough for that bread is mixed in a no-name mixer that is at least 70 years old; it then gets an initial bulk fermentation and is shaped into loaves before being retarded in a cooler overnight before baking.

When they started the bakery, Marvin and Heyn used commercial roller-milled organic flour from a small producer in Quebec. However, after a fellow baker in North Carolina overnighted them a box of freshly milled and sifted flour about seven years ago, the smell of that fresh flour, and the taste of the bread made from it, led Heyn to make his own stone mill. For the past six years they have been milling all their own flour in that mill, as well as milling a limited amount of flour for other bakers and for some of their farmer-suppliers.

Other bakers heard about Heyn's mills and asked him to

Blair Marvin at the loader in front of her marvelous wood-fired oven at Elmore Mountain Bread.

build mills for them, an endeavor that soon blew up into New American Stone Mills. That company recently moved from a large garage on the couple's land in Elmore to a commercial/industrial building in Morrisville. There, Heyn and a small but expanding crew are now building mills (more than 125 so far) that are being shipped all over the country and around the world. The fact that these mills are constructed in Vermont makes the story all the more fascinating: the welded steel frames are made by a contractor in Elmore, are locally painted, and are topped by stainless steel grain hoppers that are welded up in Chittenden County. The heart of the mill, the granite millstones, are cut by Granite Importers, in Barre, of local, fine-grained Barre Gray granite, then shaped at the facility in Morrisville using pneumatic chisels (some of them custom-designed) made by Trow and Holden in Barre.

This Vermont bakery, with a Vermont mill, baking for local Vermont stores, is part of an international revival of wood-fired baking and small-scale milling. Marvin is also part of a national group of artisan bakers committed to a project to make "approachable bread." In her case, that is a sandwich loaf made with high-extraction stone-milled white flour (retaining some natural minerals and bran usually absent from white bread) baked in conventional bread pans and sliced before packaging. That bread has only five organic ingredients (including water) and will keep for a week because of the naturally preservative nature

Andrew Heyn dresses the stones in-house at New American Stone Mills in Morrisville.

of its sourdough content. It is baked once a week so families can buy it on Sunday at an affordable price to make a week of school lunches. Now, that is thinking globally and acting locally – a philosophy that extends to buying the grain she needs.

Marvin buys from five organic farmers, including Seth Johnson of Morningstar Farm in Glover. Johnson and his family have been farming full-time for eight years in a diversified operation with 100 tillable acres. The farm is reached by a bridge that passes over a small brook and Seth is always

conscious of the flow of nutrients across that bridge, teaching his children that if things leave the farm (hay, grain, beans, cattle) they must be balanced by things coming to the farm (sunlight, water, minerals, dairy manure, bran from the wheat milled by Blair, wood ash or chips) to preserve and improve the soil.

Johnson studied agriculture in college and got the organic bug while working for the late Jack Lazor at Butterworks Farm in Westfield. Morningstar Farm is best known for its nine varieties of open-pollinated dry beans, planted on 30 acres that are rotated with both winter and spring wheat. The rotation has been essential for soil health, but the demand for local organic bread wheat is now so good that it is becoming co-dominant on the farm with the beans.

Planting the wheat is fairly straightforward, but harvesting in the Vermont climate is not. Each exposure to moisture after the grain is mature reduces the quality of the wheat – lowering protein, increasing amylase levels, and potentially leading to fungal growth that can render the crop unfit for human consumption. In a wet year, there may be only a few days that are ideal for harvesting wheat, so Johnson has invested carefully in harvesting equipment. He recently bought a large (for Vermont) used combine from the Midwest. It cost $35,000 to purchase and transport, but it's in good condition and can do the same quality work as a newer, larger, $300,000 machine. This allows him to harvest quickly at optimum times, and given that the machine can travel down the road at 20 mph, he has done enough nearby custom harvesting in the past couple of years to defray much of the expense of owning the machine.

The field work starts in April, with plowing and seeding the spring wheat, a variety called Bolles, running into May. Seth winters a beef herd of about 40 animals under cover on a "bedded pack" (the animals tromp down straw, hay and manure to develop a solid dry mass several feet thick). In the spring, he turns the cattle out to pasture and breaks up the manure pack, moving it to a composting windrow for a year before using it on the fields. That way, the nutrients are fully available, the volume and weight have been reduced, and the weed seeds have been burned out in the hot compost. Soil inputs like wood ash or compost are spread in the fields before crops are planted; this prior composting saves on time, fuel, and equipment wear and tear. Each summer the farm produces 1,500 round bales of hay, some of it sold for good profit to feed horses in New Jersey. On the backhaul, Seth, who has a CDL, picks up shipping containers at the Port of Newark to sell to other farmers back in Vermont – value added to his trucking of the hay.

The previous year's winter wheat is harvested in mid-summer; the current year's spring wheat is harvested in August. In September, winter wheat (recently Expedition or Warthog varieties) is planted before the beans are harvested in October.

The rest of the fall is devoted to drying and sorting dry beans and getting them ready for market. The entire family is involved in that time-intensive activity. The wheat harvest is in the bins and dry after pre-cleaning and will be cleaned again before shipping throughout the year, usually in one-ton bulk tote bags or smaller bags as required. Wheat, beans, beef, hay, shipping containers; there is a lot coming and going across the bridge at Morningstar Farm.
—*Dan Wing*

Seth Johnson with the large combine he brought from the Midwest to efficiently harvest grain at his Morningstar Farm in Glover.

RED HEN BAKERY

Local Loaves: Big and Small

Red Hen Bakery in Middlesex has become one of the leading artisan bakeries in the country over the last 21 years – and has been using Vermont wheat and rye for some bread varieties for most of that time. Currently, Red Hen is buying wheat kernels from Joe Hescock's diversified family farm in Shoreham. Red Hen has a new 40-inch stone mill from Andrew Heyn, which they use to process Hescock's wheat and the rye that they buy from Todd Hardy in Greensboro.

TRUKENBROD

John and Zsuzsa Mellquist have a small bakery, Trukenbrod, on their farm in Corinth. John began to bake as a teenager, baked for his family, and eventually began to grow spring wheat on a small scale in the 1980s – harvesting with a sickle bar mowing machine and processing with a threshing machine made in Vermont in 1880. In 2001, he bought a small Austrian stone mill, built two ovens, and was soon selling bread to as many as a dozen food co-ops, all while working in the software industry. Too much. Today, he has an Andrew Heyn 26-inch mill and bakes 125 loaves a week for a devoted clientele, selling locally to neighbors in Corinth and Vershire and to two farmstand stores. —*Dan Wing*

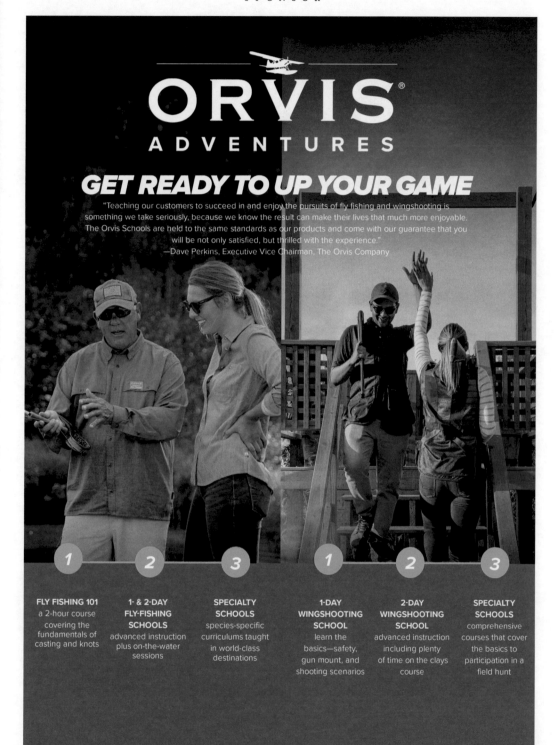

JUNE

June

In June, when the governor's pandemic restrictions began to lift, I drove from Hardwick to Greensboro with my friend Diane for two errands, each errand a kind of repair. First, we headed to a mutual friend's house to borrow tools, so Diane could plaster her mud room walls and ceiling. My friend wanted to keep her two-hundred-year-old house together, mending horsehair plaster and sealing it with brand-new gold paint.

Except for my daughters, I hadn't driven with anyone in my car for almost a year and a half. Now, vaccinated and not wearing masks, the drive seemed festive. Laughing, we remembered those summers we had driven around, our kids in the backseat of my old blue Volvo. On the way home from the beach in Greensboro, the kids tented towels over their heads, so Diane and I couldn't hear their whispering.

That early summer afternoon, we passed fields patterned with curved mounds of the first hay cutting. Low, cold mist floated and a little rain fell. We stood in our friends' open garage bay, joking and talking. June's damp gnawed into us, and I tugged the cuffs of my wool sweater over my wrists.

Then we were in the car again, borrowed tools rattling in the back of my Subaru. Where the dirt road joined the pavement, we saw a glimpse of Caspian Lake, a shimmering mirror held in the emerald earth and ringed by gently rolling hills.

Next, we stopped at the town hall in Greensboro, where a crowd was gathering. An unused school bell had been moved from beneath brushy pines where it had been largely unnoticed for years and gifted by the town to the consolidated high school, Hazen Union. The school's principal, David Perrigo, had been searching for a bell in memory of Finn Rooney, a high school student who had died a few months before the pandemic closed down the world. Bread and Puppet's band played in the rain, so the occasion was both merry and heart-wrenching.

In a few weeks, the bell would be rung at high school graduation. Had he been alive, Finn would have received a diploma that June.

When the bell had left in a red pickup, escorted by the fire department and a parade of cars, I drove us back to Hardwick. My friendship with Diane now spans two births and four toddlerhoods, the death of a stepfather, one divorce, one move, multiple jobs, and myriad cups of coffee – a whole lot of living and memories. Ahead of us lay the promise of a Vermont summer of swimming and campfires, or the challenge of woodchucks in the garden, or whatever else the world might throw at us.

Driving, Diane and I mused how the bell would be rung at soccer and baseball games. Hazen was built on a hillside, and the bell's tone will carry across the river and the village of white steeples. This bell will ring for years to come, when the story of Finn Rooney and how the bell was pulled from the shrubbery in Greensboro and escorted ceremoniously by pickup to Hazen will morph into the sticky stuff of legend, that hazy terrain of stark fact and enthralling fiction, the meat of our small towns.

As poet John Donne wrote, the bell tolls for Finn Rooney, but, in a way, for each of us, too. That June, in varying degrees, our lives had all been upended, veered far off the expected course. In one way or another, we leaned into whatever we sensed might mend some small bit of us – a sonorous bell to celebrate a baseball game, yellow paint over repaired plaster, or a field of blooming dandelions.

The world changes, and the world doesn't change – our conundrum. In June, we're enchanted with the bottomless well of Vermont's beauty. Fragrant lilacs fade as vibrant irises unfurl; spring ephemerals vanish into waist-high ferns. These are the days of swimming in pollen-sprinkled ponds, when kids bike long beyond suppertime, with no threat of imminent darkness.

More than anything, June reminds us of how profoundly we love this place and this life. Soak it up – cold rain, mosquitoes, and all – while these days last. —*Brett Ann Stanciu*

Hot and Dry

Hot summer temperatures do not usually occur until the end of June, but that was not the case this year. Record-breaking warmth came on the 6th, with highs uncomfortably into the 90s over the Champlain Valley. Montpelier reached a high of 90 on that date – shattering the record for that date by 5 degrees. The day after also offered record-breaking heat as the mercury again crested into the 90s over the valleys. A second period of record-setting heat came at the end of the month, as lows on June 28 fell only into the tropical-like lower- and mid-70s. Record highs in the 90s were observed the next day with another round of record-setting overnight lows.

The heat was accompanied by abnormally dry conditions throughout Vermont, further enhancing dry and drought conditions throughout the state. In a month that averages around 4 inches of rainfall, most sites picked up only half of that. For farmers without irrigation, this made for stressful times; it also made for busy sprinklers and hoses in many a home garden.

The hot, dry weather also made for some unhappy hay farmers, as field grasses thrive under cooler and moist conditions. The result was a later first cut of hay than usual with a lower than normal yield. The heat and lack of rainfall did make for some long windows of opportunity to mow, dry, and bale the hay. And one of Vermont's unofficial state ag products – Creemees, preferably with maple added – were in high demand as people looked for ways to beat the heat. —*Christopher Kurdek, Fairbanks Museum and Planetarium*

Temperature departure from average (°F), June 2021

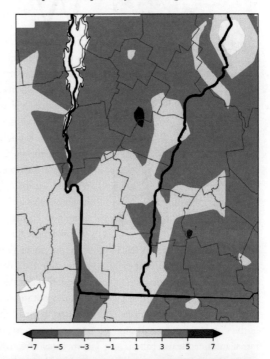

At Sweet Seasons Farm and Artisan Confections in St. Johnsbury, a dry June meant hand-watering the apple and superfood berry orchards.

SWEET SEASONS FARM AND ARTISAN CONFECTIONS

NATURE NOTES

BUNCHBERRY FLOWERS
(*Cornus canadensis*) seemed to
peak in the Green Mountain
National Forest around June 6
this year. The four showy parts
of the flower are not petals but
rather modified leaves called
sepals. The true flowers, grouped
in the middle of the showy part,
are tiny, relatively insignificant
things that contain an ingenious
pollen distribution mechanism.
When the flowers are ready
to open, the four petals stick
to each other at their tips. If a
heavy-enough insect lands on
a flower, the petals fly apart,
releasing the stamens, which
fly upward with explosive force.
The flower opens in less than
0.5 milliseconds and shoots
pollen an inch high, 10 times
the height of the flower.
—*Virginia Barlow*

Entomophaga maimaiga

What most of us know as gypsy moths are now being called LDDs – the initials of their Latin name, *Lymantria dispar dispar.*

Beginning not long after this introduced insect first escaped from captivity in 1869 in Massachusetts, LDD caterpillars have defoliated uncountable numbers of trees, especially oaks. By now, over 100 million acres in the northeastern US have been defoliated by the moth's caterpillars. Plus, a lot more acres in eastern Canada. Efforts to control them have included the introduction of *Entomophaga maimaiga*, let's just call it EM, a fungus that attacks the moths in part of their native range in Japan.

EM was brought from Japan and released here in 1910, 1911, 1985, and 1986, seemingly to no avail. In 1989, for the first time, dead LDDs were found that had been killed by EM and since then, somewhat mysteriously, it's been surprisingly effective at keeping caterpillar numbers in check. The last big outbreak in Vermont was in 1991. Before that, there were outbreaks every 6 to 10 years.

Like most fungi, EM's spores require moisture – something that was in short supply in Vermont in the spring of 2021. That may be why the LDD population took off like a rocket here, especially in the western part of the state. On more than 50,000 acres, mostly from St. Albans to Rutland, not just oaks but many other tree species were completely defoliated. Rain came too late, in mid-July, about when the fully grown caterpillars stopped feeding and began to pupate. An LDD-killing virus, called *Nucleopolyhedrosis*, is sometimes effective when the caterpillar infestation is really high.

Healthy trees can tolerate some defoliation and some drought. This year some have gotten both – not a good combination. —*Virginia Barlow*

LDD killed by Entomophaga maimaiga.

BROWN-HEADED COWBIRDS are native to the Great Plains, and the thinking is that back in the day they fed on insects kicked up by the herds of bison which dominated the landscape. When your food source is mobile, it doesn't make sense to nest in a stationary place – so they developed a strategy of laying their eggs in other birds' nests. As the bison disappeared, brown-headed cowbirds moved East into the open, agrarian landscape that European settlers created and started pawning off their children on our forest birds. Having no bison to follow, at least some of the females of the species now sit near the nest and communicate with the crying chicks. The host birds still do all the work of feeding the chicks, but the communication allows the chick to bond with the deadbeat mom.

A cowbird chick in a hermit thrush nest, June 25, 2021

TESSA MANCE

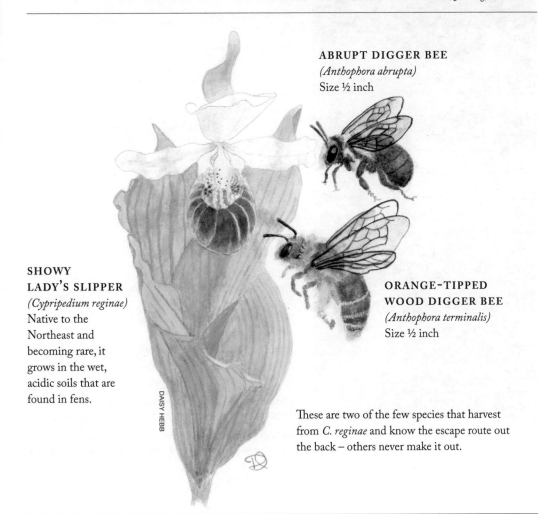

ABRUPT DIGGER BEE
(Anthophora abrupta)
Size ½ inch

**SHOWY
LADY'S SLIPPER**
(Cypripedium reginae)
Native to the
Northeast and
becoming rare, it
grows in the wet,
acidic soils that are
found in fens.

DAISY HEBB

**ORANGE-TIPPED
WOOD DIGGER BEE**
(Anthophora terminalis)
Size ½ inch

These are two of the few species that harvest from *C. reginae* and know the escape route out the back – others never make it out.

AT HOME

Shoveling Dirt

Cool earth meets hovering air.
The dirt pile grows high enough to shade
my puppy, whose muddy snout snuggles into damp shadows
along the garden wall.
My shovel wearies, and I rest on its wooden handle
rubbed shiny by a thousand gardens.

Legions of lupines and digitalis pose for
their weeding and watering
along the stone wall built by Italian masons,
who christened this farm with their sweat,
and blessed these barns with steady footings
of chiseled, gray slate.

The earth whispers of other farm women,
their herbs planted close to the hearth –
their breath light as snow on an early spring day such as this.
They pinched parsley, sage and rue for various purposes-
colds, insomnia –
to conjure teas and broths made in heaven for earthly cares.

The shovel bites into sods stillborn along
the rocks and bearded iris –
another chomp of its blade severs the clay
near burgeoning hollyhocks,
their umbrella leaves open to the black flies of June.
Another stitch into the lattice of witchgrass,
and I am nearly done.

Dirt clods drop like wet boots, and the grass recoils
like an emerald mattress.
The next shovel-full brims with treasure:
the gold spotlights of a salamander
glisten and I lower this rare piece of garden jewelry.
It slithers back into a crevice of stone.

I hold my breath as if, for a thousand Sundays,
I rest against this shovel.
I give thanks to the elements, the wind, the rain, the sun
smiling along the workdays strung like amber beads of summer.

—Diana Lischer

DIANA LISCHER

HIGH MOWING ORGANIC SEEDS

Testing Seed Viability

Have you ever considered using last year's seeds (or even older) but weren't sure if they were still viable? Try this germination test at home to see if your old seeds are worth planting, or if you should be buying new seeds.

Start with a double-thick paper towel. Moisten with water and fold in half. Open the paper towel like a book and place a minimum of 10 seeds on one side of the towel. Fold the paper towel so the seeds are covered completely. Place the paper towel in a plastic bag, or on a plate covered with plastic. It is okay to roll or fold the paper towel to fit if necessary. Do not air seal the bag shut, as you need some air for healthy germination.

Put the bag in a warm spot and check daily to make sure the towel does not dry out. Most seeds will germinate within three to ten days. Some flowers and herbs may take longer or have special germination requirements. There is a great deal of specific germination info listed online – do a simple Google search for "germination requirements for ___."

Check the seeds every few days, and monitor their appearance and germination rate. Healthy seeds have uniform germination and will not have any fungal or bacterial growth on the outside of the seed coat. If your germination rate is less than 60 percent, consider buying new seeds or sowing your seeds extra thickly to compensate for the low germination rate. —*High Mowing Organic Seeds*

SEED SHARING

You know that big shoebox full of old seeds that you meant to plant but never did? Another year passed and you bought duplicates, so now you're really never going to use them. Wouldn't it be cool if you could just exchange them with someone else in the same boat?

Julie Hutchinson-Smith was tired of just that scenario, so she started the Northshire Seed Exchange in Arlington. It's housed at the rec park, and community members can help themselves and are encouraged to donate their own leftovers. Erin and Charlotte Lyons painted the lovely seed shelf.

Soil Chemistry Primer

It's been a long time since many of us took high school chemistry, and even back then, some of us didn't pay adequate attention. Here's a refresher course built around the results of a soil test I took where I planned to put in a home vegetable garden. Special thanks to Don Ross, who retired from UVM last year after overseeing the soil-testing program for over 30 years, for his help with the annotations.

PHOSPHORUS (P) is responsible for root growth, among other things, and when your garden struggles in the early season it's often because plants have a hard time taking P up when the soil is cold. It's also the element that's largely responsible for the cyanobacteria blooms in Lake Champlain and elsewhere – a symptom of manure and fertilizer runoff from farm fields and lawns.

POTASSIUM (K) helps plants make strong stems; it's also associated with the movement of water and nutrients within the plant.

MAGNESIUM (Mg) helps plant cells function properly, and its presence or absence often depends on soil type. You might be wondering why magnesium, not nitrogen, is listed as one of the big three elements atop this soil test report, alongside P and K – the numbers on a fertilizer bag, after all, are expressed in terms of N-P-K. Well, nitrogen levels are constantly in flux, based on time of year, temperature, moisture, and microbial activity, so that figure isn't always conclusive.

SOIL PH is a measure of how acidic the soil is. Most home-garden plants do best at a pH between 6.0 and 7.2, but some, like blueberries, thrive when the soil is more acidic. To raise pH, you add limestone or wood ash. To lower it, you add elemental sulfur. The site of this soil test was at the base of the Taconic Mountains in southwestern Vermont, so the relatively high pH and comparatively high zinc and calcium measurements reflect the sweet bedrock of the area.

The **MODIFIED MORGAN** extraction test is the standard soil test that land-grant universities in New England use. It was developed by M.F. Morgan in the 1930s, using sodium acetate to dissolve minerals for measurement. (Modern practice is to use ammonium acetate, which is where the "Modified" bit comes from.) Other parts of the country use different tests.

PPM is, of course, **PARTS PER MILLION**. Some soil tests give nutrient concentrations in pounds per acre (lbs/A). To convert lbs/A to ppm, divide by 2. This conversion is based on the estimate that if you piled the top six inches of soil from an acre of land onto a scale, it would weigh 2,000,000 pounds.

The **ORGANIC MATTER PERCENTAGE** is a snapshot of the soil's physical and biological condition, as opposed to its chemical composition. Soil is an ecosystem, and the billions of microorganisms that live in it have a symbiotic relationship with the plants that grow in it. Organic matter is largely plant and animal remains that have been worked over by microbes – up to a point, more is better. It contributes in a major way to a soil's ability to retain water: for every one percent increase in the amount of organic matter, soil will retain an additional 160,000 pounds of water per acre.

CEC stands for **CATION EXCHANGE CAPACITY**. Don Ross explained it this way: "In nature, many surfaces have charge, usually a negative charge. (Maybe there is an alternate Earth somewhere with more positively charged surfaces.) Some common nutrients, such as calcium, magnesium, and potassium, are found in soils as positively charged ions (cations). These are loosely retained by the soil's negatively charged surfaces. A soil needs to have a sufficient CEC, or the nutrients will just wash through. Most soils, except for really sandy ones, have enough cation exchange capacity. If one's CEC is below 5, there can be problems."

BASE SATURATION is a concept based on the idea that there is a proper balance for the ratios of Ca, K, and Mg in soil. Ross is skeptical, saying that there's no valid science that supports this and that in practice, there's no ideal ratio – a wide range is fine. "We report saturation percentage because of customer demand," he wrote. —*Dave Mance III*

Soil Test Report

Agricultural & Environmental Testing Laboratory and UVM Extension

Sample Information:

Order #:	9898
Lab ID:	S20-02312
Mance Garden	

Area Sampled:	1800 sq ft
Received:	6/25/2020
Reported:	7/7/2020
VT County:	Bennington

Results

Nutrient	Low	Medium	Optimum	High or Excessive
Phosphorus (P):				
Potassium (K):				
Magnesium (Mg):				

Analysis	Value Found	Optimum Range ** (or Average *)	Analysis	Value Found	Optimum Range ** (or Average *)
Soil pH (2:1, water)	6.7		Boron (B)	0.3	0.3*
Modified Morgan extractable, ppm			Copper (Cu)	0.4	0.3*
Macronutrients			Zinc (Zn)	45.1	2.0*
Phosphorus (P)	2.1	4-7	Sodium (Na)	21.0	20*
Potassium (K)	64	100-130	Aluminum (Al)	27	35*
Calcium (Ca)	1935	**	**Soil Organic Matter %**	4.8	**
Magnesium (Mg)	80	50-100	**Effective CEC, meq/100g**	10.5	**
Sulfur (S)	10.0	11*	**Base Saturation, %**		
Micronutrients			Calcium Saturation	92.0	40-80
Iron (Fe)	4.0	7.0*	Potassium Saturation	1.6	2.0-7.0
Manganese (Mn)	6.2	8.0*	Magnesium Saturation	6.3	10-30

* Micronutrient and S deficiencies are rare in Vermont and optimum ranges are not defined; thus average values in Vermont soils are shown instead.
** Ranges shown are for Field Crops; Vegetable ranges are higher. Ranges for Calcium, Organic Matter, and Effective CEC vary with soil type and crop.

Soils on the Vermont Landscape

The word soil evokes a simple picture – likely a generic handful of dark loam. But as everyone who's worked the earth in Vermont knows, soil is anything but simple. There are dozens of different soil types in our small state. But we can simplify things into five categories that express a particular soil's parent material – a term soil scientists use to describe how a soil was deposited on the landscape. Let's take a deeper look.

GLACIAL TILL is a generally unsorted mix of soil textures, stones, and boulders – it's the dominant soil type in Vermont, as you might guess from the miles of stone walls that we're famous for. This material was scraped up and pushed around by advancing glaciers, then deposited unevenly back onto the ground surface. The characteristic mix of particle sizes makes glacial till soils highly compactible. One of the characteristics that stands out to people who work with glacial till is the commonly observed dense substratum, typically beginning within one to two feet of the soil surface. This layer is more colloquially referred to as hardpan. Digging in it can feel like chipping your way through a concrete floor.

Glacial till soils were deposited relatively close to where they were "picked up" by the glaciers, an idea that's supported by the fact that the mineralogy typically reflects the underlying bedrock. Examples

TIM MASTERS

A never-ending chore on Vermont's glacial till soils: clearing stones and boulders before planting.

include the coarse-textured, acidic, glacial till soils found near the granitic bedrock formations in the eastern part of Vermont, and the fine-textured, high-pH, dark-colored glacial till soils that are typically found above the fine-textured, dark-colored phyllite/interbedded limestone bedrock formation in central Vermont.

Some of the more common soil series names for glacial tills in Vermont include Cabot, Marlow, Peru, and Tunbridge, the latter being the official Vermont state soil. (That's right, we even have a legislatively approved state soil.)

GLACIOFLUVIAL soil is generally characterized by well-sorted, coarse-textured soil particles that were deposited by flowing water, most typically a result of ice melting across the receding glaciers. The mixed soil textures on and in the ice were sorted by size, with the larger soil particles (sand and gravel) settling out of the flowing meltwater first, and smaller particles (fine sand and very fine sand) being carried further and dropping out of the flowing water as its velocity decreased. This is a gross oversimplification, of course, as glacial geology is a complex science. The end result, though, is that the river valleys throughout the state are typically a complicated mix of glaciofluvial soils which overlap with glacial

Gravelly glaciofluvial soil supports crops at a farm in Shaftsbury.

tills and glaciolacustrine deposits (more on those to follow) to varying degrees. These are the landscape positions where we find most of our sand and gravel pits.

Some of the common soil series names derived from glaciofluvial soil depositions include Adams, Windsor, and Colton.

GLACIOLACUSTRINE SOILS can often occupy similar positions on the Vermont landscape as glaciofluvial soils. These soils are derived from silty and clayey sediments that settled out of the still waters of lakes and ponds. The primary source of these lacustrine sediments is the geologic Lake Vermont, which occupied much of the northwest and north-central parts of the state. These soils make up the fertile cropland in the Champlain Valley. Some of the more common soil series names for glaciolacustrine soils include Vergennes, Salmon, Covington, and Scantic. One notable feature of these soils is that they have no gravel, stones or boulders within the soil profile or on the soil surface. While these soils can make for very productive farm land, their fine textures can also create significant challenges for tillage, especially when attempts are made to work them while they are either too wet or too dry. The same field of Vergennes clay can be a soft mess in the spring and become a dry, nearly impenetrable mass later in the summer.

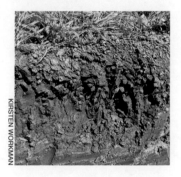

Heavy clay soil on a farm in the Champlain Valley town of Panton.

ALLUVIAL SOILS are found in the floodplains that run along most of our larger streams and rivers. Floodplain soils run the gamut of moisture regimes, from very poorly drained areas that rarely dry out to excessively well drained areas that lack the moisture needed to be productive for agriculture. In general, though, the floodplain soils in Vermont are some of our most productive farmland. Some of our more common floodplain soil series in Vermont include Rumney, Hadley, and Limerick.

Floodplain soils contain a concentration of organic matter that does not decrease regularly

The Connecticut River flows past farms in Newbury, where it continues to deposit sediment during flood events.

with depth. This is true because of the nature of the deposition of floodplain soils. They were formed, and continue to be formed even today, by sediment deposited during flood events. All of these thin sediment deposits carry similar amounts of organic material, so even relatively deep horizons in the floodplain soil profile typically have similar organic matter concentrations as the upper soil layers. This is in contrast to the glacial tills, glaciofluvial, and glaciolacustrine soils, where organic matter decreases with depth. In these soils, the organic matter in them is introduced from the soil surface as plants die and decompose, so the organic matter builds up near the soil surface and is relatively scarce in the soil horizons below the surface layer.

This brief discussion of organic matter provides us a nice transition to the organic soils that make up the **HISTOSOLS SOIL ORDER**, the last of the five soil parent materials we are looking at here. Histosols are permanently saturated soils that are composed entirely of decomposing plant material. The thickness of organic material in a Histosol can range from as little

as 16 inches to more than 30 feet. The organic material is typically underlain by mineral soil material, with textures ranging from clays to sands. These are the soils found in the bogs and fens that we value highly as the underlying support for many rare plants and animals.

While none could be considered common, some of the soil series names for Histosols in Vermont include Rifle, Markey, and Wonsqueak.

Pitcher plants flower from the permanently saturated soil of Chickering Bog in Calais.

This has been a quick sketch of some of the soils we encounter every day as we spend time traveling across the Vermont landscape. Deepening our understanding and awareness of the complexities of the soils under foot can help us develop an even deeper appreciation of the world around us, and more particularly, beneath us. —*Brad Wheeler*

Land is ...

This section is inspired by the people of color who are not always seen,
known, or recognized in Vermont. The profiles are not intended
to be representative – each individual has their own unique
perspective on the land and what it means to them.
But I hope they give a sense of the diversity of their experiences.

For Aaron Lawrence Carroll,
land transcends identity.

For Will Kasso Condry and Jennifer Herrera Condry
of Juniper Creative Arts,
land is an opportunity for engagement
with family and issues of social justice.

Sahra Ali's relationship to Vermont
is complex, very personal, and spiritual.

Land is the inspiration for Dr. Carolyn Finney's work,
which explores the intersections of place with power, race,
and so many other things that form our human identity.

And for Steffen Glen Gillom, rural southern roots inform his activism
around the inequity of land ownership in Vermont.

These profiles show us that land is personal and political, but it's also the
very thing that pulls us all together across race, class, gender, and personal
histories. I hope that after reading this, you're inspired to think about your
own rural roots and your own relationship with the land.

—*Shanta Lee Gander, June 2021*

---

*In this year of racial reckoning, in recognition of Juneteenth, we asked writer
Shanta Lee Gander to collect stories from Black Vermonters about their
relationship to the land and to Vermont. What she's assembled on the
following pages is one small step toward building a shared narrative about
where we live and who we are in which everyone finds an honorable place.*
THE EDITORS

SHANTA LEE GANDER

Land is … *an Equalizer Among People*

Aaron Lawrence Carroll is a father, entrepreneur,
photographer, writer, and farmer at Sowing Roots Farm in Underhill.

When we moved to Vermont in 2016, we got into kayaking, fishing, snowboarding, mountain biking – all types of outdoor activities. The same activities that took place in uncomfortable settings in Ohio, where I'm from. Rural areas there are often seen as more racist, conservative, all of the things someone like me is trying to avoid. But here we are, living and playing in rural Vermont every day, and feeling … not scared, but not without a watchful eye.

I don't really call myself a farmer yet, because I don't sell anything. What we grow we use for our family. Or share with other families, who more often than not turn around and share something new with us. I feel like it's valuable to create these sharing relationships with others, and it is rare that we get that opportunity. I have had that opportunity here in Vermont more than in any other place I've lived. And what it has grown are some of the strongest friendships and relationships I've had in my life. When Sowing Roots Farm begins producing larger amounts, we hope people will buy from us. I also hope they remember that I would share with them just the same as I would sell to them, because that is just the type of man I am.

A book I would love to write would be called *Free to Be*. And it would talk about the sense of freedom I feel where my boys are right now. *[Aaron gestured to the woods in the back of his house where his two boys*

Aaron, 14, and Alden, 7, were playing.] When I'm in nature, the social confines of things fall away. There's no need to be wealthy. There's no need to be proper. There's no need to be buttoned up – if you need to pee, pee over there. Do you know what I mean? So many of the social constructs that are emotionally destructive to us drop off when you are in the wilderness, right? And then the other thing I found is that when you run into someone else, especially when you are way out in the wilderness, there's a sense of respect to that. I get that feeling when my boys and I are mountain biking. When you get to the top of a mountain, there's no, 'How much money you got?' No, 'Are you Black?' Nature is an equalizer – a social equalizer, definitely an ego equalizer. I've never been judged for the clothing I was wearing when gardening.

Vermont is a great place for brushing dirty elbows with multimillionaires. You wouldn't know it, and it's not what matters, and we need more of that. We need more of these types of equalizers to break down some of those social constructs and fences that we put up around each other.

Land is supposed to be for everyone – to heal everyone – and in Vermont, sometimes it feels like that is understood. Are we all the way there? Of course not. But I've never been to any place that makes me feel the way I do in the 802.

SHANTA LEE GANDER

Land is... *a Family Affair*

Will Kasso Condry and Jennifer Herrera Condry,
founders of Juniper Creative Arts, met at Middlebury College in 2012.

WILL: Vermont is a place I never thought I'd see myself living. It was kind of like I ended up here. I'm from Trenton, New Jersey, a small, urban city. Vermont is a completely different culture. But it just felt right. I had the space to explore my own ideas, to take the time with my work. It gave me an opportunity to settle down.

I've started to research my family lineage and discovered that most of my family comes from a line of tobacco farmers – I got as far back as the 1850s. This discovery made me think that it wasn't a coincidence that I ended up in a place like Vermont. I was drawn here, and for Jennifer, it was the same thing. We come from that culture, but throughout the generations, a lot of information got lost. We have to get back to that knowledge. Land is one of the most valuable assets you can have, and it is key to generational wealth-building. I come from poverty. None of our parents finished high school. My father did some farming on the little backyard plot we had, but it was not to the point of what my ancestors were doing. A lot of stuff got lost.

JENNIFER: But it didn't, because if your father still managed to plant a little bit, have a little garden, it wasn't lost. It was the same in my family. My family came to this country just before the height of the civil rights movement. They didn't speak a lick of English, coming from Quisqueya [specifically, the Dominican Republic]. I was born and raised in Harlem. One of the things my family did was grow plants on our fire escape in the summer, and it ended up being its own garden.

Maintaining that connection to the land in my family is woven through and through. My mom made sure that we got out of the city somehow, even if it meant borrowing a friend's car to take us to do things like apple picking or pumpkin picking. My mother also made sure that we always got to the beach. She ensured that we had access to these things so that we did not feel stuck in the city and in the apartment building. This also included making sure we took bike rides, had access to parks – my mother made sure that we always had a connection to the land somehow in whatever environment we found ourselves.

The day I talked to Jennifer and Will, they'd just planted starts. Last year, they planted medicinal herbs in the front of their home in Brandon to supplement what was growing wild: "One thing that we've learned to do is to pay attention to what grows wild on our property," said Jennifer. "We get a lot of volunteer medicinal plants – nettles, yarrow, motherwort, St. John's wort. The land seems to know what we need even before we sometimes know what we need."

Land is... *a Determined and Intentional Relationship*

Sahra Ali is a Somali American writer whose relationship to the Green Mountain State has been fraught.

I initially moved to Vermont in the Fall of 2017 to work and live at a Tibetan Buddhist retreat center in the Northeast Kingdom. That was a period of time when I was in and out of monasteries – Zen monasteries, particularly. I came here for community – to build community, to live within a community.

I distinctly remember falling in love with the land. I remember I was invited to do a one-week retreat just to see if I would like the place. Chögyam Trungpa Rinpoche, a well-known Tibetan Buddhist who brought Shambala Buddhism to the West, set up camp in Barnet. A bunch of back-to-the-landers, hippies, followed him. I was having a very spiritual experience there; everything was in the context of that. The grounds were so beautiful, and I was new to rural life. I was wondering if I was going to take this job. I told myself, "I don't know what's going to happen with these people. I don't know what's going to happen with my practice. I have to explore this land. There's magic in this land."

I ended up leaving Vermont because of racism. It was a very, very clear kind of thing that happened during a public event, and I planned my exit. I could not stay somewhere where I was the exception.

I travelled to Colorado, Wyoming, Montana, Idaho, and Utah and marveled at these beautiful places while still missing those damned rolling hills, the quiet, all the green, and the slowness of Vermont. When I decided that it was time to look for a full-time job, I looked at Vermont while I prayed, meditated. I cried my eyes out. I came back.

My relationship with this land is deep, and I don't know how long it will continue. But I do know that as an immigrant who's been very nomadic all of her life, my places – Jersey City, New York, Ohio – they were all chosen for me. But I have chosen to make Vermont my American home. It is where I want to build my life, but it is not because I am fond of it. It's because I'm in love with the land.

On July 1, 2020, I wrote this poem, "When I go back to Vermont, it'll be good":

> Who can tell you where is home?
> where to lay down your burdens,
> and fall in love every day
> Who can say when it's time to hang your coat up,
> and allow the tears to cleanse and not burn?
> Who says when you go away,
> you can't come back?
> My away is here. Sometimes there.
>
> When I go back to Vermont, it'll be good.
> I will have another cabin. But this time on purpose.
> It will be mine. I will be mine.
> When I go back to Vermont, she will welcome me with open arms
> and tell me to sit down.
>
> It will be good. I miss my rolling hills, the slowness,
> the deliberate slowness of it all.
> I cannot wait for the day
> when I go back and stay.

Land is… *Personal and the Personal is the Land*

Carolyn Finney, PhD, is an artist and
scholar in residence at Middlebury College.

I grew up in New York, 30 minutes outside of New York City, in Westchester County. My parents grew up black and poor in the South. They migrated, like a lot of black folks, from the South to the North in the 1950s because my father couldn't find work after coming back from the Korean War. When they arrived in New York, my father took a job as a gardener on a 12-acre estate that was owned by a very wealthy Jewish family in an all-white neighborhood.

On this beautiful estate, I learned how to swim, run, ride my bike, do all the stuff you do in the outdoors in this beautiful state. When I was in fourth grade, nine years old, a white policeman stopped me on my way home from school and wanted to know where I was going. I was right on the corner, and I told him.

This policeman just looked at me and said, "Oh, do you work there?"

I'm thinking, "I'm nine, dude." I said, "No, I live there."

That incident was one of the first instances where I had a sense that it was unnatural for me to be in this beautiful natural space.

The house sold in the late 1990s for more than three million dollars, and my parents stayed on until 2003. At that point, they'd been there for nearly 50 years. For 50 years, that was my home. That is where I always went back to for holidays and visits. But a new owner has to find new people.

The original matriarch of the estate, to her credit, helped my parents build a lovely house on a half-acre of land in Leesburg, Virginia. But I watched my father, in particular, get depressed. He missed the land he'd cared for. A number of years after they moved, they received a copy of a letter, which I also have, that was from an organization called the Westchester Land Trust. The letter was letting everybody know that within our old neighborhood, a conservation easement had now been placed on the 12 acres. This means that generally, in perpetuity, nothing can be changed: everything is protected. That letter talked about all the environmental values of that estate, the watershed, all the wildlife, everything that's on the property. And at the end of the letter, the Conservation Trust thanked the new owner for his "conservation mindedness." The new owner at the time had been there for only five, six years. There was nothing in the letter thanking my parents, who had been laboring on that land for 50 years.

That's when I started thinking about whose ownership counts. I also started thinking about all the people in this country, across all walks of life, who've always been caring for the land, doing the work, yet getting erased from any environmental history about it.

This is how it became personal for me. This idea that a person's labor, love, and presence can be erased. The experience opened my eyes to the complexities of power, privilege, race.

SHANTA LEE GANDER

Land is…

for Everyone: Addressing Land Inequity in Vermont

*Steffen Glen Gillom holds several leadership roles across the state of Vermont
as the president of the Windham County Vermont NAACP, the acting executive director of the
Bright Leadership Institute, and a member of Governor Phil Scott's Equity Task Force.*

"My connection to land goes back to my childhood. My grandmother and my grandfather – from Mississippi and Arkansas – came from a lineage of farmers. My grandparents owned large gardens where they grew heritage crops like collard greens, maize, corn, sweet potatoes – basically all the food that the ancestors of African Americans ate when they were in different places, especially as slaves and sharecroppers.

The garden that my grandparents stewarded fed my grandmother's family – my dad and my aunts – through the summer. We had fresh greens, potatoes, and there were a couple of apple trees on their property. So I grew a connection to the land organically. I remember going to the market with my grandfather and getting the seeds, digging holes, putting the seeds in, and watering everything. I was a part of the entire process. We had a connection not only to the land but to the local animals, as well. My grandfather taught me how to skin animals, how to prepare them by taking the entrails out, but also to have respect so that they were slain in a humane way. I was also connected to the ancestral folk magic in terms of herbalism and other practices that my grandparents and great-aunts did that I did not notice until now. For example, my grandmother used to hang plastic bags of water off of the back porch to keep away flies. This is also something that is done in some communities to keep away spirits.

When we lived in the St. Louis area, most of my grandmother's family was still in Mississippi, so we would go back to Mississippi multiple times a year – "going back home," as they called it. We would go back to a cabin usually – like the one we are in now – that my cousin owned. Before that, our great-grandfather originally owned the place. I got to watch black people live in connection to the land while also hearing stories about how all of my aunts and great-aunts were connected to it. My dad talked about going to Big Mama's house, staying in the cabins, and

having to use the outhouse.

As I got older, I moved around a lot. It felt like my connection to the land became based on finding spaces that were oriented with what I remembered about land as a child. When I came to Vermont, it was so beautiful, but I felt disconnected. There was a lack of cultural infrastructure. This propelled me into doing a lot of land equity work, especially the work that led to the Vermont Land Access and Opportunity Act. In Vermont, 97.7 percent of farms are white-owned and 72 percent of homes are white-owned. My civil rights work today is based on helping people of color buy land, which builds cultural infrastructure. It also allows individuals to pass land on to their children.

A LOOK BACK

OLD STONE HOUSE MUSEUM AND HISTORIC VILLAGE

His piercing eyes catch yours as you gaze at the daguerreotype taken in the early 1850s. The corners of his mouth turn down slightly in a smirk. Or is that the beginning of a mischievous smile? His attire – coat with chevroned lapels, waist coat with mother-of-pearl buttons, white linen shirt and linen neck cloth – indicate a gentleman of comfortable means. And the quill he holds suggests learnedness. Indeed, the man – Alexander Lucius Twilight – was one of the most extraordinary and accomplished men of his time, especially when we consider that he was of African descent.

Twilight was the first identifiable person of color to receive a college degree from an American college – Middlebury College in 1823. He was arguably the first man of color to be elected to a state legislature – Vermont's in 1836. He taught and preached at several venues in Vermont and upstate New York before settling in Brownington, in Orleans County, where he served as a pastor and headmaster. Twilight's activities reveal that he was an energetic, beloved man, who earned the trust, respect, and affection of each community he served. Twilight's former students offered tributes to him long after his death, which one can read on the website (oldstonehousemuseum. org) of the Old Stone House Museum & Historic Village in Brownington. In 1888, one graduate recalled fondly Twilight's "jest-loving propensity" for "perennial fun."

Twilight's students often described their headmaster as "bronzed" and "swarthy." Yet most peers and acquaintances either ignored or remained silent about his mixed-race heritage, as did Twilight himself, perhaps to access opportunities unavailable to most phenotypically identifiable Black men. His racial ambiguity seems to have led most white Vermonters to see him as a person without race, if not as white. Twilight did not "pass" for white, which implies a deliberate, calculated, conscious effort to conceal one's Black identity to experience the privileges of whiteness. Rather, he "performed" instinctively white expectations of white identity, premised as much on who one *was* as on what one *did* – in Twilight's case, live a life of social and economic independence, learnedness, and political engagement.

Twilight was born on September 23, 1795, in

The Inscrutable
Alexander Twilight
1795–1857

Bradford. Three years earlier, his father, Ichabod, had settled his young family in Vermont, drawn most likely by the state's 1791 constitution that outlawed adult slavery. Ichabod, who was bi-racial and probably free, served in the American Revolution, at which time he was described as "colored," having a "yellow complexion." His wife, Mary – Alexander's mother – was either a white or a light-complected bi-racial woman; the 1800 census records for Corinth, where the family moved shortly after Alexander's birth, lists seven individuals in the "All other free persons, except Indians not taxed" category – the category reserved for free Blacks. The Twilight family numbered six in 1800.

Twilight was indentured around 1803 to William Bowen, a neighboring white farmer in Corinth. The 1810 census lists one "free person, except Indians" as a member of the Bowen household – most likely Twilight. While an apprentice there, Alexander learned to read, write, and cipher (do math). Apprenticing children to neighbors to be "raised up" – to learn a skill or craft, or simply to be fed and clothed – until the age of maturity (21 for men, 18 for women) was a common practice among late eighteenth- and early nineteenth-century families of limited means. Twilight must have been a hard worker, for he worked off his indentureship a year early at age 20. Shortly thereafter, he enrolled at Randolph Academy, where between 1815 and 1821 he took courses in preparation for matriculation at Middlebury College.

Twilight enrolled at Middlebury as a third-year student in 1821. He lived off campus. We do not know if the College knew or cared that Twilight was a man of color, for it had no admissions policy on admitting Black students until 1845, when local abolitionists pressured the College to educate Black men. During his two years at Middlebury, Twilight excelled in the Classical curriculum of the day, which included Greek literature, Trigonometry, Natural Philosophy (today, physics), and Natural Theology, among others. He was drawn particularly to Natural Theology, the belief that God's truths are revealed through the relationship between nature and the human anatomy. When preaching later in life, Twilight often invoked in his sermons the glories of nature and the ailing human body, which often drew criticism that his preaching was too deistic and insufficiently doctrinal.

After graduating from Middlebury in 1823, Twilight taught school in Peru, New York, where he met and married in 1826 Mercy Ladd Merrill, a white woman about ten years his junior. He continued to read Natural Theology and was eventually licensed by the Champlain Presbytery in Plattsburgh. In 1828, Alexander and Mercy relocated to Vergennes, where he taught during the week and preached in nearby towns on Sundays. The following year, Alexander and Mercy moved to Brownington, where Twilight would serve as preceptor and acting parson for roughly 22 of the next 26 years.

Twilight quickly developed the reputation as a gifted teacher. As attendance at the Orleans County Grammar School soared, averaging nearly 100 boys and girls each year, Twilight decided that the school required a dormitory to house resident students and a dependable source of funding from the county. "Athenian Hall," an expensive, massive granite structure, was built between 1834 and 1836. Worried about rumors that the residents of Craftsbury were also interested in establishing a grammar school, which would mean splitting the county's land revenues between the two towns, Twilight ran for state office in 1836 to thwart their project and won. However, he lost his battle opposing the Craftsbury school, and thus served only one one-year term in the Vermont Assembly. Nevertheless, his election stands as a singular achievement: arguably the first American of Black ancestry to be elected to a state's assembly.

In time, the trustees at the school and the church's congregation grew tired of Twilight's permissive teaching and his unorthodox preaching. In 1847, Mercy and Alexander were forced to quit the church and the school and move across the Canadian border to the small towns of Shipton and Hatley, Quebec. During his absence, the Brownington school limped along until 1851, when it closed. The school's trustees persuaded Twilight to return to Brownington the next year and resume his two posts. However, the honeymoon was short-lived; in 1853, Twilight withdrew again from the pulpit and concentrated on teaching. Despite his reduced schedule, the stress of teaching and perhaps an underlying condition – one student commented on his "pursy [short of breath], rotund form" – took their toll. In 1855, Twilight suffered a paralyzing stroke that left him incapacitated for the next two years. He died on June 19, 1857.

Mercy, who had helped run the school, tried to keep it solvent. However, after hobbling along for another two years, the school shuttered it doors permanently in 1859. Mercy then turned Athenian Hall into a boarding house and tavern. She soon fell into poverty and died in 1878. Alexander and Mercy are buried side-by-side in the cemetery of the Brownington Congregational Church. They had no children.

Alexander Twilight was an ambitious man who relied on his racial ambiguity to access opportunities closed to most Black men.

This begs the question: Should Twilight's blackness matter to us today? Or should we simply accept his racial ambiguity?

Because of a shared history of racial oppression, exclusion, and violence, many Black Americans have always claimed solidarity with bi-racial Americans of Black-White ancestry, a tradition that seems particularly essential today when Black lives are under assault. Nevertheless, I believe that Twilight's racial ambiguity can help us reflect on race and racial identities in more nuanced and critical ways beyond the absurd "one-drop rule." Racial classifications, devised by Europeans, are premised on physical features. However, race is not a biological category; it is a social construction designed to protect the privilege and power of white people. During Twilight's time, many white Americans viewed one's race as intrinsic to one's moral and social character. As such, many deemed free Blacks unworthy and incapable of exercising their full rights as citizens because they equated Black identity with dependency and indolence, rationalized by their history of enslavement and by their forced dependence on white patrons. Conversely, most white Americans deemed their whiteness as synonymous with freedom and autonomy – that is, independence and citizenship. Many early nineteenth-century white Vermonters shared this view, and thus supported colonization – the removal of free Blacks to Liberia – as a remedy to the nation's "race problem." Given this white racial thinking, one can understand why Twilight remained tacit about his racial identity.

Today, many bi-racial individuals refuse to remain silent. By claiming and celebrating their bi-racial heritage, mixed-race individuals challenge and complicate our need to classify individuals along an either/or paradigm. With the pace of the browning of America quickening – over the past fifty years, the number of bi-racial children has increased more than tenfold – the growing population of persons of mixed-racial identities will destabilize, expand, and ultimately undermine our limited and limiting concept of race. —*William B. Hart*

"Athenian Hall," built by Alexander Twilight, now houses the Old Stone House Museum and is a featured stop on Vermont's African American Heritage Trail.

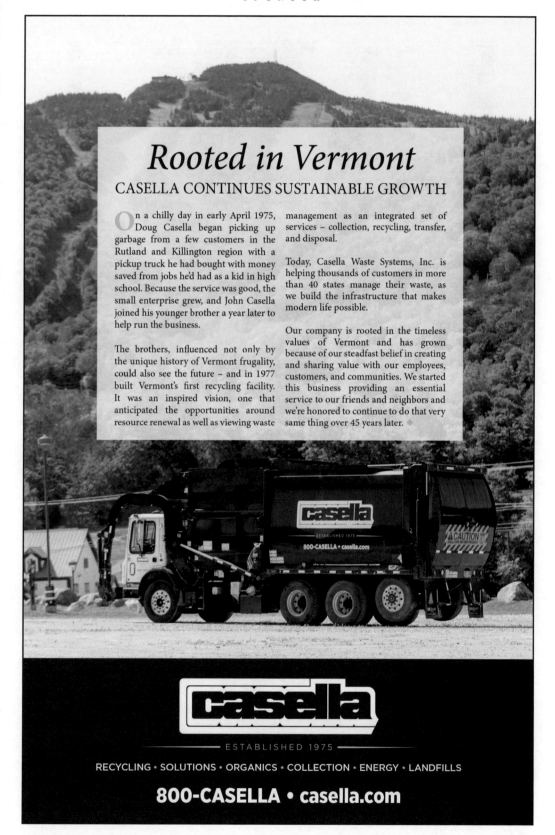

Rooted in Vermont

CASELLA CONTINUES SUSTAINABLE GROWTH

On a chilly day in early April 1975, Doug Casella began picking up garbage from a few customers in the Rutland and Killington region with a pickup truck he had bought with money saved from jobs he'd had as a kid in high school. Because the service was good, the small enterprise grew, and John Casella joined his younger brother a year later to help run the business.

The brothers, influenced not only by the unique history of Vermont frugality, could also see the future – and in 1977 built Vermont's first recycling facility. It was an inspired vision, one that anticipated the opportunities around resource renewal as well as viewing waste management as an integrated set of services – collection, recycling, transfer, and disposal.

Today, Casella Waste Systems, Inc. is helping thousands of customers in more than 40 states manage their waste, as we build the infrastructure that makes modern life possible.

Our company is rooted in the timeless values of Vermont and has grown because of our steadfast belief in creating and sharing value with our employees, customers, and communities. We started this business providing an essential service to our friends and neighbors and we're honored to continue to do that very same thing over 45 years later. ◆

casella
ESTABLISHED 1975

RECYCLING · SOLUTIONS · ORGANICS · COLLECTION · ENERGY · LANDFILLS

800-CASELLA · casella.com

JULY

July

I used to visit Locke Mathews every year or two. Once, over coffee at his kitchen table, he told me: "I come up to your parents' land in North Danville almost every year to get apples from that orchard by the old Burrough Road. My father grew up there, so I knew your folks wouldn't mind. Sometimes when I'm there, I see my father sitting under the old Wolf River tree, watching us as we pick, making sure we leave some for the deer."

❦

It's July at Cold Hollow Cider Mill in Waterbury. I'm standing with my city friends behind a railing where they press apples in every season for the visitors. It's a large room with a cement floor and a huge cider press. We watch as last year's crop is brought by forklift from its dark, perpetual October. The apples are shredded, the apple-slurry being pumped into trays that get stacked beneath the metal pad that does the pressing.

The brown juice trickles, then, as the steel elbow flexes, it flows like muddied spring rain, puddling, gathering, flooding down the chute. The pulp exhales to its exhaustion. In the gift shop, we buy a gallon jug, then browse mustards, jellies, salsas, helpful objects made of wood and wool.

Our friends seem impressed, just as they were meant to be. But I want Locke to show up – tell them about his father; tell them how, for a few days, fallen apples are the ones with the best flavor; how the bruises can be even sweeter; how wasps and hornets cluster, slowed, drunk with fermented juice; how they can help you find the apples farther from the tree, nestled in the grass.

We wander out to the parking lot. As I start the car, I notice blue-green black raspberry vines in a jumble of fallen trees and brush beside the parking lot. They're studded with loose pyramids of fruit, crowned with the ripe, purple berries at the top with red replacements ripening around the base. I jump out and start picking, calling to my startled friends, who don't understand that in the Vermont I grew up in, the finder of wild berries has an immediate assignment – Pick!

Myra McCrillis was church treasurer for years in East St. Johnsbury. But in another part of her life, she was the berry lady. She somehow always knew where they grew. She emerged each summer from her orderly red home, dressed in denim, with a red-and-white bandanna on her head. Anyone smart enough to follow her would have learned what wonders could be foraged.

Every fall, she filled a table at the Lord's Acre Auction with the random goodness of the land – jams and jellies gleaned from roadsides, old pastures, clearings in the neighbors' woods. She smiled secretly, receiving her neighbors' cash and exclamations. Everything she earned went to the church.

Her spirit possesses me when I see the black raspberries. My friends are baffled. I'm breaking many rules they've learned. I tell them to pick and eat, reassuring them that this is special food. We even start to fill a paper coffee cup.

❦

Across the fence, men are playing horseshoes. The iron shoes clink against the pipes. They're drinking beer and arguing about the score. A dead branch snaps as I climb farther into the thicket after berries.

There's a sudden silence, then a voice from behind the screen of brush: "What the hell is going on over there?"

"We're picking berries, on your land, I guess; do you mind?"

"You pay taxes here? You think this is your land? Want me to come and part your hair for you?"

My friends hastily decide it's time to leave. I want to stay. I want to see his face, tell him I do pay taxes, ask how many generations since his family farmed. I want to ask if he ever played basketball against the Lynaugh boys from North Danville, maybe suggest a contest cutting firewood, reminisce about haying. I know he understands this crop is here for sharing. The real injury lies elsewhere. But suddenly, I've become a stranger.

My friends are in the car, gesturing to me. So is my wife. I stand at the car door, a few berries in a paper cup, next to a patch of wild fruit in front of me that we will leave unpicked.

I can hardly bear it. But we leave. —*Scudder Parker*

Unprecedented Rain

Dr. Jason Shafer, an old professor and friend from my time at Lyndon State College (now Northern Vermont University), used to say one person's trough is another person's ridge where it pertains to weather in the upper atmosphere. July 2021 bore this out. The prolonged upper-level ridge over the western United States that made for record-shattering heat and exacerbated drought conditions in that part of the country created an abnormally active northern jet stream here that soaked much of the Northeast with needed rains.

A dry spring and even drier June allowed for moderate drought and abnormally dry conditions to cover almost all of the state. Although droughts typically do not become as extreme in Vermont as they can in western parts of the nation due to the fact that the ground here acts pretty much like a giant sponge as trees and undergrowth retain lots of water, dry spells do certainly develop. While it's not possible to guarantee that droughts here will always be mitigated, historical records show that our dry spells, when we do have them, gradually go away. This year, in the southern parts of our region, the drought conditions went away suddenly.

The month started out with the remnants of Hurricane Elsa moving through New England. That turned out to be just the first of multiple waves of rain that came throughout the month, making for tropical-like monthly totals. On average, 40 to 50 inches of precipitation fall throughout the year in Vermont. The far southern Green Mountains saw a major percentage of that fall just during July. Putney, for example, saw almost 18 inches of rain, or over a third of the annual rainfall – in just one month. Double-digit totals were the rule over most areas south of Rutland. As you headed north, rainfall totals were still above average, but not as extreme (St. Johnsbury and Burlington each received 6 inches).

It wasn't just the rain that was falling in July; the temperatures dropped, too. Although Vermont's summers are very short, much of the weather throughout the month felt like the calendar rolled back to the start of spring, as overall it was very gloomy and cool with highs some days struggling to make it out of the 60s over the valleys and highs in the 50s over the elevated terrain. Some cool and cloudy mornings offered the unwanted opportunity to have to get the woodstove going during the height of summer. Plants and vegetables were just as discouraged, with warm-season vegetables such as summer squash, tomatoes, and peppers struggling due to the prolonged wet weather. Cooler-season vegetables were perhaps the only things in the state that thrived this month. —*Christopher Kurdek, Fairbanks Museum and Planetarium*

This is pretty much what the sky looked like all month in southern Vermont. On the bright side, look at those Clearbrook Farm onions!

NATURE NOTES

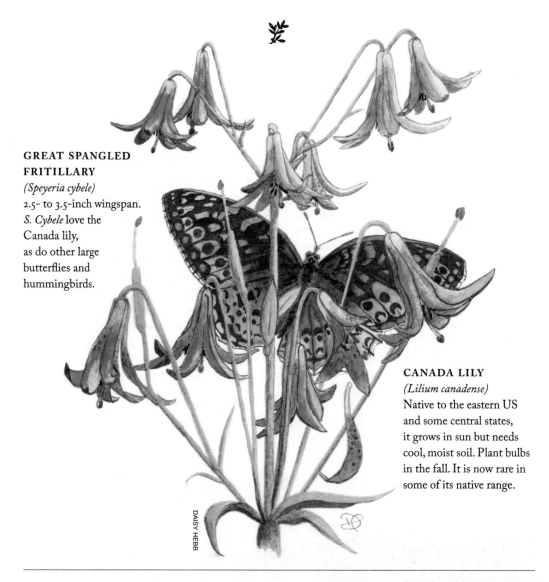

GREAT SPANGLED FRITILLARY
(Speyeria cybele)
2.5- to 3.5-inch wingspan.
S. Cybele love the
Canada lily,
as do other large
butterflies and
hummingbirds.

CANADA LILY
(Lilium canadense)
Native to the eastern US
and some central states,
it grows in sun but needs
cool, moist soil. Plant bulbs
in the fall. It is now rare in
some of its native range.

DAISY HEBB

IN A JAPANESE STUDY PUBLISHED in the *Journal of Medical Entomology*, researchers document that mosquitos landed on people with Type-O blood twice as often as they landed on people with Type-A. Who knew that most people secrete a chemical signal through their skin that indicates which blood type they have? If you're Type-A but still a mosquito magnet, you might have a "higher abundance but lower diversity of bacteria on [your] skin" – that quote from a Dutch study. Or you might be pregnant. Pregnant women emit more carbon dioxide and are on average about 1.26 degrees F warmer than the rest of us.

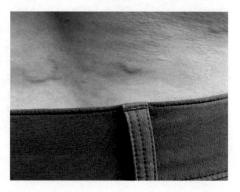

Kestrel Banding

Between the first Vermont Breeding Bird Atlas survey in the late 1970s and the most recent one, which was undertaken 25 years later, the American kestrel population in Vermont declined by roughly 26 percent. These little hawks, the smallest hawks in North America, just about the size of a blue jay, do best in open land and the reforestation of Vermont, as well as habitat fragmentation and possibly increased predation from Cooper's hawks, have taken a toll.

To help decrease the loss of this strikingly beautiful bird, kestrel friends have put up specially made kestrel boxes. They are on poles 10 to 30 feet above the ground and can be lowered temporarily so that the chicks can be checked on and banded. They are banded when they are fairly large but before they are likely to fledge. The not-so-very-happy-looking chick in this photo was banded by Sebastian Lousada in Vershire on July 4, 2021. The American Kestrel Project keeps track of nest box fledgling successes and failures throughout North America. Ⓥ

AMERICAN CHESTNUT is functionally extinct in Vermont, but some trees persist in a weakened state. Finding one is like finding a ghost, and since they flower in July, when no other forest tree is flowering, now's a great time to find one. This picture was taken on July 8.

ERIN DONAHUE

SMOOTH PATCH on ash *(Aleurodiscus sp., Dendrothele sp.)* continues to be reported across the state in conjunction with suspected emerald ash borer reports. Smooth patch is caused by a fungus that creates irregular, smooth, sunken areas that appear on the bole and branches of ash trees. This fungus only consumes dead bark tissue and therefore has minimal effect on the overall health of the infected tree. The presence of smooth patch is not an indicator of an emerald ash borer infestation.
—*Vermont Forests, Parks, and Recreation*

AT HOME

✹

KIM SONGSAK

I GAVE UP LISTENING TO THE NEWS

I gave up listening to the news.

To start each day with a walk through the fields with two brown dogs.

To hold a cup of something dark and warm while leaning on the porch rail.

To look at the river.

To listen to the vireo and wren and robin and bunting.

To watch for fledglings and foraging and feedings.

To see if the doe and fawn would come down to drink.

To study the habits of the groundhog and her pups in the brush.

To think about the world of this yard.

While cuddling furry brown dogs who snore when not worrying.

As we sit on the old velvet couch.

I do not miss the news.

But am deeply in love with the morning.

MICKI COLBECK, JULY 2021

Just Use a Fan

After 45 years of living on this earth, I finally put two and two together this summer. Everyone knows, of course, that breezy days keep mosquitoes and blackflies at bay. They have tiny flight muscles so it doesn't take much to throw them off. But outdoor dining in July – especially wet Julys like this one – can be brutal when the wind is still. After years of wasting money on citronella candles that don't work, and slathering on the DEET, which does work but has a smell that doesn't exactly complement food, someone finally said to me: just point a fan at the outdoor dinner table. I share this embarrassingly obvious revelation with joy, knowing that for everyone who's rolling their eyes at my cluelessness, there are two more who are thinking: you just changed my life. —*Dave Mance III*

Making a Bouquet at Morey Hill Farm

The first thing you should know about arranging flowers is that there is no one right way. "A bouquet is your own interpretation," said David Johnson at Morey Hill Farm (see profile on page 232). "Each person's looks different."

That said, it helps to start with the right ingredients. For David that includes a good mix of showy focal flowers, sturdy structural flowers, airy filler flowers, with a diversity of textures and sizes and colors. Make sure you cut tall and strip the bottom third of fronds and leaves. Then group them by kind, laid out flat on a long table or spread around the edge of a large bucket or vase. From there, you can go several different routes.

His partner, Hilary Maynard, likes to begin assembling a bouquet by building the structure. She gathers a diverse bundle and holds it loosely upside down, adjusting the stems so blooms are balanced and sit at varying heights. Her favorite aspect, a signature feature, is letting one or two smaller blossoms – coreopsis or cosmos or agrostemma – curl out of the top. She tucks in the focal flowers last, settling them snugly like a jewel in a velvet case. When finished, she cuts the ends of the stems to even them.

David has a different process. He holds his bunch upright and starts with a few tall stems that catch his eye. He builds his bouquet from the inside out like a spiral, spinning it in his hand to see different angles and decide which texture and color should come next.

Their differing processes means that a discerning customer can often pick out who made which bouquet. David's tend to be more cone-shaped; Hilary's have a more open, rounded top, with those stray blossoms that nod and wink.

Having another set of eyes nearby can often help, or simply talking out loud. "What does this need?" David asks aloud while working one Friday morning. They both look appraisingly. "More forget-me-nots," they both said, almost at the same time.

Once you build your bouquet, you need to find the right vase. The flowers should be close together, but not crowded.

If you want your work to last more than a few days, be sure to change the water and rinse out the vase regularly, at least every other day. When you do, snip off the bottom inch or two of stems. Take off more if the bottoms feel soft. Be sure to continue to strip off any leaves or branching stems from the portion that will sit in the water.

At some point, this trimming will mean you need to find a smaller vase. Then, you may want to separate out the flowers and start the bouquet-making process over again. —*Kristen Fountain*

A LOOK BACK

The Breakenridge Standoff

VERMONT AS WE KNOW IT TODAY WAS BORN IN JULY, 250 YEARS AGO.

In the mid-1700s, New Hampshire Royal Governor Benning Wentworth chartered 130 towns in the disputed territory between New Hampshire and New York, land that is today Vermont. The settlers in the area were sustaining small homesteads in this wilderness under New Hampshire law, but they were challenged by New York's claims to the territory.

At the time, New York marched in lockstep with the King of England and his policies. With a smaller population than Massachusetts or Connecticut, New York had not been as successful as those states in populating its frontier lands. As a result, New York royal officials coveted the disputed territory, and sought to control the settlers and capitalize on their hard work of improving the land.

Reviving the dormant Duke of York claim after 75 years, New York's governor obtained an order from the King giving New York jurisdiction of the disputed territory. Settlers living there were required to pay for a new survey, then repurchase the land and pay rents. They balked.

Things escalated when the settlers created petitions and sought recognition from the King, while New York filed lawsuits designed to remove those who were reluctant to repurchase or rent their land. New Hampshire support for these settlers in the wilderness was evaporating, and in desperation, Samuel Robinson – the founder of Bennington – went to London to plead the settlers' cause. He would die there, but an order by the King intending to curtail the New York government's granting of lands was passed in 1767.

Still, New York's efforts to resurvey the land

This 1937 mural by artist Stephen J. Belaski depicts the Breakenridge Standoff in Bennington.
It is one of six oil on canvas pieces depicting the early history of Vermont
that hang in the Robert T. Stafford US Post Office & Courthouse in Rutland.

continued. If a settler refused to have his land surveyed, then his lands could be regranted. Many poor settlers were extended credit to purchase the land but could not afford the surveys and/or the associated "damages" fees that they were charged. Eventually, New York created entirely new towns and town lines that contrasted with the New Hampshire surveys.

When the New Hampshire settlers were brought to court in 1770, New York had so much at stake that it hand-picked jury members and witnesses who were partial to their cause. The judges who were directly involved had financial interests in the now overlapping land claims. Not surprisingly, the New Hampshire Grants settlers lost. The settlers that appeared in Albany for the trials had intended to argue that New York had no jurisdiction in the case, but simply by appearing in court, they unwittingly acknowledged the opposite. After the verdict, Ethan Allen warned the New Yorkers cryptically that "the Gods of the valleys were not the Gods of the hills."

New York then sent sheriffs and magistrates, accompanied by militia, to the disputed territory to enforce the court's biased judgements. These attempts included arresting the leaders of the Bennington community who resisted the regranting process in Albany.

In Bennington, residents considered the New York court unfair and were determined to maintain their possessions until a final ruling by the King. New Hampshire's Benning Wentworth had been the longest-serving colonial governor, so certainly, they reasoned, he had the power to grant the lands in question. They also prepared for the worst. In a town meeting, Jedidiah Dewey, the pastor of Bennington's Separatist church, suggested taking all the farms under the town's protection.

The decisive confrontation occurred on July 19, 1771, at James Breakenridge's farm in Bennington. A 300-person New York sheriff's posse, including the Mayor of Albany's lawyers, magistrates, and militia, came to serve Breakenridge an eviction notice. They were confronted by the Green Mountain Boys at Henry Bridge. The New Yorkers read the Bennington mob the riot act and demanded that they disperse. They did not. Negotiating began.

The New York sheriff and 20 men continued to James Breakenridge's farm – within site of the bridge – to parley. The house was defended, and the New York militia determined it would not assist the sheriff. There

This 1775 map reflects conflicting claims by New York and New Hampshire on the land that lay between them.

GERARD BANCKER

was a standoff, but the sheriff and his posse eventually retreated without a shot fired. Their discomfiture would lead to Breakenridge Farm becoming known as the Birthplace of Vermont.

The resolve of the Bennington residents served as a model for the other townships in the New Hampshire Grants territory. Had the New York sheriff's posse been successful, these other settlers knew, similar judgements would have been rendered against all of them. Had the Breakenridge group not stood its ground, it is possible that Vermont might never have come into existence, and we would all be New Yorkers today.

The event was just the first of many that would establish Vermont's legacy of picking up the fight against unfair taxation and slavery while becoming a home for religious groups and poor farmers during the period of the American Revolution. —*Robert Hoar*

Farming Flowers

Fridays on Morey Hill Farm in Craftsbury, David Johnson and Hilary Maynard are up early cutting blooms for their local customers' joy and delight. By July, their 10-week summer flower CSA is in full swing. They offer paper-wrapped bouquets, or buckets of loose flowers so you can make your own. There is just one location for pick-up: the covered side porch of Craftsbury General Store.

July begins with snapdragons the color of sunrise and scrambled eggs, lacey white orlaya, pale pink lisianthus, and lavender rust-freckled foxglove. In the weeks to come, the offerings turn deeper colored. There are bright red and orange poppies, tiger lilies, mustard yarrow, square-stemmed purple salvia, maroon bee balm, bachelor button's electric blue, and the bells of Ireland, a tall stem with sticky green whorls. By the month's humid end, you'll find shapes rugged and strange: stiff cockscomb amaranth and giant sunflowers poking out of clouds of spiky nigella, fiery dahlias, and blushing lime zinnias. For contrast, paper-thin white delphinium and – because they can, thanks to a new walk-in cooler – one of New England's last available fresh peonies.

It's the great variety that turned Johnson toward flowers in 2015, two years after buying a former dairy farm near the top of a hillside west of the village. By that time, he had already planted rows of fruit and nut trees, which are a passion. But he knew it would be a decade before they would provide any significant crop. Vegetables didn't make much sense. He'd done that before, and the market was already well served in and around Craftsbury, the home of Pete's Greens and several smaller farms. Growing flowers and decorative foliage inspired him, and does still.

"Of all the things I am into, flower farming has limitless boundaries," David said. "Designers want uniqueness." With a crop house for seedlings, three greenhouses that can produce a rotating cast of annuals, and acres of upper and lower fields planted with perennials, uniqueness is what Morey Hill Farm aims to provide.

During our plague summers, small-scale flower CSAs have launched everywhere across the state, either as add-ons to the vegetables or as stand-alone weekly bouquets. While it does offer a CSA, Morey Hill Farm has a wholesale focus, and it shows in the breadth, depth, and pop of what they grow and sell.

Hilary Maynard shows Karen Taylor
where to snip sweet pea blooms.

PHOTOS BY KRISTEN FOUNTAIN

Above: Karen Taylor and David Johnson prepare flowers for bouquet-making.
Below: Morey Hill Farm CSA bouquets and buckets ready for pick-up.

David and Hilary keep a large garden and raise pigs for themselves and friends. But their commercial focus is supplying fresh and then dried blooms, berries, and boughs to regional boutique florists, event designers, and wreath-makers. They will grow to order, though mostly it's farmer's choice.

The weekly CSA is the smallest part of their business, and its customers benefit from that. Morey Hill sells a popular four-week spring share starring tulips, daffodils, irises, and ranunculus and will ship bouquets for Mother's Day. By summertime, though, subscriptions fall to 20 customers, so it's not a big moneymaker. The point of offering a CSA was to connect the community to what was happening on the farm, but Hilary points out that the process has turned out to have other benefits, too.

"It helps us understand what it is like to work with the flowers," she said. The CSA provides a place to test out new products, some of which are hits and some that are not (like a new type of scarlet snapdragon that loses its petals at the slightest tap – they won't get planted again). It also provides a venue for selling small experimental harvests, and an appreciative home for the remarkable odds and ends still in the field after big event orders are filled.

The summer weeks follow a predictable rhythm on the farm. The couple and part-time help harvest

on Sundays and Mondays for regular delivery to shops in Morrisville and Stowe. Mid-week is devoted to preparing event orders with the final pick-ups on Thursdays. The Friday CSA is dropped off by 3 p.m. Then, sometimes, they rest.

"Farming is a huge commitment no matter what, whether it's cabbages or flowers," David said. "It may seem more romantic than other types of farming, but, you know, I'm in it for the farming."
—*Kristen Fountain*

Produce Farm Roundup, 2021

*Editor's Note: There are around 1,000 produce farms in Vermont
that generate over $50 million in annual sales, employ thousands of seasonal
workers, and give us healthy, locally produced food. We checked in with a
handful from around the state to see how their 2021 season went.*

BLOODROOT FARM
Nancy Witherill, Susan Brace, Chester

The weather this year was nuts. Way too hot in June, rained all of July, and then August all over the map. So, lettuce, broccoli, and peas were very unhappy. Tomatoes were slow to turn red; eggplant has taken forever to set fruit. Forget the carrot germination. Cukes croaked early. We had slugs for the first time in a long while. On the plus side, the warm spring meant the peaches and plums did well, as did the strawberries. And our second cut of hay didn't happen until the end of August – a whole month late!

RUSTY BIRD FARM
Jennifer Jones and Caleb Fisher, East Hardwick

The early dry weather meant a lot of dragging irrigation around to get crops established. We have minimal water available to distribute, so this was a stressful time, but luckily the rains returned just about the time our pond went dry. We finally set up a rainwater catchment system from the barn roof, which has been on the list for a while, and we'd like to dig another pond when we are able. Most crops seemed to have a fair amount of resilience, perhaps our attempts to build organic matter in the soil are creating a buffer. I think that the more prepared we can be as a community for weather fluctuations, the better. The first several years we farmed this land were spent trying to provide better drainage, so this is definitely a switch.

CROSSROAD FARM
Tim Taylor, Post Mills

I am often asked how one season compares to another in light of climate change. Even with 41 years of experience, this questions perplexes me. It is a life's work but barely a blink in time.

Every year presents challenges growing vegetables in Vermont, and this year was no different. When we first started farming in 1980, we could count on June frosts. We had limited irrigation to use to protect frost-sensitive plants. Therefore, we grew only small amounts of frost-sensitive vegetables until later in the season. We built many greenhouses – we now have 18 – to help buffer the vagaries of the growing season. Now, in 2021, we have plenty of irrigation and June frosts are the exception. In fact, we seem to be frost free by around the third week of May and often earlier.

This past June was noteworthy for its dryness. Personally, I like a dry June. We have plenty of irrigation and we used it. Crops grew beautifully and quickly. (See June 7 harvest photo at right.) Often June is wet and it is difficult to get on our heavier, more fertile soils. July was a strange month. Instead of the driest month of the year, it was perhaps the wettest. We received at least 10 inches of rain. However, we were far better than many of our farmer friends south of us. We had just moved back into some historically wet fields and crops drowned. We lost a lot of cole crops. I kept predicting the weather would dry out and get hot, but it never did until August, which was hot but with the right amount of nighttime rain mixed in. The corn grew great and had fantastic flavor.

DUTCHESS FARM
Stephen Chamberlain, Castleton

The water was a mixed blessing. The rainwater kept our stream full, and we have been able to fully irrigate our five acres of vegetables and seven greenhouses. The past two years we had to idle the pump in September due to low stream levels. On the other hand, we lost or had reduced germination on a few beds of newly seeded root crops.

Finding help was something of a challenge this year. We worked hard to recruit a crew leader, who was great for a couple of months. But she had her own farm, and couldn't manage both, so quit suddenly. Luckily my 22-year-old son stepped up to the vacancy and the farm has been doing better since. We also have a few part-time folks who are working out well.

RIVER BERRY FARM
David Marchant and Jane Sorenson, Fairfax
Early heat got the season going well, but it was extremely dry. It seems to be a pattern for us, that it is quite dry in the spring and then it gets wet in the summer. We irrigated a lot. I can't say it was all that much different than in past years, just longer stretches of heat and dry and then longer stretches of cool and wet. We luckily missed most of the torrential rains this year.

Grace Derksen (driving) and Grace Davis, longtime crew members at Crossroad Farm in Post Mills.

We were fortunate to have an amazing crew, for yet another year. Sure, we could use a few more hands and have made a few attempts, via Indeed and craigslist. There has been a fair bit of interest in the advertised end of the season work, but no real fits. With inflation, we do suspect that the pay range will be more of an issue for hiring and/or retaining folks next year, and we will likely need to tweak up our pay rate. But ultimately, we find that many employees willing to work on fruit and vegetable farms are explicitly looking for such work, hoping to learn about the field for pursuing their own farm dream or for determining if farming may suit them as a career. Ⓥ

PAUL REEVES

All Food Comes from Somewhere

The hardware store sent me an automated text, letting me know that my special order had arrived. I went into town, picked up the box – surprisingly heavy given its small size – and thanked the cashier for hefting it onto the counter. "What's in the box?" she inquired.

"Woodchuck traps," I said.

When I started selling commercial vegetables from my farm in White River Junction 20 years ago, I was pretty green when it came to animal control. I don't believe I had killed anything larger than a mouse up to that point, and even then, I held the standard metal-and-wood mousetrap at arm's length and tried to look away whenever I was called upon to release the metal spring. Friends from high school still tease me about a trip to a White Mountain camp in which I refused to come within a broom handle of a dried mouse husk under a bed.

In the suburbs, where I grew up, squeamishness is an affectation. On a farm, it's a mal-adaptation.

My first species of concern was the whitetail deer. Deer could hardly have improved upon our farm if they had designed it themselves: abundant red and white oak on steep south-facing slopes, hemlock glens in the sheltered ravines, thick mixedwoods to the north, and glorious farm pastures below it all.

That first year, the deer mowed everything but the peas. Fortunately, I still had a day job.

But deer are an easy problem to solve if you throw a little money around: in year two, I installed the first of a series of electric fences that have been 100 percent effective at excluding deer for more than 20 years now. I didn't even need to take up deer hunting.

Fencing is great – you aren't out-and-out killing anything with it, and though you're appropriating key habitat and undoubtedly reducing the number of wild animals in your neighborhood, you can convince yourself that "live and let live" is a workable strategy. I've got mine; they've got theirs. An electric fence keeps fox from chicken, deer from lettuce, and bear from bee.

Which brings up the rodent family, a platoon of fence-indifferent, fast-breeding prey animals that vary from the mouse, rat, and meadow vole up to the hissing and tooth-clacking woodchuck. Rodents eat curing sweet potatoes in the basement of our barn, they eat ripe tomatoes wherever they can find them, they mow down germinating spinach in the greenhouse, and they take sample bites out of every eggplant in the row. A few years back, we transplanted 1000 row-feet of Brussels sprouts and carefully covered them in a polyester blanket to protect them from flea beetles. Two days later, when we lifted the blanket to check on them, we found not a single stem remaining. 700 plants gone. We looked around to see if maybe we had checked under the wrong cover.

We trap rodents diligently, constantly, and incessantly, using snap traps, peanut butter, sticky cards, dark cardboard tubes, Juicy Fruit gum, and a vitamin D poison that's allowed in organic production under limited circumstances. I've crushed nests of babies under my boot heel, nailed fleeing mice with shovel handles, and fruitlessly thrown all manner of knives, gloves, and buckets in their general direction. This spring, I hired a professional trapper to deal with the burgeoning woodchuck population, which my two house-fed dogs were not taking particularly seriously, and after watching the trapper successfully place a half-dozen sets, I ordered my own traps.

Crushing a woodchuck in a steel trap gets your attention. It's a relatively large animal, and there's strength and technique involved in setting the trap in the first place. Then you're face to face with it as you compress the springs and dispose of the lifeless body. It's very hard to pretend that you weren't the agent of this clever animal's destruction, and it's in no way like the tiny mouse underfoot or the deer grazing outside the fence.

Why not a Havahart trap, you ask? No farmer suffers from the delusion that releasing a prey animal onto unfamiliar ground some distance away will result in anything other than that animal's imminent demise. The blood is on your hands either way, and who has time for theater?

A few years back, during a spring open house on our farm when we were showing off our new crop of lambs, I found myself in the barn with a couple of twentysomethings from the city. They asked all kinds of fun questions until they came to: "What happens to all these lambs?"

"Meat," I said. "We slaughter them in the fall for meat."

After a quick pause, one of them blurted out, "Don't worry, lambs. We're vegans!"

I was too polite to say anything in the moment, but what I would have said was, "Don't talk that way in front of the children!"

Sheep, of course, take a dim view of vegans, and not just because sheep take a dim view of ideology generally. Under the vegan project, sheep would be forced into extinction. A lucky few might be relegated to the zoo. This is not the bargain sheep signed up for many millennia ago when they agreed to be docile and we agreed to protect them and together we fanned out across the globe. Stotting across green Vermont pastures, eating grass and clover, and ruminating together inside the safety of a fence are not a sheep's idea of a bad time – even were they to know that the day will come, which they don't.

All food comes from somewhere, and nowhere does it emerge immaculately or uncompromised. The woodchuck's blood is under all of our fingernails. We've spent the better part of the past century building sterile supermarkets with separate meat and vegetable aisles, with everything sealed up in Saran Wrap and Styrofoam, while out in the fields, we use ever-larger tractors to blow through hedges, drainage ditches, and even whole farmsteads in an effort to turn the natural world into a rootless monoculture of Nowhereville. And yet, despite our sustained efforts at self-deception, stories remain. Food still comes from the earth.

Here in Vermont, we're just lucky enough to still know some of the stories. —*Chuck Wooster*

On Haying

FARMING AS CONNECTION

Haying can be seen as a lyrical exercise, composed of simple, sun-baked work while immersed in fragrance and pastoral beauty.

Not quite my recollection. Haying was real farming, consisting more of sweat, dehydration, sunburn, aching forearms, back, and neck, and clothes that began the day unadorned but by evening had been seared by sunlight and dressed in a coarse shell of chaff and dust. Then again tomorrow.

On our farm, the act of haying began in May. Lambing was long done, the grasses were up, and the sheep were sheared. Time to look over the haying equipment, clean and grease it, inflate a few soft tires, and make a few repairs. It was time to walk the edge of the fields, throwing tree limbs

back into the brush and stone walls. I like walking where several generations of earlier farmers walked before; see what they saw; share some of the same activities and observations. Mingling my footsteps with theirs seems to renew an important connection with the land.

Haying is composed of three cuts. For this first cut, we wanted the hay to be 12 to 16 inches high and not too "stalky." Our goal was to cut the hay before, or just as, the seed heads were developing, but prior to the formation of seeds. In May, it is often a fine balance between cutting the hay when it is ready and soil moisture. A damp soil makes drying harder, and I didn't want to tear up the fields with the weight of my equipment.

In a good year, with frequent

three-day drying periods, we would be back in the same fields at the end of June or early July. This second cut would have more leaf content, and a bit more protein than the first. It was more fragrant as well, capturing both leaf and blossoming flowers. The yields in the second cuts were less than in Spring, but it felt somehow more meaningful: a mix of hard work and both visual and sensory reward.

With a third cut, I always felt we were getting something rare. Third cuts come late in the summer and involve a mixture of skill and experience, since the hay is short and thick. The drying time is shorter with the declining sunlight and the heavy dew lingers on the grasses until late in the morning. With the shorter day, we had to ted and rake the hay as soon as it had dried sufficiently. The reward was a darker green hay, rich in protein and fatty acids. In mid-Winter, you would never stand between a hungry flock and a lush, third cut, unless you were looking for bruised legs.

There is a certain art to haying, especially with older, affordable equipment. Our farm operation had two new pieces of equipment – a new baler and a Massey Ferguson diesel tractor – but all the rest was old: an International, an Allis Chalmers, and Ferguson tractors; G.H. Grimm tedder, Hesston mower conditioners, and Gehl hay wagons. Like many farmers, I am a believer in big and little innovations on the farm.

PHOTOS COURTESY CHANDLER POND FARM

Repair this with a weld or some bolts and nuts and a metal plate or an upturned coffee can over an exhaust stack. Put more air into a leaking loaded tire. Baling wire, hoses, and clamps will fix (nearly) anything.

Depending on the mix and types of hay grasses – timothy, alfalfa, red clover, orchard grass – you cut the hay either close to the ground or higher up if the hay is stalky or the underlying soil damp. When tedding, you *luft* the hay grasses into broad windrows with considerable care in order to improve drying. You are trying to avoid both shattering the leaves and losing protein (by "wuffling" too fast) and bleaching the nutrients out of the hay from too much sunlight. At the end of the day, in the shade just inside the barn door, you want to see the hay as a light green. The smell should be fragrant enough to remind you, in mid-winter, of the contrast to both the greys and browns of your barn and the snow and sharp cold that cling to you. A reward for hard Summer work.

You apply the same degree of care to raking, when you form tighter, curled windrows for feeding the tines of your baler.

Our haying operation relied on 40-pound rectangular bales – I could never figure round bales. Maybe it's my impecunious Scotch-Irish heritage, but after a little observation, it seemed to me that round bales are wasteful. Why would a farmer waste part of a hay crop into which he had sunk so much time, effort, and expense? Farming is hard enough.

Our finished hay was green and fragrant – never wet. The center of a wet bale of hay can reach temperatures of 190 degrees and spontaneously combust. Further, rain leaches out nutrients and increases the risk of mold, which is particularly injurious to livestock. I did know a farmer in East Barre who put up wet hay. Between each course of stacked bales, he would spread a thick coating of rock salt. He claimed the salt drew the moisture out and that his cows loved the hay. I liked how he fixed my chainsaw; not so much his approach to haying.

We sold hay as far away as Cape Cod, but mostly to local small and medium-sized farms – horses, sheep, goats, and some dairy.

Hundreds of acres of our hay land was leased, mostly from "retired" old farmers who had held their land for generations and, one way or another, succumbed to bulk milk tank costs, herd size economies, and limited capital problems. It is hard to bring a break-even farm operation to a point of accumulating surplus capital in order to invest in "modern agriculture."

Those old-timers were the best. They would greet us with a small wave from their porches, dressed in work denims from decades ago. Their sensible wives would then pull them back into the house. Some would call out, *"He wants to work with you, but he can't."*

In the early afternoon, I would get off my tractor and walk up to the farmhouse. He'd be sitting in a rocking chair on a worn porch, with faded white clapboards as a background. As I approached the steps, he'd say, *"The wife has prepared some switchel for you"* and she would appear with a pitcher in hand. Usually it was apple cider vinegar, maple syrup, ginger, and black strap molasses. Depending on the proportions, it was good or foul.

On days when we baled, treasured stories would follow, but not until all the day's hay was in the barn. —*C. E. Crowell*

JL DAMON

A PLACE FOR ALL OCCASIONS AND ALL SEASONS

Social House (SoHo) is a Mediterranean based restaurant with sharing and family-style options. Serving dinner with two private rooms, outdoor seating, and off-site catering options. Led by restaurateur Luis Pazos and his wife of 11 years, Debbie Pazos, who combined have 25 years of experience in the food and hospitality industry, including working together in the world-renowned French-Seafood restaurant Le-Bernardin.

1716 Depot St, Manchester Center, VT

A cozy GastroPub with Vermont vibes in a rustic, industrial atmosphere – all underground in the heart of Manchester Center. Known for its great food and drinks, as well as frequent live music and events, Union Underground is a great place to relax and grab a bite. Savor fresh cuisine with ingredients provided by local farms, and a variety of drafts on tap from breweries around the area.

4928 Main St, Manchester Center, VT

A local coffee shop to fill all your coffee, baked goods, breakfast and lunch needs! Featuring locally roasted, Mocha Joe's coffee and espresso. Stop in for specialty coffee drinks, fresh baked goods, grab-and-go sandwiches, salads and more.

39 Bonnet St, Manchester Center, VT

AUGUST

August

The truck thermometer said 95 degrees in town – the hazy air thick enough you could chew it. By the time we turned off Route 7A onto a dirt road it said 90. Twenty minutes later, surrounded by green at the cul-de-sac at the end of the hollow road, it said 86. We took a jeep trail farther into the woods, and by the time we'd parked beside the stream it said 80.

My brother, his wife and kids and I followed the small stream as it meandered through a hardwood glen full of ash, yellow birch, and maple. The occasional red oak. In places, the streambank was lined with stacked stones – at one place there was evidence of a dam and base for a water wheel. We wondered how old it was. The 100-plus-year-old trees and lack of any cement put us back in the 1800s. The stones showed no quarry marks. Our best guess, based on the pre-industrial boom cycle in this area, was pre-Civil War. 1840s, maybe.

Can you picture it? A rudimentary structure perched at the edge of the stream amidst a hacked clearing, the stumps that were too large to pull, some of them wide enough to lie down on, still rising irregularly from the bony earth. A man in a wide-brimmed straw hat, and an ox pulling a sawlog, picking a path through the clearing toward the mill. Outside the structure water passing over a flutter wheel. Inside the structure a sawyer in a linen shirt and light wool pants. A vertical, six-foot steel sawblade with coarse teeth on one side suspended in a wooden sash frame sliding up and down between two grooved fender posts. A log on a crude carriage being gigged forward by a rack-and-pinion gear with every downstroke of the saw. It's moderately loud, but perhaps slower than you're imagining. Hum Aretha Franklin's "Respect" – "Re, re, re, re, re, re, re, re, spect (Just a little bit)." That's the rhythm of the machine. It's slow enough that on big logs the sawyer walks out to escape the noise and stickers a modest lumber pile.

See him visiting now with his wife who's come by. She wears a bell-shaped wool skirt despite the heat, and a brimless bonnet, the ribbons untied at the nape of her neck. She has their two children with her – a little boy and a little girl. Five and seven. The man who'd been working the ox joins them, and they all walk together upstream to a worn spot on the bank where there's lunch and cider. The stream here curls around and falls through a limestone rock formation, the walls green with moss, the streambed a macadam of whorled bedrock and marble-flecked loose stone.

We sit on the worn spot and talk about time passing. The father and his kids and his brother walk in the stream through the limestone gorge; phoebe nests amidst layer cake stones that, were they sentient, could tell stories of prehistoric oceans and continental collisions. Here the temperature drops further – it might be upper 60s in the shade and damp air. The kids wear swimsuits made out of nylon and spandex. Polyester sun hats. Water shoes made out of rubber and neoprene. They take turns sitting in a plunge pool, the stream falling on their shoulders and heads, the rush of water in their ears, cooled, and exhilarated, and unsettled by the power in that water, the relentlessness that drives it to the sea. —*Dave Mance III*

Record-high Lows

"Record-high lows" might sound like a tongue-twister, but it's what early August 2021 had in store for Vermont. For five consecutive days, from August 9-13, temperatures in Burlington didn't drop below 70 degrees. That's the first time that's happened in Vermont, in any month, since 1901. Two of those nights never dropped below 75 degrees, setting daily record-high lows. High humidity during this stretch made nights (and days) all the more uncomfortable. Jarringly, by August 15, nighttime lows had dropped into the 40s in many parts of the state.

Strong late-afternoon/early-evening thunderstorms were a common occurrence, as they often are this time of year in Vermont when warm, humid air masses meet with our mountainous topography.

Precipitation in August 2021 was close to normal, as between 3 and 4.5 inches of rain fell throughout the state. Although a couple tropical storms moved through southern New England, they had little impact on the Green Mountain State. The biggest single rain event throughout the month came right in the middle, as thunderstorms broke the daily rainfall record in Burlington with 1.26 inches of rain falling on August 14. —*Christopher Kurdek, Fairbanks Museum and Planetarium*

After a pandemic year without fairs, these annual rites returned to Vermont this summer. Here, a glorious August evening at the Vermont State Fair in Rutland.

DONNA WILKINS

NATURE NOTES

BASSWOODS HAVE beautiful nectar-rich flowers, abundant seeds (as you might have noticed this year), and very cute seedlings. Yet despite this, most full-sized basswoods originate from stump sprouts. This helps explain why they are so often found growing in clumps. In many hardwood species the ability for a stump to produce sprouts declines with age, but stumps from 100+-year-old basswoods still have this ability. Unlike a seedling, a sprout is born with an extensive root system that's ready to get to work. Older oaks also can produce sprouts.

Basswood seeds litter the foreground in this picture, but the double trunk indicates that these two trees grew from stump sprouts, not seed.

MONARDA SHORTFACE
(Dufourea monardae)
Size ⅓ inch

D. monardae harvests from just a few species of beebalm, unlike other short-faced bees in the same genus that have a wide range of hosts.

Wild bergamot *(Monarda fistulosa)* is native to almost all of the continental US. It grows in sun and part shade on almost any soil that's not wet. Early autumn is a good time to divide and share.

DAISY HEBB

Burying Beetles

If you have a dead mouse handy, you should have no trouble finding a round neck sexton beetle. They can smell dead creatures from far, far away and small carcasses other than mice will also attract these carrion eaters. These common beetles are active beginning in late May.

About 1.5 cm (0.6 inches long), they are handsome: shiny black with two bright orange patches on each wing and antennae that are tipped with orange.

Their remarkable ability to locate dead animals is only one of their notable features. It's long been known that both parents feed the larvae and that they work together to completely remodel their carcass home. If their mouse is on a stump or a rock, they will push it off, millimeter by millimeter, so they can bury it. Rather like one of our species moving an elephant.

Early naturalists thought that burying beetles might be capable of reason. If they knew as much about burying beetle behavior then as we know now, they wouldn't have had a doubt.

A mouse will provide food for the parents and their larvae right up until the larvae pupate. Most of the carcasses these beetles occupy are only big enough to feed one family, and competing carrion feeders, both beetles and flies, are likely to pick up on the same malodorous scents. That's a problem, as a mouse will only feed one family.

It's long been known that the beetles change the microbial population within their chosen carcass, and it used to be thought that they were sterilizing it to preserve it. But it turns out that this is not what they are doing at all. Steven T. Trumbo and colleagues at the University of Connecticut discovered that they change the microbial community in order to deceive other insects so that they can keep the place entirely for themselves.

Exactly how they do this is not known. But soon after a pair of beetles arrives at a carcass, there's a 20-fold reduction in methyl thiocyanate, a sulfur-based product of decay that produces the familiar onion-egg like odors that signal death and attract beetles. In addition, a beetle-prepared carcass emits an increased amount of dimethyl trisulfide, which is a beetle deterrent. Trumbo calls this "an active disinformation campaign" to mislead rivals. And it works. Far fewer beetles discovered prepared carcasses compared to fresh, uninhabited ones. Flies are put off the trail as well.

The eggs are laid in the soil near the carcass, and regurgitated food is fed to the hatchlings by both parents in much the same way as a bird feeds its chicks, at first two or three times an hour. This is most unusual behavior for insects and is limited to those in the family of carrion eating beetles. —*Virginia Barlow*

ADELAIDE TYROL

Tomato Fruitworm

C. WATTS / CC

The ability of plants to signal other plants and to call in predatory insects when attacked is getting more and more attention, these days. Insects, too, are paying attention and researchers at Penn State discovered that the saliva of a caterpillar that feeds on tomato plants (the tomato fruitworm) secretes an enzyme that causes the host plant to close its stomata, thus silencing the plant's calls for help. The enzyme is effective within five minutes and keeps the plants from signaling for help for 48 hours. The caterpillars can chomp away in peace. Ⓥ

AT HOME

❧

Is it Cyanobacteria . . . or Something Else?

Cyanobacteria – formerly and inaccurately called blue-green algae – are photosynthetic bacteria that can easily be identified. A simple way to do this is the "stick test." If you put a long stick into a green surface mat on a lake or pond and it picks up threads of green hair, it's not cyanobacteria. It's harmless filamentous green algae.

If you suspect that cyanobacteria might be present in a pond or lake, fill a mason jar three-quarters of the way with the water and let it sit in the fridge overnight. Next morning, if the organisms have settled to the bottom, they are not cyanobacteria. If they're floating, they might be. But these bacteria, among the first organisms on earth to fix nitrogen, are not always a cause for concern. Problems occur when they are overly abundant.

Carbon, nitrogen, and phosphorus – plus heat and light

– cause population blooms and that's when they produce toxins. Usually it's phosphorus that's the limiting factor and recent strategies to limit phosphorus inputs have had the intended effect. But there's phosphorus in lake and pond sediments and it's released all the time, especially as the environment heats up. Cyanobacteria blooms are increasing despite lowered phosphorus inputs.

The toxins produced by cyanobacteria when they

are abundant are dangerous. Don't swim in or eat fish from scummy water. And do what you can to reduce the amount of phosphorus – whether it's from laundry detergent or manure – from getting into a stream, pond, or lake near you. If you want to learn more, the Lake Champlain Committee (lakechamplaincommittee. org) offers many cyanobacteria resources and services, including sampling, reporting, and monitoring. —*Virginia Barlow*

Plant Those Fall Food Plots Now

If you'd like to grow a high-quality food plot this coming fall, early August is the right time to plant seed.

The advantage of summer planting is that warm soil and fewer weeds mean that new crops can grow very quickly compared to those from an early-spring seeding. The risk is that water is needed for good germination, and August and September can be dry months. Watch the weather and wait until hot dry spells have passed and showers are expected.

You'll want to do a soil test ahead of time and amend the soil with lime before any planting. A pH between 6 and 7 is ideal to start. Fertilizer is also required at planting if you want a productive crop. You can find more information about wildlife food plot nutrient requirements at https://go.uvm.edu/ag-testing

The seeding rates in the instructions below are in pounds per acre of pure live seed, so adjust the seeding rate according to the percentage of seed germination, seed coating material, and your food plot's size. I like to plant these mixes either in separate plots or side by side in a long strip plot right at the end of July or in the first week of August.

COOL SEASON PERENNIAL: 8 pounds clover mix plus 4 pounds chicory per acre. Add 30 pounds of oats as a nurse crop (and to keep the bears busy) while the clover gets good roots established.

COOL SEASON ANNUAL: 6 pounds Brassica mix, plus 2 pounds radish per acre. Overseed 100 pounds of winter wheat-winter rye mix in early September for a tasty treat in late fall that provides for winter feed and also spring green-up.

TOWARD THE END OF AUGUST, TRY THIS MIX: 50 pounds oats plus 50 pounds winter peas. Add 100 pounds of wheat or rye in early September for an extra boost of feed. —*Jeff Carter*

Oats and winter peas

PEOPLE IN MANY PARTS OF VERMONT were reminded this summer that water bars are an essential part of forest roads. In this photo, Vermont Forests, Parks and Recreation foresters Rick Dyer (left) and Nathan Tapper (right) look at an existing sugarbush road to determine the best location to install a water bar. The wooden gauge is set to 30 degrees relative to the road and represents the ideal angle to both divert runoff and prevent erosion.

MARK ISSELHARDT

We are All Related

AN ABENAKI GLOSSARY ON LAND AS KIN

When a language disappears, how can we reclaim its essential concepts and values? When I was a child, several languages were spoken in our family: English, French, and a few strange words and phrases that I never quite understood. These Abenaki words explained the core concepts and values I grew up with. Sometimes, a single word spoken in one language would require a paragraph in another. When the concepts are untranslatable, I begin to understand what has been lost from my heritage. As a teacher, I've struggled to find the right words to preserve and share our sense of kinship with the land. My students crave a sense of reciprocity and belonging. During our era of climate crisis, I share these healing concepts in our original language.

As a child, I learned that **AKI**, *soil or land, was the place of birth, the beginning of life*. We needed to feed the soil. Offal from fish and seaweed gave back the exact nutrients to support birth. "Soil" in English does not necessarily carry a sacred meaning. In the Abenaki language **AKI** *is a word that could represent the whole earth.*

MOWKAWOGAN *represents the spine of the land, home to the community of all life.* Community embraces everything: insects, plants, birds, fish, humans, and those beings in between. The community protects the land to keep the spine connected in every way. This connection allows the place of birth to continue to

give life and health to the community. The spine of the land, being sentient, understands the importance of this relationship. **WOIGAN** *is the word for spine.*

MOWI *means together.*

MOWKANNOAK *means they travel in a group together.*

MOWIGOBOAK *means they stand together, or they stand as a group.*

All of these words signify that the community will move and stand strong together to protect aki, at all costs. After all, it is their place of birth.

MOWKAWIK *means the band's homeland,* the area within which the community or band travels together to protect aki, and themselves. This is the watershed, the place where the waters feed the spine of the land that loves and cares for aki.

A community never stays in one place long enough to damage aki or bakabagw, the clear water. The group moves throughout the watershed to preserve the clear water for the community. This is true conservation.

GOGASSIGAMIGWZOAK *translates to "there are many families living together."*

This is the Nation, the place where everyone speaks the same language. It is the place where the spine of the land comes together in one mind and one being.

GOGASSOMKWAKI *means so many thousands,* referring to the people who care for water, community, and aki. This is the place where Mowkawogan, or the spine, continues to grow.

GEDAKINA *means our world, or our worldview.* This is the place where one reaches an understanding of the cycle of life within their own community, in relation to other communities. This is the place one reaches to form new relationships and learn together. It is the responsibility of the people to show respect and reverence to aki, to learn to treat aki as our sacred relation, and to educate those who don't understand.

Once these values are learned, the community will know how to reciprocate with aki in a proper way. Traditionally, Abenaki children are raised with this wisdom; they build on it during their lifetime, and teach their children so the relationship will continue.

The community knows Wadagwobagezi: we are all related to one another. Reciprocity sustains us: treat the land as kin so aki will continue to care for us forever.

—Judy Dow

IN RELATIONSHIP

Gedakina
our world, worldview

Gogassigamigwzoak
nation land

Mowkawik
watershed
the "band lands"

Mowkawogan
community
spine of the land

Aki
soil

Wadagwobagezi
to be related to

A LOOK BACK

Ten Years After Irene

Saturday, August 28, marked 10 years since Tropical Storm Irene hit Vermont, causing so much destruction to so many homes, businesses, and towns, and most tragically some loss of life. It rerouted the Mill River just north of the railroad trestle in East Wallingford and took our first farm with it. In the 10 years since then, with the help of more people than we could possibly list, my partner

Before, during, after Irene.

Ryan and I rebuilt Evening Song Farm on land off Shunpike Road.

We take a moment every year at this time to find stillness and reflect on that experience. The first couple of years after the storm were incredibly difficult, especially emotionally. It took a long time before I was able to look out the window at the backyard without crying. Ten years out, it's no longer gut-wrenching to think about that loss and the years of burnout that it took to rebuild.

Those of you who pick up your veggies at the farm know how lucky we are to farm in such a beautiful place. The views of the ridgeline on the other side of the highway, the surrounding forest, the towering trees that line the road are like a fairy tale. A common sentiment that we share with others is how we would not have had the good fortune of being here without Irene. Our original farm site was essential for us when we were new to the area, because so many people would drive by, see what we were doing, and feel some connection with us when they saw us at the farmers market or signed up for a CSA share. Now that we have become more established in this community, we don't need the high level of visibility that Route 103 offered. We're grateful to be on this quiet, dead-end road, among the trees, with more growing space to produce food for more people, enabling us to employ a larger team of farmers.

And yet, 10 years later, the gratitude we feel is complex and multi-dimensional. It's mixed with the memory of ourselves on August 29, 2011, driving back to that land and feeling kicked hard in the stomach at the sight of those precious fields of crops made unrecognizable by the most jarring natural transformation of land we had ever personally witnessed. It includes memories of the impossibility of our farm's recovery – the feeling of being a hollow shell of ourselves every autumn, overworked from simultaneously building and running a farm, the end of the chaos both vaguely in sight but unreachable.

The fields at Evening Song Farm before and after Irene passed through.

EVENING SONG FARM

It includes memories of the painful uncertainty of our partnership's ability to heal from that loss and weather the ongoing stress, which sometimes felt like it might never end.

But we also remember the beautiful generosity of so many people, who over years and in countless ways expressed their care and desire for us to continue to grow food for this community. Shortly after Irene, neighbors, family, and friends came by our farm to help in any possible way – pulling broken irrigation lines from the sand, digging out old equipment, shoveling mud out of the barn, clipping the garlic that was safely drying in the barn, singing to us, taking out the trash, feeding us, hugging us, burning through chainsaw chains cutting up downed, sand-covered trees, offering land, taking us on walks. Our gratitude is woven with all the joyful memories of

the past decade: sunny days spent in the abundance of beautiful crops, laughing with our farm crew, and watching our kids learn to open irrigation valves, harvest cucumbers with the crew, and run up and down the towering rows of tomato plants playing tag.

I wish the young adults we were – naive and full of energy – didn't have to go through the exhausting marathon of losing and rebuilding a new farm. But we're grateful for the lessons. We learned about humility, vulnerability, and resiliency. These are often just buzzwords, but we felt them in a deep body way. We learned to accept help and even ask for it. We learned that we are capable of doing hard things, and we got a little better at not sweating the small stuff. (Punctured tractor tire? That's ok, we rebuilt a farm after a hurricane.) We got introduced to the idea that we have limits, and that it's wise to heed them. We learned how humans are tremendously beautiful and compassionate and can be good at caring for each other. We added to our climate resiliency toolbox by personally experiencing climate trauma.

And I think the loudest thing I learned from that experience is that everyone is carrying something hard at some point in life, and to always, always approach people with grace and gentleness. For the first year after Irene, it felt nearly impossible to do some very mundane, basic things, like buying groceries. I would

have to hold back my tears at farming conferences when fellow farmers would fret over pest issues. (I would think: I wish I had a farm to have pests to stress about. Give me flea beetles!) But in moving through all of that, it's clear that we are all holding something tender, and to just always offer compassion.

When we returned home to the farm that Monday morning 10 years ago, we felt pretty clearly that we were done being farmers, that it was time to shift into new jobs, grow a little garden behind our house, and move on. But little by little, neighbors and strangers would stop by, asking how they could help, wondering what the next steps were, planning a big community fundraiser. So in the aftermath, it felt like the only choice was to keep farming, buoyed by the support of our community.

What we had started building before Irene, and grew rapidly afterwards with everyone's generosity, was invisible layers of community support. That invisible community foundation is what we need more than ever in our world, and we hope that this farm can continue being a part of that for years to come. —*Kara Fitzbeauchamp*

Top: Kara and Ryan Fitzbeauchamp working to move equipment and small structures to higher ground during the storm. Left: A 2021 visit back to the river where they once grew garlic. Below: Evening Song Farm in August 2021; a new home in a splendid location 10 years after destruction.

JERRY HIAM

Irene's Impact on Ag

ON AUGUST 28, 2011, Tropical Storm Irene dumped as much as a foot of rain as it traveled through Vermont. The subsequent flooding, erosion, and property damage was more than anything most of us could remember. Farms on riverbottom land were especially hard hit (see accompanying table).

"Damage was reported from every county, although it was minimal in Grand Isle and Essex," reported UVM Extension in January 2012, after four months had passed and it was possible to fully take stock of the event. "The intensity of the flood ranged from fast-moving waters moving debris and soil to slow moving water that simply covered fields and crops for a short time. Unofficial estimates place economic losses by farms at about $20 million."

At the time, one of the major concerns in agricultural circles had to do with the food safety of flooded crops. Accepted practice for typical summer flooding is to destroy tender crops but allow durable storage crops that survived to mature and harvest, as long as they are thoroughly washed prior to sale. The scale of Irene was so severe, though, that the Agency of Agriculture mandated that any edible crop "that had come in contact with flood waters in any way, for any length of time" would have to be left unharvested and/or destroyed. The decision was based on the large number of sewage treatment plants, septic systems, and hazardous waste sites that were underwater.

There was considerable pushback from growers on this ruling, who asked for scientific evidence to support it. In response, the state sent seven paired groups of carrots, potatoes, and winter squash to a food lab in Texas for testing. Though it was a limited sample size, contamination was not ubiquitous. Tests for nine heavy metals found the only one present was copper, and that at very low levels in every sample. None of the organochlorine pesticides analyzed for were found, and the only hydrocarbons found were "background levels" in three samples. Salmonella was not found in any samples, and generic *E.coli* showed up on two flooded and two unflooded samples.

Perhaps this evidence may help guide future decisions in the event Vermont farms suffer another large-scale flood event comparable to Irene. Ⓥ

STATEWIDE AGRICULTURE DAMAGE REPORT

Producers affected	476
Corn acres damaged	6,065
Soybean acres damaged	225
Hay acres damaged	7,268
Fruit/vegetable acres damaged	596
Pasture acres damaged	1,752
Maple acres (wind damaged)	1,402
Acres of land damage	9,093

SOURCE: USDA, FSA VERMONT STATE OFFICE

INDUSTRY

UVM EXTENSION

Bitter Sweet

THE HOPS RENAISSANCE IN VERMONT

One of the few things we can probably all agree upon these days is that the only stable thing is change. Agriculture is especially rife with reinvention, and the evolution of hop farming in the state is part of a much larger story that originates in ancient times. Give or take a few centuries, the taste of hops got married to beer as a preservative about a thousand years ago. Ever since, even though in some circles it may have led a less ballyhooed parallel life as a medicinal plant, the history of hops has remained yoked to beer. And nowadays, Vermont has become yoked to craft beer.

Hops in Vermont isn't new. Little known fact: in the 1800s, Vermont was the second largest producer of hops in the country, second only to New York. Toward the end of the nineteenth century, along with lots of

other farms and industries that abandoned Vermont, hops cultivation followed the Great Expansion out to the drier valleys of Washington, Oregon, and Idaho. There, downy mildew, the biggest threat to successful harvests in the east, isn't such a problem, and the Pacific Northwest still generates something like 96 percent of all hops produced in the US.

Before the recent upsurge in craft beer production, hops were a mere remnant perennial found in the wild and in many Vermont gardens, creeping up trellises, poles, anything the bines can twine around clockwise. (Botanically speaking, a bine wraps its stem around an object, a vine uses tendrils to attach itself to an object.) Because it's a vigorous plant with heavenly scented flowers that can also be used to treat anxiety, insomnia, and ADHD, it's fun to grow in temperate climates. *Humulus lupulus* – incidentally in the same family as cannabis – likes to climb high. Fast. Tended to and trained, the bines will use every second of our latitude's sixteen hours of daylight in June to grow up to two feet in a week, or six inches in a day. One planter even made an unverified claim of twelve inches.

In 2021, according to the *Bangor Daily News* in Maine, Vermont had 72 breweries. One brewery for every 8,672 people. So, for Vermont brewers, an ancillary business of farms has emerged to produce high-quality hops. The plant is making a comeback as a crop and can thrive here, but it also has many enemies.

For the love of beer, and in lockstep with the agricultural trend, the UVM extension specifically designed a program to help hopyards navigate the well-documented risks. And another organization, the Vermont Hops Project, is collaborating with Vermont microbreweries to study Vermont-grown cultivars that create Vermont IPAs and ales. Terroir is a fancy French word lifted from winemaking that identifies and manages individually distinctive flavors specific to a region. It gets used a lot with hops in New England, as aspiring hop farms and beer afficionados refine regional knowledge.

From the UVM extension website, growers can download a Virtual Reality game to help learn how to identify the pests and employ Integrated Pest Management. Potato leaf hoppers may be mitigated by planting alfalfa and red clover as tasty culinary diversions. Aphids can be combatted with natural enemy arthropods, two-spotted spider mites with biological warfare, Japanese beetles with nematodes, pesticides, or milky spore bacterium. Downy mildew, the curse that sent nineteenth-century hop farmers out west, can be controlled by bio-fungicides and improved airflow.

Even though it's a risky endeavor, amateur and serious hopyards have been popping up all over our brave little state. If you've ever spotted the curious sight of what looks like a field of telephone poles linked by top wires, it was a hopyard, not giraffe fencing. —*Tania Aebi*

MEDICINAL USES OF HOPS

Pillows filled with hops have been used as a remedy for sleeplessness for centuries. Other traditional uses for hops, not counting improvements to beer, range widely but mostly have centered on reducing nervousness, irritability, and restlessness. Like many other plants, it's been employed to treat most all of the problems that we humans are heir to: cancers of all kinds, indigestion, infections, baldness, tuberculosis, and more.

Until recently, scientific findings for the medicinal value of hops have tended to the tentative and laced with caveats, almost always including something along the lines of "more research is needed."

But over the past 20 years several new hop-based compounds have been found to be helpful in treating conditions not on the old folk-remedy list. A recently discovered substance in hops called xanthohumol may help prevent diet-induced obesity and diabetes. Perhaps it will be coming to a pharmacy near you before too long.

No bad side effects have been identified from using hops for any and all of the things it's been tried on. Even bathing in cold brewery sludge, which, according to legend, was believed by King Wenceslas to have rejuvenating effects. —*Virginia Barlow*

Verdant Valley

Champlain Valley Hops in Starksboro is set in the loveliest of Addison County valleys, one blessed by soil left behind by retreating glaciers. The operation is headquartered in an old farmhouse ready for change, a relic from another era, tired and unsteady on her footings. The faded white paint, paired with green shutters and a cool portico, lend a touch of faded grandeur from when the farm was flush on dairy success. The dooryard leads to barns, sheds, and buildings full of familiar traditional farming vehicles and accessories like Gators, tractors, and brush hogs. Then, there's all the specialized planting, harvesting, drying, and baling equipment that's unique to growing hops.

Standing at the edge of this 37-acre hopyard, you gaze down row upon irrigated, plowed, weeded, trellised row of 18-foot-high poles, a line of sight that disappears below a faraway dip. The sheds full of mechanical advantages make this infrastructure no less daunting. Hundreds of poles are buried at least three-feet deep so they remain straight and true. Barbed wire runs from pole top to pole top; hanging from the barbed wire are coconut coir lines anchored to the ground below. In May, the view is of a forest of

Julian Post (left) and Peter Briggs co-founded Champlain Valley Hops in 2018.

poles and lines. At the base of each line are four hops crowns, each of which can live up to twenty years, that will bud, shoot, and get trained to climb into a jungle of green by August.

Champlain Valley Hops cultivars are "old school" varieties: Cascade, Centennial, Willamette, Magnum, Nugget, Chinook, and Crystal. Each one has been studied, analyzed, and monitored, optimized for local pest, weed, and fungal control. The clusters of green papery scales on the 67,000 cones will ripen to a yellowish color. The small lupulin glands at the base of the scales are what make hops hoppy, and determining when the ideal ratio of alpha to beta acid has been achieved is key. Harvest typically occurs between mid-August and mid-September.

Amazingly, many home- and micro-brewers have never even seen a hops cone. Once harvested, more specialized equipment processes and delivers the cones to the beer-makers as pellets. The whole effort requires a massive capital and infrastructure investment for such a risky niche crop. And yet, this group of farmers has plunged all in, assumably driven by a collective love of both agriculture and beer.

—Tania Aebi

Hop cones recently stripped from the bine. CVH has two German-made Wolf hop pickers that do that work and separate the cones from the other material. Quality control is then done by hand to pick out any leaves or stems that the machine didn't remove. [1]

Coir strings are fed into the arms of hop harvesters after being cut. "We cut and strip bines in continuous batches throughout the day," explains Max Licker, CVH's director of sales. "The bines are also very rough and can irritate skin, which is why operators use gloves and long sleeves/long pants to cover exposed skin." [2]

Waste wagon: all the plant material other than the cones is moved into this wagon via a conveyor belt from inside the processing barn; it's then composted on site. [3]

A member of the harvest team rides in the picking wagon. The wagon has an arm which cuts the string and bines, and a mechanical floor, which helps to unload the strings in a neat pile in the processing barn. 4

CVH's two Wolf hop-pickers inside the processing barn. "We run both all day since picking is our biggest bottleneck during the roughly 40-day hop harvest," explains Max Licker. 5

In spring 2021, CVH planted experimental varieties to see how they would grow on the farm before committing to planting larger quantities. The experimental varieties included Triumph, Comet, Cashmere, and Saaz. [6]

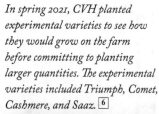

Most of the crop is dried, ground into powder, and formed into pellets which are then vacuum-sealed and frozen. This keeps them fresh for years. [7]

A delivery of 300 pounds (150 pounds per bin) of wet hops (fresh, unprocessed) at Foam Brewers in Hinesburg. Wet hops are only available during harvest time and contribute unique herbal qualities to beer. "Think about the differences between cooking with fresh versus dried basil or other herbs," says Licker. "East Coast brewers have had very limited access to wet hops because of the lack of commercial hop farms in the region. We are proud to offer local brewers wet hops during harvest time." [8]

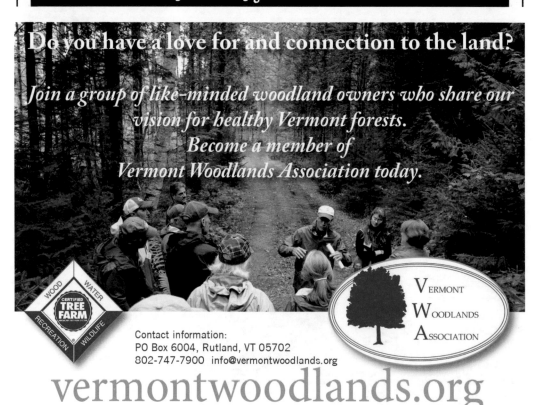

SEPTEMBER

September

Watching, in a state of near hypnosis, a steady stream of fragrant, bright-green haylage, unloading from the wagon onto the conveyor belt on the Ag-Bagger or into the blower for the silo. The roar of the tractor, the rocking motion of the seat as the power take-off runs at top speed. On and on and on, the steady flow of green, mesmerizing. Alertness dulls: 5:00 a.m. was long ago, and last night was late, looking for a newborn calf out in the back pasture. Finally, the flow slows, another load finished, and off to the field for another. Repeat, today, times 10.

Tomorrow will be clear and misty, at first. Full of dew. But when it burns off, there'll be dry hay to ted, the same sea of fragrant green spread over the land. Around and around and around on the tractor, the same hot late-summer sun. Always glad for the hot in September. Glad for the days before the cold really sets in. Looking back over my shoulder, a perpetual state of watching, ever watching to see that no green wad of hay has clogged the tedder tines, dragging a snowball of green, unable to be thrown out far and wide. A somnolent state, around and around and around the field.

Another season, another, this time quiet: long evenings stretching into night in the sugarhouse. Filled with steam, the rolling boil, on and on and on. Interrupted only by the screech of the arch door, opened to fill the roaring fire again; the lifting of the scoop to let the syrup run off into an "apron"; the heavy, sweet steam settling over all. The rolling boil, on and on and on.

I remember this today as I stand in front of the candy machine. Watching, in a state of near hypnosis, a steady stream of fragrant maple candy syrup running from the tilted pan above. Into the trough with the turning auger, out the valve, and into the molds.

On it comes, ready or not, a steady flow to keep pace with. I cannot look up: no time now for fetching more molds, the unending flow of candy hardening almost instantly. Almost hypnotic, this echo repeating today, just like yesterday and the day before. On and on and on it flows.

Farming of every kind is rooted in monotony – almost lulled into a dreamy state. But wait. There is always, always, in the back of the mind, an alertness to the moment. A looking, a listening for a plugged blower pipe, an almost imperceptible change in sound announcing impending calamity. A clogged gutter cleaner, the smell of scorching syrup, a teat cup sucking air. A sudden shutting off, running to make things right.

Autopilot/ready alert. —*Bette Lambert*

No Frost in Sight

For most Vermonters, September is a very busy time of year, as gardens need to be harvested and put to bed, wood needs to be moved in or stacked, and a dozen other outdoor projects need to be buttoned up before the snow arrives. It doesn't help that there's less time to get things done, as we lose about one full hour of daylight during this transition month. Lots of anxiety can come during this in-between season, as we make sure we're ready for the long winter ahead.

When will the fall colors really pop? Conditions that are too wet, too dry, too warm, or too cold through September can all have an impact on the changing of the leaves. Last year, a stretch of record cold in the middle of the month, combined with dry conditions, led to some of the best late September foliage in memory.

This year, not so much.

September 2021 got off to a somewhat soggy, cool, and breezy start. Labor Day cookout plans were thwarted by thunderstorms that were widespread across the state. Wind gusts reached 40 mph over many areas that day, and pea-size hail was reported from St. Albans to Brandon. More storms and rain in the following days led to some flood warnings, including in Chittenden County on September 8. The storms and moisture continued into mid-month, even as temperatures warmed into the 70s. Burlington reached 84 degrees on September 23, some 15 degrees above average for that date.

An extended stretch of dry, more seasonable weather ended the month, but as of October 1, most places in the state had yet to experience a frost. —*Christopher Kurdek, Fairbanks Museum and Planetarium*

Early September and the garden is at its peak.

Bearing Witness

The national news in 2021 was dominated by severe weather stories. A million people in the south lost power during Hurricane Ida, which proceeded to plow up toward the Northeast and drown people in their basements in New York City. Tens of thousands of people fled wildfires in the West. Hundreds perished in a spring heat wave in parts of the Northwest, where high temperatures are not supposed to exceed 120 degrees (but did). This came just four months after people froze in Texas, where temperatures are not supposed to fall below zero for extended stretches (which nonetheless happened). Editorial pages in newspapers were full of op-eds by scientists basically saying, *"We told you that as CO_2 levels rose, the weather was going to become more severe."*

We didn't have massive loss of life here in Vermont, or any once-in-500-year heat waves or cold spells. But compared to our established baselines, the weather here has been extraordinary. Our monthly weather recaps are a key part of the historic value of this *Almanac* project, because they provide us a record with which to remember. With the publication of Volume II, we now have two years worth of records. So let's remember.

As detailed in Volume I, in October 2019, the Missisquoi set an all-time record level of 14.72 feet in North Troy after a 5-inch rainfall on Halloween. This was followed up, that November, by the coldest month in Vermont records (6.6 degrees below the mean). Two months later, January 2020 was 6 degrees warmer than normal – roughly equal to the mean temperature in Roanoke, Virginia. May snow is not uncommon in Vermont, but the 10 inches of snow that fell just north of Bennington on Mother's Day 2020 certainly was. The Burlington area saw heat in July 2020 that was seven degrees hotter than normal, shattering the temperature record in the city

(they've been keeping records there for 130 years). The 25-day dry spell in September 2020, after a dry July and August, was not unprecedented, but it did contribute to a long-term drought record in the spring of 2021.

You can skim through the pages of this *Almanac* to note that the weirdness has continued over the past 12 months. In November 2020 it was 6 degrees above normal in Burlington, then 5.5 degrees above normal in the month of December. We had a 44-inch snowfall in 24 hours in the southern Greens, the most ever recorded in a single day in Vermont. The northeastern part of the state saw a drought stretch into summer that in total lasted 60 weeks. In July 2021, when crops were struggling to grow because of dry weather near the Canadian border, it rained for 21 days in parts of southern Vermont. Putney got almost 18 inches of rain – essentially a third of a year's worth falling in one month.

The concept of climate change has always been hard to grasp because it's often couched in terms of warming. And it has, on average, gotten warmer. If we look at National Weather Service records from the years 1980-1990, the mean July temp in Burlington was 70.6 and the mean December temp was 24.6. That's the weather us Gen-Xers who grew up here remember from our summer and winter school vacations. The mean July and December temps in Burlington for the years between 2010 and 2020 were 73.5 and 29.1 degrees, respectively, so kids who are coming of age today are doing so in a significantly warmer place. But none of us feel mean temperature, so the concept doesn't communicate well.

All of us understand extremes, though. And for the last two years we've been getting a steady dose of them.
—*Dave Mance III*

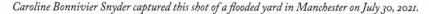

Caroline Bonnivier Snyder captured this shot of a flooded yard in Manchester on July 30, 2021.

NATURE NOTES

SARAH HINA

Monarch Wing Clap

Butterflies have huge wings compared to their small bodies and their fluttery flying, though charming to us, does not appear to be at all efficient. Who among us hasn't found it almost impossible to believe that monarchs fly from Vermont to Mexico?

It's been known for 50 or so years that on the upstroke butterfly wings clap together. Recent studies of butterflies in a wind tunnel have revealed that the upward moving wings take on a cup shape with an air-filled pocket between them. When the wings clap together air is forced out at the back in a jet that sends the butterfly forward. The downward stroke keeps the butterfly aloft.

The scientists who studied these butterflies concluded that their flight is much more efficient than it looks. Plus, the clapping mechanism allows them to take off rapidly to escape predators. 🅥

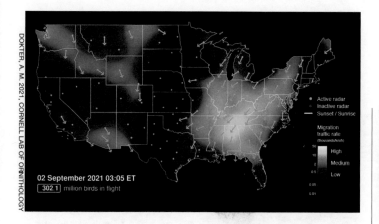

DOKTER, A. M. 2021, CORNELL LAB OF ORNITHOLOGY

02 September 2021 03:05 ET
302.1 million birds in flight

Active radar
Inactive radar
Sunset / Sunrise

Migration
traffic rate
(thousands/km/h)

50 High
10
2 Medium
0.5
Low
0.05
0.01

Bird Migration Forecast

That many birds that spend their summers in the north leave for the winter is not surprising – a fair number of us do the same. But since most of them travel at night, an astonishing number pass over us unnoticed. You can eavesdrop on them now online, in real time, thanks to the Cornell Lab of Ornithology and Colorado State University.

The Cornell Lab uses the US weather surveillance radar network to map migration as it happens, live, from local sunset to sunrise, across the country. The orange arrows on this map indicate the direction the birds are flying. The large black area in the Northeast that shows no expected migration on September 2 is thanks to Hurricane Ida.

A bird migration alerts tool on the same page lets you enter the name of a city – or even some towns – and find out how many birds are expected to pass over that night. The results are reported as the number of birds that fly across a one-kilometer-long line perpendicular to their direction of flight.

Realizing that the Connecticut River is a known flyway, I entered Norwich, Vermont on this page and learned that on September 1 migration there was expected to be 3,000 to 7,000 birds/kilometer; on the 2nd and 3rd, high migration would see more than 7,000 birds per kilometer!

You can try it yourself, and find all sorts of additional information at https://birdcast.info —*Joan Waltermire*

EVER WONDER WHY CHICKENS constantly bob their heads? It's because their eyes don't reflexively focus like ours do. We – along with most animals – have what's called a *vestibulo-ocular reflex* (VOR); it's a reflex that allows us to maintain focus on something even while our head moves. When we rotate our head to the left, our eyes rotate right to compensate. Chickens lack the reflex, so they need to manually move their heads to accomplish the same thing.

THE RIBBONS OF FIGURE in this red maple board running perpendicular to the growth rings are called pith rays. In the tree, they're pathways along which nutrients move from the periphery of the trunk to the center. In the sawmill, they're revealed in wood by sawing it radially. In the shop, they're brought out with planing, sanding, and a coat of teak oil.

AT HOME

❦

Chelsea Barn Quilt Project

Accessible art, art that does not discriminate, can spur a sort of human connection that is sometimes hard to come by, particularly these days.

Carrie Caouette-De Lallo knew this when she pulled two large pieces of plywood out from the scrap wood pile behind her house with the intention of making art. It was not the first time she had repurposed her husband Tim's building materials, and it certainly would not be the last.

First came a layer of plain white paint, covering the grain from edge to edge. Then upon that layer she envisioned patterns. Flowers emerged. Purples, blues, and reds set against a yellow checkered background.

The image was borrowed and reimagined, just like the idea Carrie had, as she went about painting a second piece of plywood. An iris this time, and tribute to one of her favorite flowers growing in her gardens, a pastime, like painting, she finally had time for now she was officially retired from teaching.

With two pieces completed, she solicited her builder-husband to hang these sizable pieces on the outside of two of the buildings they owned in Chelsea Village. She already had acquired a bit of a reputation for hanging art on her front porch, upon out-building doors, and in her gardens. In her opinion, the environment and weather made the artwork more interesting. She also

PHOTOS BY SARAH E. CAOUETTE.

enjoyed sharing her art with others, and hanging it outside was just easier than inviting everyone inside.

People started talking, as they do in small communities. Some commented about the new roadside art they had been admiring in passing on the way to the post office, the bank, and to Will's General Store.

Others asked, "Did you get a permit for that?" Or said: "Art's not gonna fix a town."

Carrie was not looking to fix anything about Chelsea. She simply believed she had something to offer that could potentially help elevate the spirit of the town where she had made a home for nearly 20 years. At least it was worth trying. And maybe, she thought, there would be others, like herself, who would want to join in sharing a piece of themselves in the hopes that it would inspire more neighborly connection. More connection between neighbors may even lead to a more optimistic outlook for the community.

It has been three years since Carrie put into motion the Chelsea Barn Quilt Project, and there are now 100 quilts in the area. Looking back, she could not have imagined the response she was met with. "The best part," she says, "are the stories that come with the art-making." How people she once only knew by name or in passing now invite her into their homes to see and share the art they have made.

Collectively the Barn Quilt Project has brightened Chelsea's facades and connected neighbors to one another. Though these changes may be more subtle in nature, it is small ideas and acts like these that can grow into something fundamentally beautiful and good. —*Sarah E. Caouette*

Carrie Caouette-De Lallo

Steam Juicer

If someone had suggested 15 years ago that I buy an expensive, bulky, stainless steel cooking contraption that I would use just five or six times a year, I would have been quietly disdainful. But I borrowed one of these things, called a steam juicer, from a friend and now I lend my own to other friends and neighbors during the summer.

We use it to make juice from rhubarb, pears, grapes, and occasionally elderberries, because that's what we have too much of. Peaches, plums, and cherries make good juice, too. No peeling required!

The juicer is in three sections: at the bottom is a water-filled pot that sits on a stove burner. Next up is something that looks like an oversized angel food cake pan. Above that is a large colander-like section that holds the fruit. A lot of fruit, usually layered with some sugar. Steam rises from the bottom pot through the center hole and permeates the fruit. After two or more hours of simmering, the fruit has collapsed into a mat and all its juices have run into the central section.

Canning the juice is simple. A flexible tube with a shut-off clip near its end comes out of the juice section and is used to fill canning jars. We preheat the jars in a 200-degree oven and don't process them since they get quickly filled and quickly capped. You can do whatever you want with the juice. It's completely clear and ready to use to make jelly. Next year I think I'll try crabapple jelly. Just think – no cheesecloth.

Our steam juicer holds roughly 10-12 quarts of fruit which yields about 4 quarts of quite concentrated juice.

A few marbles in the bottom pan will rattle noisily and will let you know if the water level gets perilously low. If you ever need distilled water, it will make that, too.

These gadgets, made in Finland and Germany for a long time, are now made by many manufacturers, some even in China. —*Virginia Barlow*

Solvitur Fodiendo

(IT IS SOLVED BY DIGGING)

Imagine a scene from Louis Sachar's novel *Holes*. A dozen teens in face masks squint and sweat, hurling shovels downward against unyielding ground. It's mid-September 2020, and we're deep in record-breaking drought, our parking lot baked solid like desert caliche. The atmosphere bearing down on us at East Burke School's campus – the weight of pandemic, social inequity, and political strife – seems only to confirm the dystopian image in our parking lot. But our students are here by choice. They're learning that when the weight of the world comes crashing down on you, you must dig down to rise up.

A student pops out of a shallow hole she's been chiseling for over an hour. "I think there was a fire here!" She holds up bits of charcoal from several inches down. Another student recalls that, a century ago, children were paid five cents per day to keep the school's wood stove running. "Maybe this is where they dumped the wood ash," he speculates.

EBS's parking lot has borne generations of village history. Horse-drawn carts, games of kickball and basketball, cars and school buses, Kingdom Trails bikes and Vermont Association of Snow Travelers

(VAST) snowmobiles, snow plows and sand trucks, and five generations of foot traffic have all crushed down this patch of land. From soil samples in ecology class, students learn that what they're working with isn't actually soil any longer: it's completely dead.

After 150 years of nothing but being trodden under foot, hoof, and tire, it's no wonder our little lot is so unyielding.

⁂

It's nearly fall when our students start toiling to transform 1,000 square feet of this dead parking lot into a thriving food forest. Mimicking the ecology of a natural woodland ecosystem, our garden will ultimately produce perennial edibles at every vertical level of a forest ecosystem, from root tip to treetop, while actively restoring the soil. The idea is not a new one, but examples of regenerative food production remain limited in cold climates like ours. Our students are creating a model that others in the Kingdom can follow.

Beyond the observable resurrection of dead ground, the food forest serves to resurrect spirits as well. After a spring of mandated school closure and social isolation, our students – like so many of us – were not okay. Anxiety and depression skyrocketed among adolescents. Many of these students, expressing feelings of despair, begged to come back to school. They need a sense of purpose, a reminder of their individual and collective ability to have a meaningful impact. They need to rediscover that most precious treasure: hope. The treasure they seek is not buried in the ground, yet the digging will guide them to it. Their work will create a legacy for them and a resource for generations to come.

After weeks of digging, conducting

First dig with students

Newly planted rose bushes, courtesy of Elmore Roots Nursery

percolation tests, and hauling in compost from Black Dirt Farm for mulching, students and faculty cover the surface of the lot with whatever is immediately available: an abundance of maple leaves and twigs, manure from nearby farms, compost from our school's kitchen, and coffee grounds from Café Lotti. Then, we wait. Hope doesn't grow all at once.

In spring, when the ground begins to thaw and it comes time to purchase plants, we get an astounding response from followers on Facebook. Donations pour in from as far south as Mississippi and as far west as Washington, helping us reach our fundraising goal in just three days. With a matching gift from Elmore Roots Nursery, we're able to plant over $1,600 worth of trees, shrubs, and perennials in our first year.

Sunchokes now tower over young pawpaws, seaberries, and cherries. Field peas and clover, planted as nitrogen-fixing cover crops, mingle with pumpkins, peppers, kale, and cabbage donated by Firefly Farm.

Amazingly, weeds spill over the plot's borders into the unfertilized driveway, helping stabilize the sand that has been eroding there for a century. Nature picks up where we've left off, reclaiming ground that, only a year ago, was too damaged to sustain life.

The story told by our neglected, callused, uninviting parking lot is very much the story that our students will have to play out in their lives. To build themselves up, they will need to dig down – to do the work of hauling in what will nourish and sustain growth, to learn and plan the cultivation of something better, to pour in hours upon days upon weeks of seemingly thankless work, and to wait patiently through spiritual winters. Now, as they look out on a patch of dead land resurrected, the pride that they feel is written all over their faces, and their minds just might be turning to what else they can build. The surfaces of their lives, too, looked pretty bleak a year ago. But now that they know how much power they have, they just might be ready to reclaim what so many others have given up for lost. They might begin, within themselves, to dig.
—*Megan Durling and Nathan Bradshaw*

A LOOK BACK

Into the Light Cellar

Beginning in 1972, Suzanne Opton photographed just about everybody in Chelsea, but she was particularly drawn to the people who slept in the same bed all their lives and were rarely seen in the village. Many of the eight families portrayed in new her book, *Into the Light Cellar*, struggled to keep their farms going and took care of their parents after their siblings left for the wider world.

The farms were mostly off the grid, as we now call it, and had very few amenities. But Suzanne's experience was that "poverty was not the focus of their lives." Kenneth O'Donnell, as well as many of the others, just wanted to live from day to day and "let the rest of the world go by."

Into the Light Cellar is available through the Norwich Bookstore and Suzanne Opton's website: www. suzanneopton.com.

KENNETH O'DONNELL

I don't make no money. I don't know as anybody's makin' any money now, are they? A lot o' money changes hands, but I don't think there's very much stickin anywhere. Well, they say an honest man don't get nowhere, and I think it's true. But if you was brought up honest, it's kind of hard to be anything else. You'll see a revolution right here in this country 'fore you get done. Be another civil war. It's just what it's building up to every damn day. Keep crowding the poor man out. And the rich get richer. It ain't gonna take forever.

Leone Thorne cared for her parents and three siblings on the farm which had been in the family for four generations. When only she and her brother Earle remained, they moved to Chelsea village to be more among people. The Thorne Family farm had it all – cows, pigs, turkeys, chickens, bees, preserves in the dark cellar, apples in the light cellar. Leone remembered butchering days when all the doorknobs in the house were greasy.

LEONE THORNE

I didn't enjoy raising turkeys too much cause they're delicate creatures. At night you'd have to get them into the barn. They can't stand wet weather. When they're little, you know, the mother will take them out in the deep grass. You couldn't see them, couldn't tell where they were. And I'd have to climb up the ridge of the pasture a little way so's I could look down over the field and see the mother turkey's head come up above the grass. And then I'd spot her in my mind and go to her. But she could get away in the meantime. It surely took time to work those little turkeys out of the grass.

INDUSTRY

Green Mountain Grapes

The box arrived from a nursery in western New York in April 1999. Seeing the skeptical look on my face, my supervisor, the University's professor of pomology, said, "Look, Terry, they're just little apples. We can grow these here."

So it went that the first vineyard since the 1980s was planted at the University of Vermont Horticulture Research and Education Center. I felt my skepticism was justified. My own pomology professor had convinced me just a few years earlier that our climate was too cold for high-quality winegrapes, but there was something afoot in the region. Just up the road from the orchard I had been managing in Charlotte, I regularly drove past a man I'd assumed a fool, planting rows of vines on a couple of acres near the lake, and I'd been hearing of some lawyer up in the Islands who was also taking on this fool's errand. Little did I know that over twenty years later, those vineyards would still be producing as part of Vermont's now maturing wine industry.

When most consumers think of wine, varieties like Chardonnay, Cabernet Sauvignon, or Merlot come to mind. These "old world" grapes are members of the species *Vitis vinifera*, which evolved in the Mediterranean region, on the Balkan peninsula, and in southwestern Asia. While well known for the quality of the wine they produce, *V. vinifera* grapes generally are not considered hardy enough to survive Vermont's cold winter temperatures, and are highly susceptible to disease in our humid summer climate.

However, there are other grape species that evolved in North America. One such species is *V. labrusca*, which has been grown successfully and commercially for fresh eating, juice, and jelly production for over a century, especially in neighboring New York and Pennsylvania. Concord is the variety we most think of among such grapes, but Delaware, Catawba, and Himrod are also commercially important. While these varieties are reliable producers, they prefer a slightly warmer environment – not so much in order to survive as to properly ripen.

Most of the wild grapes found in Vermont and similarly cold regions – areas with temperatures that reliably dip below -20°F – are usually from the species *V. riparia*. Riparia grapes are very cold-hardy (some wild selections have shown hardiness to temperatures

as low as -70°F), but they have a major drawback in that their juice is far too acidic to make palatable, much less quality, wine.

But grapes have an astounding ability to hybridize. Among those first varieties that showed up at the UVM farm and were planted in the first Vermont vineyards were French-American hybrids that were bred in the late-ninteenth through mid-twentieth centuries to withstand New World diseases that were plaguing the French wine industry. While many of these early hybrids were still just a bit too cold-sensitive to succeed in our state, newer hybrids released from breeding programs in the upper Midwest, including from the University of Minnesota and from private breeders like Elmer Swenson and Tom Plocher, found the formula for cold hardiness, disease resistance, and wine quality.

Wine regions typically take time to settle on the best varieties to grow and the management systems best suited to local soils, climates, and markets. Classic wine regions like Burgundy in France have had centuries to experiment and settle on their best varieties; it took many decades for California's vineyards and wineries to develop their own distinctive style. Vermont is now on its own journey; the state currently hosts about 175 acres of vineyards that provide grapes to 24 licensed wineries in the state. As the industry here has matured over the last two decades, we have seen changes in the makeup of the vineyards: of those original Vinifera varieties, only a few Riesling exist in the most protected sites along Lake Champlain, and the French-American hybrids now make up a relatively small portion of Vermont-grown grapes. Instead, it has been the "Minnesota varieties" that spurred a real jump in planting from around 2004 to 2010. Breeding and evaluation of new varieties continues, and the best winegrape for Vermont, and even for the specific micro-climates within the state, may not have been released yet.

Vineyard work is hard, with a long payback period after the initial investment of planting, installing trellis, and training vines. A recent economic analysis of grape production in Vermont concluded that a producer could expect to break even after about 20 years. Management of the vineyard for optimum yield and wine quality requires handling every vine from tip to tip six to eight times per year. There's also spraying, mowing, and harvest. The idea of growing grapes will seem romantic to some, but grape production is not a

Sheep are in the vineyard and on the bottles at Ellison Estate Vineyard in Grand Isle. At left, the vineyard's Louise Swenson grapes.

glamorous or easy endeavor. The reward comes when those grapes are transformed into wine.

In just a few short years, Vermont wineries have distinguished themselves in the region. Our cool climate supports production of crisp white wines from La Crescent, Prairie Star, Louise Swenson, and for the brave growers on the best sites, Riesling and Cayuga grape varieties. Red grape varieties include the French-American hybrids Leon Millot and Baco Noir but are dominated by more cold-hardy varieties such as Frontenac, St Croix, Petite Pearl, and the current favorite, Marquette.

Over the course of these past two decades, my mind has changed completely. A successful grape industry has developed in Vermont. Vineyards here now regularly win national awards and receive accolades. We've proven not only that the right grapes can survive in the state, but that we can be leaders in the production of excellent wines. —*Terence Bradshaw*

Grapevine Pruning

rapes are climbers. Botanically considered a liana, grapes are a woody, climbing vine that uses other structures, usually trees in the wild, to reach the top of the forest canopy in a search for sunlight. Grape growers take advantage of this climbing habit, coupled with the plasticity of the vines, to train plants to a trellis. A typical grape trellis spreads growing structures, either annually renewed canes or semi-permanent cordons, horizontally and at a consistent height to make management easier and the vines more productive. By spreading vine growth laterally rather than allowing the vine to climb vertically, the apical dominance of the vine – the trait that discourages formation of branching and fruiting until the plant reaches the forest canopy height – is broken, and the vine can be contained within a smaller space. When this happens, the plant's production shifts more toward fruit, which is formed from those lateral shoots, rather than vegetative growth.

Grapevines are pruned in winter and early spring, after they have reached dormancy. During pruning, as much as 80 percent of the growth from the vine may be removed. Growers tend to prune to a certain number of buds, located where leaves and fruit grew on previous years' canes. We commonly seek to retain four to six buds per foot of canopy. Where I first stumbled in understanding pruning was with the inverse concept that a vigorous vine needs to be pruned less heavily than a more weakly growing one. This is because a certain amount of growth can be expected from a grapevine, and that growth can be spread among shoots that emerge from the retained buds after pruning.

Leaving more buds on a vigorous vine gives more shoots to spread the growth around, and therefore the shoots are more balanced. Conversely, less-vigorous vines can have their growth distributed among fewer shoots, thereby increasing each one's vigor.

One wild card in grapevine pruning is the amount of cold damage that retained buds may have experienced over the winter. The plants growing in Vermont have a remarkable adaptation for surviving winter temperatures in that each compound bud actually contains three separate buds that are easily seen with even the slightest magnification. The primary bud is the largest and most fruitful, but the least cold-hardy. Secondary buds are somewhat more cold hardy and can produce a smaller crop that is often delayed in development. Finally, the most cold-hardy tertiary buds typically will produce no crop, but can produce shoots in the event that the other two buds are damaged, potentially helping to keep the plant alive. Growers commonly dissect some buds before and during pruning and may adjust their strategy by retaining more buds if cold damage is observed.

Most of our vineyards are grown on a bilateral

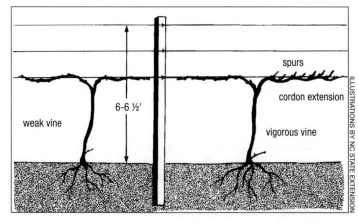

ILLUSTRATIONS BY NC STATE EXTENSION

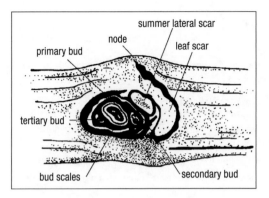

summer lateral scar

node

primary bud

leaf scar

tertiary bud

bud scales

secondary bud

At left: Dormant bud and node of the one-year-old cane. The compound bud has been cut cross-sectionally to reveal the arrangement of the bud's inner structures.

cordon or cane system. This means they have a trunk from the ground to the trellis wire, then growth that extends in both directions down the wire from which all annual growth is produced. Pruning grapevines tends to follow a general formula. I like to start at the base of the vine and select a single renewal shoot to retain, then remove all other shoots from the base. Grapevine trunks face a variety of threats including cold temperatures, bacterial infection known as crown gall, and "tractor blight" from careless operators; it is important, therefore, to maintain a shoot growing from the base to retrain a vine if such damage occurs. I then clean all shoots off the trunk until I reach the "head" – this is the area at the top of the trunk (or trunks, as many growers retain two trunks, and spread each in an opposite direction down the trellis wire) from which the lateral growth is produced. Then, working out from the center down one "arm," I remove the prior year's wood, retaining the four to six buds per foot that I want to maintain a balanced vine.

There are two ways to maintain that bud number. Some growers prune to a certain number of two-bud spurs along the length of the cordon. Because the buds closer to the base of last year's shoot are more cold-hardy and productive than buds farther out on the shoot, this method is more reliable than cane pruning, where a whole cane (the term used for a one-year old woody shoot from the previous year) is selected and laid down on the trellis. Because inoculum for certain diseases like phomopsis and anthracnose can build up on older woody tissues, this method is more commonly used in organic production systems, but at the expense of some productivity.

Ideally, one shoot will emerge sometime in May from each retained bud. In reality, buds either don't produce a shoot or, more commonly, the primary and secondary buds both produce shoots. Growers will

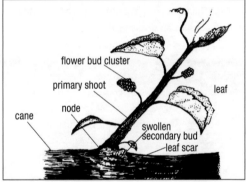

flower bud cluster

primary shoot

leaf

node

cane

swollen secondary bud

leaf scar

then thin shoots when they are just a few inches long to the desired number. This allows for the selection of evenly spaced shoots along the canopy, and for the removal of delayed and under-vigorous shoots that emerge from secondary buds. During summer, growers have a few more passes to make through the vineyard. One of the most important happens after July 4, when shoots have lignified enough to handle. The shoots are separated from one another and "combed" to a training habit. The goal is to place fruit at a consistent height on the trellis and expose them as early as possible to sunlight, which promotes even ripening and optimum fruit quality. —*Terence Bradshaw*

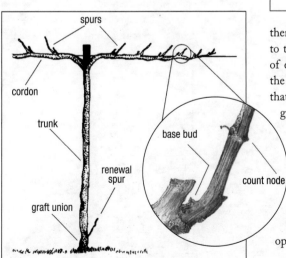

spurs

cordon

trunk

renewal spur

graft union

base bud

count node

Working Vermont's Vineyards

It's a beautiful morning at the start of the second week of September. At Shelburne Vineyard, the day's harvesting crew – Josh Stecker, Kate Cartwright, Casey Pitcher, Katharine Sherrer, and Julian Wise – is deep in the rows of St. Croix vines, picking berries, which, technically, is what grapes are.

The grapes are plump, a deep, hazy purple in the sun that warms the vineyard, just off Route 7, about a half-mile south of Shelburne Museum. The pickers' fingers are soon dripping purple juice as they gradually fill a big yellow plastic bin.

The growing season that culminates today for these vines has been "all over the place," according to chief winegrower Ethan Joseph, who has been with the vineyard since graduating from UVM with a degree in natural resources in 2008.

There was some spring frost, Joseph said, then it was "nice and hot," though an early dry spell threatened to reduce pollination. July was wet in many parts of the state, but not to the extreme in this part of the Champlain Valley. And the late summer days have been warm, helping to ripen the grapes, although at times it got up to 95 degrees, which can interfere with photosynthesis. "It's not necessarily ideal," said Joseph, "but it does mean that it pushed the ripening along." Yields have been on the low side in 2021, he said, but grape quality has been excellent.

The weather may vary year to year, said Joseph, but the winemaker's year always follows a similar pattern: December to March: pruning, along with indoor chores such as barreling, aging, and bottling; April and May: mowing, trellis repair, and preparing for the growing season; June and July: out among the vines, mowing, and moving, and trimming foliage to ensure the grapes get as much sun as possible; August: a bit of a breather; September and October: harvesting, pressing, starting fermentation, and monitoring the wine's progress.

"For the most part," says Joseph, "you're just taking it as it comes." —*John Lazenby*

PHOTOS BY JOHN LAZENBY

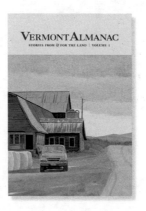

Did you miss Volume I of Vermont Almanac?

Complete your collection at **VERMONTALMANAC.ORG** or buy a copy from your local indie bookstore.